ISLAM, CHARITY, AND ACTIVISM

Indiana Series in Middle East Studies
Mark Tessler, general editor

Islam, Charity, and Activism

Middle-Class Networks and Social Welfare in Egypt, Jordan, and Yemen

JANINE A. CLARK

INDIANA
University Press
Bloomington & Indianapolis

This book is a publication of

Indiana University Press
601 North Morton Street
Bloomington, IN 47404-3797 USA

http://iupress.indiana.edu

Telephone orders   800-842-6796
Fax orders   812-855-7931
Orders by e-mail   iuporder@indiana.edu

The paper used in this publication meets the minimum
requirements of American National Standard for Information
Sciences—Permanence of Paper for Printed Library Materials,
ANSI Z39.48-1984.

MANUFACTURED IN THE UNITED STATES OF AMERICA

Library of Congress Cataloging-in-Publication Data

Clark, Janine A.
  Islam, charity, and activism : middle-class networks and social
welfare in Egypt, Jordan, and Yemen / Janine A. Clark.
    p. cm. — (Indiana series in Middle East studies)
Includes bibliographical references and index.
  ISBN 0-253-34306-2 — ISBN 0-253-21626-5 (pbk.)
  1. Social institutions—Egypt. 2. Social institutions—Jordan. 3.
Social institutions—Yemen. 4. Charities—Egypt.
5. Charities—Jordan. 6. Charities—Yemen. 7. Middle class—
Egypt. 8. Middle class—Jordan. 9. Middle class—Yemen. 10.
Islam—Charities. I. Title. II. Series.
  HN786.A8C53 2004
  301—dc21

                                        2003008461

1 2 3 4 5 09 08 07 06 05 04

For John, Astrid,
Martha,
Eric, Ella,
and
John

CONTENTS

TABLES AND CHARTS

PREFACE AND ACKNOWLEDGMENTS

This book originated from a Ph.D. thesis on Egypt and slowly expanded to include two more case studies, those of Yemen and Jordan. It has thus been approximately a ten-year effort, during which time I have relied on many institutions and people. I am indebted to the Social Science and Humanities Research Council of Canada; the American Institute for Yemeni Studies in Ardmore, Pennsylvania; and the Council for the Humanities at the University of New Hampshire for the financial support and the ability to leave for the field when it was necessary. I would also like to express my thanks to the Department of Political Science at the University of Guelph for granting me the time to complete the manuscript. Without this institutional support, this book would not have been possible.

I also owe my gratitude to the many Egyptians, Yemenis, Jordanians, and Palestinians who aided me in the field, befriended me, and granted me time-consuming interviews. Their help was invaluable. As this book centers not just on Islamic social institutions but on the social networks in which they are embedded, I am especially indebted to those who brought me into those social circles, had me over for meals, invited me to family weddings, let me spend the night at their homes, and brought me into their confidence. In particular, I need to thank the many women I met and befriended. It was their networks that not only aided me in accessing interviews, but, by bringing me into them, granted me my greatest insights. Their friendships were the most rewarding aspect of my field work.

As my research concerns both Islamic social institutions (ISIs) and their institutional and, primarily, social networks, my interviews extended far beyond site visits to the ISIs and with Islamists. I interviewed Islamists and non-Islamists working in the entire spectrum of society. This included men and women in the Muslim Brotherhood, the Islamic Action Front and the Hizb al-Islah Party; Islamists and non-Islamists working in Islamic social institutions other than the ones under study and in other nongovernmental organizations; and Islamists engaged in different activities, such as university student councils and the elected boards of directors of various syndicates such as the doctors' and the engineers' syndicates. I also visited numerous Islamic cultural centers and regularly attended weekly Qur'anic study groups and lectures. In total, I conducted several hundred interviews.

While in some of these interviews I used fixed questionnaires, I primarily relied on open-ended one-on-one interviews and participant observation. In order to study the networks that interested me, I had to develop a bond of trust with the people I interviewed and to ensure that I did not break or betray that trust by always being forthright about the purpose and nature of my research. I found this easier with other women, both Islamists and non-Islamists, who fairly rapidly allowed me into their homes and social circles. In most cases, however, my sex did not prevent me from being brought into the confidence of the men I interviewed. While Yemeni women, for example, are culturally prohibited from attending or are unwelcome at men's afternoon social sessions, I was often invited to sessions when the interviewees I met felt I would benefit from the discussions. As a colleague once stated to me, to a certain extent Western women are a third sex—one that is unbound by many of the social customs to which Yemeni women in particular generally must adhere. Having stated this, in Yemen and Jordan, where the respective charities and Islamic parties have many active women, I relied primarily on the women I met, and with whom I gained trust, both for interviews and to further my connections with other men and women. In Egypt, I relied quite heavily on my research assistant, whose sex, personality, and credentials created a strong bond of confidence and trust during the interviews. Respecting this trust while at the same time critically interpreting my research findings was sometimes a difficult task. Some interviewees assumed that this trust included only stating the positive. While not all of the people with whom I had interviews will agree with or even like what I have to say in this book, I strove for honesty in my interviews and hope that this fact is respected and appreciated. I like to think that the fact that I am still in touch with many of the people I met and am on good terms with them—despite the fact that some of them have read some work of mine that is critical of their activities—means that I achieved this difficult and fine balance.

I gathered the field data on Cairo's Islamic medical clinics during three extended trips, beginning in 1991. During the first two trips, I conducted the interviews together with one assistant; however, during the final trip, I employed thirty-six research assistants (all of whom were students at the University of Cairo and who had responded to an announcement made by a colleague in his classes) in order to be able to interview at a larger number of clinics. To be considered an "Islamic" clinic, clinics had to be located in a mosque or mosque complex. This site requirement was necessary because many associations and clinics wholly secular in orientation and practice often adopt Islamic names to gain greater credibility and legitimacy. In this regard, the required mosque affiliation guaranteed a religious affiliation. Without a master list from which to choose clinics (the Ministry of Social

Affairs in Egypt, with which all associations must register, does not have a category for Islamic associations), my assistants and I randomly chose clinics of all sizes and from both the most populous areas of Cairo and the city's newer outlying areas by literally choosing a geographical district, driving to it, and interviewing the first clinic spotted. We did not exclude any clinic that adhered to our criteria, including, for example, clinics that may have been run by groups labeled as radical. In total, we independently conducted interviews with directors, doctors, nurses, and former patients in over seventy different Islamic associations. The interviews were conducted one on one; however, in many cases, other doctors, nurses, patients, directors, and community members would join us and the interviews would be quite lively affairs going on late into the night.

Naturally, any researcher in a foreign country and culture confronts cultural barriers as well as suspicions, particularly in the Egyptian context of growing violence between Islamist extremists and the state. I was concerned that in addition to my nationality, my sex and religion would present a barrier to the necessary trust and rapport needed for the interviews. While I soon found that many of the doctors were not Islamists, I wanted to show respect for a religion which, in its strictest legalistic interpretation, forbids members of the opposite sex to be alone in a room together unless related by blood. I therefore decided to conduct my interviews with a form of chaperone with me. With the help of sociologist Saad Eddin Ibrahim, I located an Egyptian Muslim male graduate student at the American University in Cairo to be my research assistant. Certainly, there was at least one case in which a doctor, out of religious conviction, did not want to shake my hand (only that of my male assistant) and averted his eyes while speaking to me.

The trust my research assistant (actually, research partner) was able to engender in many of the directors and doctors was due not only to his own warm and honest disposition but also to the fact (unbeknownst to me when I first hired him) that his elderly father and uncle (deceased) had both been active members of the early Muslim Brotherhood and that his brother was a doctor known to some of the doctors we interviewed. The fact that his uncle had spent several years in jail under former President Nasser for his Brotherhood activities lent credibility to my assistant and created trust in some of the interviews. My assistant was not a Brother; in fact, although not politically active, he considered himself a Communist. Without a doubt, the necessary trust which developed during the interviews was predominantly obtained as a result of my interview partner's presence and credibility.

Of the thirty-six students who assisted me during the third trip, twenty-one were male and fifteen were female. Two of the men and one woman were Coptic, and eight of the Muslim women wore a *hijab* (head-scarf). The diversity of students proved to be educational in and of itself. On the whole, the researchers all felt that they had equal access to the clinics and received similar receptions regardless of sex or religion. Indeed, not one of the researchers was ever asked about his/her religion. As I had found during my first two field trips, the researchers complained that their biggest obstacle to getting interviews was not the directors or doctors but the *ba-wabeen* (doormen) who prevented our entry for no reason other than to exert their presumed authority.

I conducted my field work in Yemen during the course of three field trips between 1996 and 1999; a fellow researcher, Marina de Regt, conducted additional work for me in 2002. I decided to focus strictly on the Women's Committee in the Society. Based on custom (not law), Yemen is an almost wholly segregated society in which men and women socialize separately. I decided that I would most easily be able to gain access to and the trust of my interviewees if I worked within this societal arrangement. I felt that instead of its being a disadvantage, being a woman granted me certain potential opportunities to gain access to women's friendship circles.

Once I had decided upon the Women's Committee of the Islah Charitable Society as my Islamic social institution for research, the choice of sites for interviewing was relatively easy. I went to all the major towns and cities in Yemen where the Society has an active Women's Committee. In most cases, the women did not have their own facilities and indeed constituted a relatively small number of women who were largely engaged in raising donations for the main headquarters and distributing money, food, and clothing. Finding out if in fact there was a Women's Committee (there was always one on paper; the question was whether it existed in reality) and who these women were was really a matter of learning through word of mouth. Women in Sana'a were particularly helpful in providing me with names in other towns and cities. In both Sana'a and Hodeidah, however, there are impressive facilities in which various services, such as literacy classes, are also offered. I conducted the most in-depth interviews there, and visited not only the facilities but also the various Society projects located throughout the two cities. I was also fortunate enough to be invited to a variety of Society events, such as fund-raising events.

Once again, in Yemen serendipity played an important role in my interviews. When I told a fellow researcher that I was interested in women in the Islamist movement, she brought me along with her to a women's Qur'anic study group that she had attended in the past. She was familiar to the hostess and had personal friends in the study group, so I was welcomed. I soon came to attend this as well as other Qur'anic study groups on a regular basis. It was at these study groups that I was able to further certain friendships and gain greater insights into Islamist women's informal networks. I was regularly invited to their homes for meals and introduced to their families and friends, often other women also in the Society or Hizb al-Islah Party. (Indeed, I was also given names of friends in Jordan to whom I was to pay my respects. These were friends that they had met at Muslim women's conferences outside Yemen.) Most important, I soon learned that for many women in the Society and Party, Qur'anic study groups are an important form of social gathering.

My field work for Jordan was conducted during a lengthy field trip in 1998. Unfortunately, my trip was cut short by the *mukhabarat,* the internal security, which (because of factors such as King Hussein's failing health, the U.S. bombing of Iraq, and tensions mounting in the Palestinian Authority) felt inclined to question me for several days before asking me to leave the country. In this case, serendipity worked against me. I was in one of the larger Palestinian refugee camps and asked the first person I saw if my car could remain where I had parked it. That person turned out to be internal security and he decided I should submit myself to some questioning. I owe the Canadian ambassador tremendous thanks for bringing a relatively swift end to the questioning and bringing some laughter and levity to the situation. In 2001 and 2002, I had a research assistant, Rana Taha, a graduate student I trusted and respected, gather additional data for me on the clinics and tie up loose ends I had not been able to complete. All interviews conducted in Jordan for this book in 2001 and 2002 were done by Rana Taha.

In addition to its main headquarters in Amman, the Islamic Center Charity Society (ICCS) has four regional branches and thirty-two centers in twelve governorates, or provinces (*muhafazat*), around the country. Therefore, as in the case of Egypt, I ensured representativeness by controlling for size and location (although this time I had a list of all facilities from the ICCS main headquarters). This included a balance between urban and rural sites, Palestinian-dominated and Jordanian-dominated locations, and areas of varying degrees of affluence. I visited a total of fourteen ICCS branches, centers, and services or projects located in six different governorates. As in Yemen, I considered all centers or services that were affiliated with the ICCS as "Islamic" and as valid for the case study.

I originally chose both the ICCS and the Islah Charitable Society as case studies precisely because they are both, to one degree or another, affiliated with the two countries' respective Islamic political parties and because they are by far the two largest ISIs, indeed, NGOs (nongovernmental organizations), in their respective countries. In other words, if vertical recruitment is occurring, this is precisely where one would logically find it. In order to control for any selection bias in the cases of Yemen and Jordan, I conducted in-depth interviews in other NGOs and ISIs. In these two countries, I interviewed ten additional NGOs and ISIs. I found no significant difference in my results. Similarly, I chose Islamic medical clinics in Cairo, as opposed to day cares located in mosques, for example, because most Islamic associations prioritize medical clinics as the first project they usually establish, and because of the attention in the literature on medical clinics and the recruitment role they presumably play among the poor. In Egypt, due to state restrictions, only a limited number of ISIs has been permitted to establish nationwide institutions. Those that do have a "mother" association with branches are significantly smaller than that of either the ICCS or the Islah Society. Since there is no comparable ISI that is large in size and linked to a moderate Islamist political party, I randomly chose clinics from throughout the city.

Innumerable people, in small and large ways, made my research in all three countries possible. For those whose names I have inadvertently overlooked in the writing of this preface, I hope you forgive me. In Egypt, I would like to thank Saad Eddin Ibrahim for his suggestions and assistance in finding me a research partner and Amira El-Azhary Sonbol, Raymond Baker, Noha El-Mikawy, and Hassan Hanafi for their advice and guidance. Ahmed Khaled also played a very important role in arranging and organizing research assistants for me. For providing me a safe haven to which I could retreat, I must thank Sally and Daniel Gabriel. And for all the wonderful times we spent in Cairo, I thank Abir, Fadya, Amal, Enas, Nadr, Carolyn, Heni, and Debbie. Most important, I must thank the person who played the most crucial role in the completion of my field work, my research partner, Abdel Rahman Hillel Zaki.

In Yemen, the list is perhaps even longer. I thank Sheila Carapico for originally inspiring me to go to Yemen and do work on Islamists, particularly Islamist women. For getting me started and supporting me throughout my field work, I must acknowledge Lucine Taminian. I am indebted to Steve Day for introducing me to a wonderful circle of Yemeni friends and for opening various doors for me. Amin, Mohammed, Khalid, and Abdul Nasr, thank you for keeping me laughing! For always being willing to listen to me, I thank Delores Walters. Maria Ellis, Noha Sadek, and Marta Colburn at the American Institute for Yemeni Studies also ensured that my living and working conditions went smoothly. Of the many wonderful Yemeni who helped me, I must acknowledge Amat al-Alim as-Suswa, Raufa Hassan, Waheeba Fariah, Azah Ghanam, Bilquis al-Hadrani, Abdel Karim al-Aug, and Rashida, Misk, Samira and the many generous women who invited me into their homes for *nadawat* (pl.; sing. *nadwa*) and who I met at *nadawat*, whose privacy I would like to respect. Arwa and Alawiyya, I cannot begin to express my gratitude for your friendship, warmth, and endless efforts on my behalf. Finally, I cannot forget to mention Marina de Regt, who not only aided me tremendously in my field research in Yemen but has also become one of my dearest friends.

In Jordan, Hana and Khalil provided a wonderful living environment for me. Thank you, Hana, for your stimulating discussions and Khalil for introducing me to the hidden Amman. And to Rania, Dalia, and their families, I do now know how to express my thanks; you became my substitute family abroad. Huda, Dima, Dr. Tariq, and Abir were all extremely helpful to me. Most important, I am indebted to Rana Taha, not only for her friendship but also for the ongoing work she did for me in Jordan. Without her tireless efforts, I could not have completed my field work in Jordan.

There are, of course, people in Canada and the United States who have been there since the very beginning of this long process, discussing ideas, reading drafts, and endlessly supporting me in a variety of ways. Marie Joelle Zahar, Paul Kingston, Jillian Schwedler, Charlie Kurzman, Denis Sullivan, Remonda Bensabat Kleinberg, and particularly Quintan Wiktorowicz are among those who have spent much time unselfishly helping me. I would like to thank Fred Lawson for his ongoing encouragement. In addition, I owe my gratitude to Indiana University Press, in particular to Janet Rabinowitch, Rebecca Tolen, and Mark Tessler and to the reviewers. To Diane Singerman, thank you. Your conscientious and detailed comments were invaluable. Finally, I would like to thank Josh Adams, Lesley Burns, Sara Hartley, and Michelle Crawley at the University of Guelph for doing all the dirty work! I am indebted particularly to Jordan DeCoste for his careful proofreading of the manuscript. Brent and John, thank you for your help with the graphics. All the strengths of this book I owe to these many people and friends. All the weaknesses are due to myself.

ISLAM, CHARITY,
AND ACTIVISM

ONE

Islamic Social Institutions, Social Movement Theory, and the Middle Classes

---

My first contact with an Islamic social institution (ISI) was a health clinic located in a relatively wealthy but crowded part of Cairo. After I was misdiagnosed by the private doctors I had visited, an Egyptian friend insisted I go to the nearby Islamic medical clinic. My friend had heard the clinic was new and clean and that it had excellent doctors and facilities. I knew little about the clinic other than that it was located in the basement of a mosque, but when I arrived later that evening I realized that I had assumed that the clinic would be small, dark, relatively unsanitary, and very basic. I had also assumed that the clinic would be only for the very poor and was unsure, if not apprehensive, about how a Western, non-Muslim, and comparatively wealthy woman would be greeted.

I became aware of my prejudices only when I saw how wrong they were. Although the clinic was by no means luxurious or even "hospital clean," it was brightly lit, large, busy and had a definite aura of efficiency. There was a large waiting room when one first entered with simple wooden benches along the sides and a list of the doctors and specializations written on a large cardboard sheet on the wall. Otherwise, the walls were simple bare painted plaster. Opposite the entrance at the other end of the room was the counter where one purchased a ticket to see a doctor. The waiting room was T-shaped, and the doctors' offices were located along the stem of the T. There seemed to be three or four offices on either side of the stem and a laboratory and bathrooms (which were Turkish style and not the most inviting!) at the end.

My friend went to the counter and bought the ticket (under $1.00 US at that time) and received a number for me. My number was somewhere in the seventies. The room was overflowing with patients—young, old, male, and female—and their families waiting to see the doctor. I soon also noticed that the patients were not limited to the poor and, more to the point, that, judging by appearances, relatively economically secure middle-class patients formed the majority of people waiting to see the doctors. After a wait of an hour or two, I was able to see the doctor. He was young and had a strong command of English; he soon sent me home with a correct diagnosis and the order to sleep.

It was only when I was back in Canada that I gave any additional thought to my observations and experiences in the clinic. Too sick to think of much else, I had not paid attention to the fact that the clinic I had visited represented just one of hundreds of Islamic social institutions throughout Cairo and the Middle East. It was one of many nongovernmental or private institutions aimed at addressing the socioeconomic needs of its society within, at least theoretically, a stated Islamic framework.[1] Months later, when I came across an article on this growing phenomenon, I began to question the greater social and political significance of the clinic and similar institutions. What role do Islamic social institutions, such as medical clinics, play in terms of the larger Islamist "movement" or collective action? What role do they play in terms of movement participation? What significance do they have for moderate Islamic activism? What can Islamic social institutions tell us about the nature of moderate Islamism as a whole? What is the relationship between social activism and political activism? Using the case studies of Islamic medical clinics in Egypt, the Islamic Center Charity Society in Jordan, and the Islah Charitable Society in Yemen, this book represents the outcome of this questioning.

RETHINKING ISLAMIC SOCIAL INSTITUTIONS

Upon returning to Canada, I found that scholars examining Islamic social institutions such as the medical clinic I had visited and the role they play within the Islamist movement generally examine them with the explicit or implicit assumption of vertical clientelist ties within the institutions. Islamic social institutions are regarded as arenas for cross-class recruitment in which middle-class Islamist professionals actively and successfully recruit and mobilize the poor on behalf of the Islamist movement. Sami Zubaida states that the criteria for enjoying the opportunities and benefits in Islamic welfare institutions include not only "adherence to Islam (including the codes of social and family morality) but also networks of patronage and clientship, communal membership and loyalty, and possibly political allegiance."[2] According to Zubaida, Islamic associations treat the masses as simple objects of religious reform and control.[3] Similarly, Alain Roussillon argues that Cairene Islamic institutions are fronts for "missionarism" promulgating Islamist ideology and are crucial outposts in the battle against the state for the minds, souls, and institutions of Egyptian civil society.[4] He argues that Islamic associations, such as those that run Islamic medical clinics, are attempting to gain control of Cairo's urban quarters from the traditional local elites by establishing clientelistic networks, mediating with authorities, enforcing rules of morality, and settling disputes.[5] Mustapha al-Sayyid agrees.[6] Indeed, within much of the literature, the mere successful provision of services by the middle class to the poor is generally assumed to result in a growing number of adherents to the Islamist movement in the streets and/or at the ballot box.

Yet this was not my experience within the clinic I visited. In fact, upon first reading some of the literature, I did not immediately recognize that it was discussing the same type of institution I had visited when I was ill. As a Christian, I had certainly not observed "adherence to Islam" to be a criteria for entry, nor had I witnessed the provision of health care to the poor only. While there were certainly patients of what appeared to be all socioeconomic classes at the clinic, I had not witnessed a predominance of poor patients. It further occurred to me that if the clinic's goal was to serve the poor, it had not chosen a neighborhood with direct access to the poor; while mixed, the neighborhood was dominated by people from the middle classes. It seemed to me that if cross-class ties were developing between Islamist professionals and the poor, they were weak at best. Upon reflection, my first visit to an Islamic clinic made me question the degree to which Islamic clinics were vehicles for cross-class recruitment and/or mobilization. Rather than vertical ties, I had witnessed what appeared to be the development and strengthening of horizontal ties—ties between peoples of relatively similar socioeconomic categories. If ties or networks were being created in Islamic clinics, they were between those who worked in the clinics and patients of a relatively similar class base. While I recognized the difficulties of defining classes, never mind the difficulties in determining classes based upon appearances, I wondered if in fact health services in Islamic clinics were being provided *by* and *for* the middle classes. The middle classes seemed to be benefiting as employer, employee, and client. To what extent were the middle classes, and not the poor, benefiting from Islamic social services and what was the political significance of these horizontal networks?

Social movement theorists have long dealt with the role and significance of horizontal ties in social movements. Although they use the concepts differently, the two most influential schools within social movement theory, the resource mobilization perspective and the new social movement perspective, conceptualize social movements as webs or networks of institutional and social linkages in which their associated institutions are embedded. Increasing numbers of resource mobilization theorists refer to social

movements as "multi-organizational fields"[7] or "social movement industries"[8] or "loosely structured collective action"[9] or collective events in which
institutions and groups are loosely bound by the same (broadly defined)
ideology and symbols and are connected by overlapping, primarily social,
networks. Social movement organizations, such as Islamic clinics, are embedded in amorphous horizontal networks connecting largely homogenous
circles of friends together. According to social movement theory, these social or friendship networks—which are usually of like-minded or relatively
similar peoples—are pivotal to movement participation and recruitment.
Using such a framework, the focus of analysis becomes the horizontal connections within social networks, between social networks and institutions,
and between individual institutions.

Only a limited number of scholars of the Middle East have employed
social movement theory in their study of Islamist movements.[10] Yet the recasting of Islamic social institutions as part of a larger uncoordinated network is an important reconceptualization. It shifts the gaze of researcher
and student away from the presumed vertical ties that permeate and control
the "Islamic movement" and toward the horizontal ties created by the establishment and ongoing functioning of the institutions. The object of research expands to include the horizontal ties between like-minded and
generally homogeneous peoples that form social networks. This recasting
thus redirects the object of inquiry to the horizontal ties within which Islamic social institutions are embedded and their significance for the movement as a whole.

This book is an examination of why and how Islamic social institutions
establish middle-class ties and the political significance of these institutions
and their middle-class networks. In undertaking this study, I employ social
movement theory not only as a means of further understanding the dynamics of Islamic movements but also as an attempt to contribute theoretically to the body of research on social movements. Based on the three case
studies of Egypt, Jordan, and Yemen, I argue that Islamic social institutions
are run by and for the middle class. As a consequence of both the operational dictates of the institutions and the instrumental needs of the Islamist
movement of which the institutions are part, Islamic social institutions
cater to and benefit the educated or professional middle class. This process
not only neglects the poor, it often comes at the expense of the poor. Rather
than vertical recruitment or mobilization of the poor, Islamic social institutions play an important role in the strengthening of horizontal networks
binding middle-class doctors, directors, donors, volunteers, patients, and
clients together. Ties of trust, solidarity, and teamwork develop along these
horizontal lines, indirectly leading to the development of new social networks and, potentially, the diffusion of new ideas.

ISLAMIC SOCIAL INSTITUTIONS: PRODUCTS AND AGENTS OF POLITICAL AND SOCIAL CHANGE

ISIs can be understood to be situated at the confluence of two distinct but intimately related histories or contexts. The first is the rise of nongovernmental organizations in the region in the context of a changing economy on the one hand, and on the other, the growth of the secular state in the nineteenth and twentieth centuries, largely in response to the former context. Economic upheavals produced a local bourgeoisie that had not existed before. At the same time, beginning in the nineteenth century, the state gradually expanded its purview to include social welfare services that had previously been conducted largely by religious authorities and wealthy notables. In the context of this transition, during which neither traditional authorities nor the state were adequately providing social welfare services, it was this local bourgeoisie that established the region's first nongovernmental organizations to meet its own economic and political demands as well as those of the poor. The rise of the middle class is thus pivotal to the establishment of nongovernmental organizations. Then, as now, the middle class established nongovernmental organizations in response to state weaknesses.

The second context in which Islamic social institutions (ISIs) can be placed is in terms of the rise of Islamic activism or Islamism in the region. While most of the Western world did not become aware of Islamism until the assassination of former Egyptian president Anwar Sadat in 1981, the roots of Islamism go back much earlier, beginning with the *salafiyya* movement at the end of the nineteenth century, but they are most commonly associated with the establishment of the Muslim Brotherhood in 1928. The rise of Islamist groups, both moderate and violent, can be seen in a broad historical perspective as a response to the secular state's increasing encroachment on the domain of religious authorities and the role of religion in society. Today's moderate Islamist groups thus assert that Islam is the solution to the socioeconomic and political ills of the Middle East. In this regard, Islamists actively attempt to establish alternative institutions, such as Islamic hospitals, to those of the secular state in order to demonstrate the viability and the superiority of Islamism in the face of a struggling secular state, particularly with regard to the provision of social welfare services of all kinds. It is once again the middle class, and increasingly the professional or new middle class, that has responded to the call of moderate Islamism.

Located at the intersection of these two histories, ISIs are more than just a challenge to the state's ability to do its job; they are a challenge to the secular state itself. They represent an alternative organization of state and society—a potentially revolutionary one—based on Islam. They furthermore represent a class pushing for greater political power. What happens within (and between) ISIs as a locus of social change and political change is therefore of interest to Middle Eastern states and of interest to researchers. It is crucial to understand the networks in which ISIs are embedded—to whom and to what they are linked—and their social and political roles.

NONGOVERNMENTAL ORGANIZATIONS
AND THE MIDDLE CLASSES

From as early as the seventeenth century, one can trace a gradual process whereby the Middle East was integrated into the European-dominated world, particularly its markets and economy.[11] While historians disagree about the magnitude of the transformation resulting from European penetration and the degree to which the Middle East had been a subsistence economy and has only now moved to an export-oriented economy, there is a general consensus that capitalism was introduced to the region by Europeans during the nineteenth century.[12]

As Alan Richards and John Waterbury state, there is no gainsaying the fact that the mid-to-late nineteenth century is a watershed in state and class formation in the Middle East. Although European penetration and its impact upon the region could be felt prior to the nineteenth century, the processes leading to the social transformation of the region were greatly accelerated in the nineteenth century as the increasingly mature industrial societies of Europe contended for geopolitical and economic advantage in the Middle East.[13] The impact of the increasing growth and economic dominance of European trade and of the Middle Eastern state's response to that phenomenon was multifold. Most important for the purposes of this book was the rise of new classes in the Middle East.

According to most sociologists, class in the Middle East has historically been defined by three economic and social criteria: landownership, wealth, and status.[14] Prior to the nineteenth century, land belonged to the state and the ruler; however, the state granted temporary rights to certain individuals to appropriate the produce of the land. While these rights could be and were at times revoked, in many cases this practice evolved into a form of hereditary access to state-granted land or the right to collect tribute in the state's name. Thus an early stratum of tax-farmers, tribute-gatherers, and rural notables who gained their wealth and status from landownership developed.[15] Class position was also determined by wealth as capital. Trade, originally overland trade, created an early class of wealthy merchants composed of urban elites and notables. Status, on the other hand, is the result of belonging to or claiming descent from a prominent family. This would include descendants of the Prophet Mohammed, but also prominent religious scholars or tribal heads. The result is that social structure in the Middle East cannot be said to be based on class defined strictly in Marxian economic terms. Rather, we have an historical interplay of social and economic factors relating to wealth, prestige, family, and tribe—although these "noneconomic" factors do enable one to acquire land and wealth. Political scientists James Bill and Robert Springborg conceptualize social structure in the Middle East as an intricate web of vertical and horizontal stratifications—those based on groups that include family and tribe (vertical stratification) and those based on class (horizontal stratification), which they define in terms of power and employment position.[16] Historically, the class system in Egypt has been (and continues to be) highly complex and permeable.

The class system in the Middle East also cannot be considered static. As elsewhere, new classes in the Middle East are created and rise to ascendancy while others decline. With the Middle East's integration into the world economic system as a result of European economic penetration, new trade routes were created, new products were imported, and the region developed new exports suited to European demands. Large numbers of rural inhabitants flocked to the major cities of the region as domestic overland economic systems were dislocated and new opportunities arose elsewhere. In her study of civil society in Yemen, for example, Sheila Carapico notes that the influences of the world economy had their greatest impact on the port cities, such as Aden. Aden attracted youths from a more than 100-kilometer radius, and this burgeoning population created new demands for food and other necessities. In this manner, increasing numbers of Yemenis became involved in the cash economy through industry and trade, both in the cities and in the countryside that fed the cities.[17] The result was a new local bourgeoisie directly linked to the West that served as a mediator between the local consumer and the European producers.[18] We therefore see the rise of various forms of middlemen such as private moneylenders, real estate banks, and buyers and brokers of export crops.[19]

However, the creation of a new local bourgeoisie could not have been possible without the state and its policies in response to the European economic and military threat. Beginning with the restructuring and transformation of its military along European lines, by the mid-nineteenth century the Ottoman Empire embarked upon a full-scale reform program, the Tanzimat, that was emulated in the outskirts of the empire as well. In addition to the modernization of the army, the Tanzimat involved the restructuring of the state along European lines with the creation of new ministries and attendant bureaucracies. Seeking capital to fund these reforms, the Ottomans embarked upon a new taxation system. Both private property and a new taxation system were introduced. This not only freed individuals from the land and allowed them to move to the cities (as land became alienable, it could serve as collateral against loans), it also brought investment in agriculture and began, in parts of the empire, to attract foreign capital to export agriculture.[20] The result in the cities was that the "public bureaucratic function increased in importance, as did the bureaucrats themselves; the military establishment became more elaborate; and a new merchant bourgeoisie . . . took root."[21]

Notwithstanding country variation, it was this local bourgeoisie that established the region's first nongovernmental organizations (NGOs) in the late nineteenth and early twentieth centuries, many of which offered charity or social welfare services. Two of the earliest social welfare NGOs in Egypt were the Geography Society and the Association of Islamic Benevolence, created in 1875 and 1878, respectively.[22] However, it must be borne in mind that charity efforts have always been an important aspect of Muslim life; they were not new. *Zakat* (alms), entailing the giving of a percentage of an individual's wealth to the poor, is one of the five pillars of Islam and as such is an obligation. The rules of *zakat* and the collection of *zakat* began during Mohammed's lifetime. *Sadaqa,* a personal form of charity in which meat or clothing, for example, is donated directly to poor families, is also encouraged in Islam. Finally, *waqf* (literally meaning confinement, prohibition, or restraint) has also been in existence since the time of Mohammed. *Waqf* (pl. *awqaf*) is a form of endowment, usually land or buildings, that is donated in perpetuity for philanthropic purposes, such as for the benefit of mosques, schools, orphanages, or charities (alternatively, the proceeds from the endowment are used for these purposes).[23] Historically, therefore, public services and works were established and endowed by the leaders, elders, and notables of the relatively autonomous social formations—for example, religious sects, ethnic groups, tribes, villages—that constituted the region. Amira el-Azhary Sonbol notes the impressive hospitals or *maristans* established by endowments throughout Cairo and built as early as the ninth century.[24] *Waqf* properties were historically controlled by the independent mosques themselves. And *zakat,* while ultimately headed for the state, was collected and redistributed by the *ulema* (religious scholars) through mosque-based *zakat* committees. The nineteenth-century reforms, however, ushered in a slow process of increasing state control. The state began to command increasingly greater areas of responsibility at the expense of other societal groups, particularly religious authorities. With the Tanzimat, therefore, the responsibility for society's social welfare slowly came under the prerogative of the state. In Egypt, for example, the reforms go back to Muhammad Ali, who confiscated much of the *waqf* land and in

1851 created a central administration (as opposed to the mosques) to regulate the administration of *awqaf.*

What make the nongovernmental organizations of the late nineteenth and twentieth centuries and today different from these earlier charity efforts are both the conditions under which NGOs are established and who is establishing and working in them. It was this new local bourgeoisie, not religious clerics or notable elders, who began organizing themselves in the context of the breakdown of traditional societal arrangements and the state's failure to adequately provide. They created organizations in collective efforts to address their own needs as well as those of others. As opposed to earlier charity efforts, these were collective grassroots efforts, not philanthropic endowments. While their actual function was a relatively familiar continuation of early charity efforts, those who provided the charity differed.

It is thus largely the middle class, which many scholars refer to as the petit bourgeoisie, that stepped in and, by establishing NGOs, filled in where the state was lacking.[25] To a large extent this has remained the same today—NGOs continue to be practical responses to the inadequately addressed socioeconomic ills associated with industrialization, migration, and urbanization. However, the petit bourgeoisie has been joined, if not supplanted, by a new middle class or new petit bourgeoisie whose status is not based on birth, blood, or income but on its secular education. While the old petit bourgeoisie is made up of small traders, shopkeepers, self-employed artisans, and small and independent farmers, the new petit bourgeoisie generally consists of white-collar workers engaged in technical, professional, and administrative occupations. They are teachers, bureaucrats, professors, students, technocrats, engineers, physicians, writers, journalists, and middle-ranking army officers. In a historical perspective, the centralizing, standardizing, and secularizing reforms instituted first by Ottoman rulers were continued by the colonial powers and finally by post-independence powers. The policies of the colonial powers after the collapse of the Ottoman Empire after World War I and of the post-colonial independent states continued to play a highly influential role by further expanding state powers, chipping away at the powers of the religious authorities and creating new classes. From the perspective of this book, the most important changes that were introduced by the colonial powers and vastly accelerated by the post-colonial powers were the establishment and broadening of public education and the promotion of the professional civil service. The colonial powers introduced these changes in order to create an educated civil service to carry out its directives. The newly independent states further entrenched these changes both in reaction to the discriminatory policies of the colonial powers and to the elites who helped keep the colonial powers (or colonial puppet powers) in charge.[26] The introduction of mass educa-tion, for example, expanded public education far beyond that which the colonial powers had introduced. The post-colonial powers thus further re-drafted the class map of the region. A new educated white-collared and salaried class began to emerge in the early to mid-twentieth century. This process—the creation of a new middle class—was furthered by the under-mining of other classes because of state policies such as land reform.

By the mid-twentieth century, the old and new petit bourgeoisie were situated between the dominant class, which is largely determined by the ownership of land and large businesses, and the working class made up of workers, peasants, and outcasts. With relatively little land or wealth, the new middle class seeks to advance itself through its education and profes-sional skills. Its members are largely the product of capitalist development, the extension of the market, the development of mass secular schooling, and the intensification of the state in social and economic life.[27]

Indeed, it is precisely this understanding of the new middle class that guides my use of the term "middle class" throughout this book. Adapting a definition used by Dietrich Rueschemeyer, Evelyn Stephens, and John Stephens, I define a class as a group of people who by virtue of what they possess—tangible property, intangible skills—are compelled to engage in the same activities if they want to make the best use of their endowments.[28] Furthermore, united by their similar "possessions," members of a class, as a result, are united by similar status or power positions in society. However, a class need not feel or act as a unit. As Hanna Batatu states, it need not be an organized and self-conscious group: "The members of a class may not be class-conscious in their behaviour but their behaviour could nonetheless be class-conditioned."[29] When I refer to the middle class, I mean specifically the new educated middle class that is distinguished by its secular (as op-posed to religious) higher education. Its "possessions" are its education, which is usually professional. Members of this new class seek to advance themselves through their professional skills and talents as opposed to the use of wealth, land, kinship, or personal connections. This new educated class is most strongly related to the growth of the state in the Middle East and the tremendous expansion of education that occurred during the latter half of the twentieth century. In Egypt, for example, this is most closely as-sociated with the rise and rule of President Jamal Abdel Nasser, the coun-try's first president. As I define the term, members of the new middle class are not defined by occupation per se—for example, by earning one's liveli-hood as a teacher, physician, or engineer—but by possessing the education or skills (or by acquiring the education), and the attendant prestige that should enable one to earn his/her livelihood as a teacher, physician, or engi-neer. In Egypt, for example, we find medical doctors driving taxis. They continue to belong to the new middle class despite the fact that they are only practicing their profession part-time or may have relatively low incomes.

Conversely, using the above definition, the term "the poor" is defined as those who have inadequate "possessions" and as a result are unable to effectively participate in the marketplace, broadly defined. The poor are those who cannot, due to their lack of "possessions," meet their daily needs. They are unable to meet the minimum monthly expenditures per household required to cover the costs of food and other necessary items. It is for this reason that they turn to charity in ISIs and other NGOs.

The new middle class, permeated by members of the old petit bourgeoisie, dominates the creation of NGOs today. The boundaries between the new middle class, or new petit bourgeoisie, and the old petit bourgeoisie remain highly fluid and to a certain extent overlap. The lower echelons of the new middle class, for example, blur the boundaries between the new and old petit bourgeoisie. Studies indicate that the members of the new middle class may be the offspring of members of the old petit bourgeoisie, particularly those from rural areas.[30] Although NGOs are also created by members of the old petit bourgeoisie, they are increasingly being established by the new middle class.

In her study of private voluntary organizations (PVOs) throughout the Arab world, Amani Kandil states that "PVOs have been established by the higher middle-class professionals, who are mainly urban."[31] Similarly, in his study of Egyptian PVOs, Robert Latowsky notes that "Egypt's private, non-profit associations are—like nearly all of their counterparts in other, less developed countries—*middle class* in character and members."[32] The same can be said for both Yemeni and Jordanian voluntary associations. Marina de Regt's study of NGOs in Yemen found that nearly all NGOs are run by the middle class—in particular, by middle-class civil servants who are government employees during the day and association volunteers in the afternoon.[33] Throughout the Arab world, even when their declared objective is to serve the less privileged, NGOs or PVOs[34] are dominated by educated middle-class professionals, including doctors, engineers, and schoolteachers.[35]

Islamic social institutions, therefore, must be put in the context of a changing economy, the growth of the state, and the rise of the middle classes. It is not surprising that the number of ISIs have increased dramatically in recent years as governments of the Middle East have instituted policies of political liberalization, including greater freedoms of association. Concomitant with these political changes have been International Monetary Fund and World Bank economic restructuring programs that have resulted in the "downsizing" of states and state withdrawal from areas

of social concern such as health care. Unable to adequately provide sufficient social welfare services and saddled with massive debts, Middle Eastern
states have been slowly retreating from areas they claimed over 100 years
ago; this process was most intense during the first half of the twentieth
century. Nongovernmental associations and, particularly, Islamic social institutions have been highly successful in filling in the resulting gap. Studies
conservatively estimate the number of Islamic voluntary associations is
2,457 out of a total of 12,832 voluntary associations in Egypt.[36] This
number represents the largest category of PVO in the country.[37] While
exact figures are not available, in Yemen, there are over 2,000 registered
NGOs, approximately 70 percent of which are estimated to be highly conservative or religiously motivated.[38] In Jordan, the largest NGO is the Islamic Center Charity Society (ICCS), run by the Muslim Brotherhood. In
1998, it alone ran forty-two schools and day care centers and a community
college and managed forty-five health clinics and two commercial hospitals.[39] Twelve thousand students attend the Islamic Center Charity Society's
schools and day care centers.[40] In the case of Egypt, this increase in NGOs,
particularly ISIs, occurred after 1976, when former president Anwar Sadat
initiated his economic-opening (*infitah*) policy. In the cases of Jordan and
Yemen, the growth of Islamic institutions, in terms of number and type,
has been more recent—since 1989 in the case of the former and 1990 in
the case of the latter—with the introduction of political liberalization and
democracy.

ISLAMIC ACTIVISM
AND ISLAMIC SOCIAL INSTITUTIONS

The changes wrought by the Tanzimat, however, did not end with the creation of new classes. To a large extent, the growth of the state came at the
expense of religious authority. This in turn has had its own repercussions,
one of which is the rise of Islamic activism, or Islamism. While the roots of
Islamism are complex, in a broad historical perspective, the rise of Islamism
can be understood as a reaction to state encroachment on religious authority; the takeover of mosque-based social welfare services by the state is just
one example. Today the reaction can be seen in two broad responses—radical Islamism and moderate Islamism, the latter of which includes the phenomenon of ISIs. Both of these responses stand in opposition to the secular
state and strive, at least in their stated aims, not just for a change in government but for a change in state type. Within this context, ISIs represent a
moderate response not only to the secular state's inability to provide social
welfare services but against the secular state itself. They represent an "ideology through action"—institutional alternatives to those of the secular state.

In an effort to reform and stave off European domination, Tanzimat reforms involved an attempt to substantially restructure state institutions, largely along European lines. Although these reforms had an initial centralizing effect on Ottoman Islam, they eventually did serious damage to the traditional institutional roots of its authority. Public schools sponsored by the state that used a curriculum based upon technical and scientific—rather than religious—knowledge were created alongside the religious school (*madrassa*). Secular courts using legal codes from the West were introduced which, as their mandates expanded, led to the shrinkage of the jurisdiction of the once-dominant religious courts, eventually confining their authority to issues of personal status. The participation of the *ulema* in the affairs of state was gradually replaced by that of Western-trained technocrats at the highest levels. And where religious institutions and personnel maintained their connections with the state, it was in a subordinate role and was relegated by such state agencies to the departments of religious affairs and/or departments of religious endowments.

The centralizing, standardizing, and secularizing thrust of the Tanzimat reforms thus relegated Islamic authority, the *ulema,* to the sidelines under control of the state. This process was continued and advanced with colonial and post-colonial powers as secular states modeled along European lines asserted themselves. The initial response by Muslim intellectuals to this assault on religious authority and institutions came in the form of the *salafiyya* movement, which sought to tap into the roots of Western power to reform what they saw as a deterioration of the Islamic tradition. Subsequent responses to the perceived increasing domination of Western power and the secularization of state institutions, however, took on an increasingly defensive and antagonistic tone. Rather than striving to seek the revitalization of Islam through Western methods of rational inquiry, this new response refused to be apologetic for Islam and located the roots of the problem in Western secularism and materialism. The secular state, with its attendant relegation of religion to the private sphere, and the Western political thought and powers that upheld the secular state were the problem. The solution lay in the elimination of the secular state and the establishment of a state and societal institutions based on Islamic law and principles.

The Islamist challenge is thus rooted in what Dale Eickelman and James Piscatori refer to as the "invention of tradition."[41] Islamists generally regard the period of the Prophet Mohammed and his first four successors, the "rightly guided caliphs," as one in which there was little divergence between ideals and reality. It is regarded as a period of ideological inspiration or guidance. Islamists thus refer to their project as one of re-Islamization—reimplementing the ideals of Islam as they are believed to have been during the Golden Era of Mohammed and the Rightly Guided Caliphs. Central to this project is the argument that the divergence of ideals from reality following the period of the Rightly Guided is associated with the gradual but increasing separation of church and state, as it were. In the twentieth century, this progressed, Islamists argue, to the emasculation of religious authorities by the state. Islamists' appropriation of what they believe to be this tradition therefore includes the assertion that Islam is *din wa-dawla*—religion and state—that Islam is a comprehensive system encompassing all things material, spiritual, societal, individual, political, and personal.[42]

It is this understanding of Islamism that guides my use of the term throughout this book. I define an Islamic activist, or "Islamist," as a Muslim who attempts to re-Islamize society by encouraging individuals to practice Islam in daily life and to bridge the perceived gap between religious discourse and practical realities.[43] He or she is a Muslim who seeks to actively extend and apply Islam beyond what is commonly regarded in liberal political thought as the private realm and into the public realm. In doing so, Islamic activism (Islamism) promotes the idea of regarding Islam as a complete system, a body of ideas, values, beliefs, and practices encompassing all spheres of life.

This effort to implement Islam is captured in the Islamist conception of *da'wa* (call). In the Islamist's "invention of tradition," the concept of *da'wa* becomes central.[44] Beyond simply proselytizing or preaching (as traditionally operationalized), *da'wa* becomes the very act of "activating" Islam through deed in all spheres of life. As stated by Egyptian Muslim Brother Member of Parliament Ahmad al-Bis, for example, working for politics is working for Islam.[45] *Da'wa* becomes a vital component of practicing Islam. Indeed, *da'wa*—working in a free medical clinic, for example—becomes incumbent upon all Muslims. The Islamist project, therefore, is an attempt to create a seemingly seamless web between religion, politics, and charity and all forms of activism. All of these realms should reinforce each other and promote public virtue and personal piety. Islamic social institutions are thus a form of putting *da'wa* into practice. More important, working or volunteering for or donating to an Islamic social institution as a form of activist *da'wa* (ideology through activism) is an important component of Islamist identity.

An essential aspect of Islamist identity therefore is the creation of alternative institutions to those of the state, particularly social welfare ones. While the Muslim Brotherhood by no means accounts for all of moderate Islamism (nor were the first examples of Islamic social institutions in Egypt, Yemen, and Jordan necessarily established by the Brotherhood), a brief examination of the early Brotherhood in Egypt is instructive.[46] Since its establishment in 1928, the constitution of the Egyptian Muslim Brotherhood has stated its purpose as achieving social justice; providing social security to every citizen; contributing to popular service; resisting ignorance, disease, poverty, and vice; and encouraging charity work.[47] It established numerous private schools, medical services, and charity services —which provided money, food, and clothes—for the poor, aged, orphaned and homeless, to name just a few; it also established a bureau of charity and social services that was responsible for these initiatives. Thousands of Egyptians were affected by its services. One Brotherhood hospital alone treated 51,300 patients in 1947.[48] However, these socioeconomic programs were not ends in themselves. Ideally they would lead to the creation of a harmonious Islamic society without exploitation or oppression.[49] Then, as now, the Brotherhood emphasizes that a society based on Islamic precepts would "promote social security for citizens, narrow the socioeconomic gap between classes, undertake welfare spending to assist those in need, encourage economic solidarity among citizens, respect private property, and enforce the requisite that each able-bodied person must be economically productive."[50]

ISIs are thus not only an alternative to state institutions; they represent the foundations of an alternative society. They stand in direct contrast to secular states that appear to have lost their concern for the poor. By offering successful social welfare services in the name of Islam to their fellow citizens, they represent an ideological and concrete or practical alternative to the present system. As institutions, ISIs are more than just representative of a populist ideology; they are that ideology put into practice and are central to the Islamist vision of a new society and Islamist identity.

Today, as stated above, the Islamist response to the decline of traditional religious authority can be categorized into two broad types, that of "moderate" and "radical" (also called "violent" or "militant") Islamism.[51] A hard-and-fast distinction between moderate and radical or violent Islamism is difficult to make, given that an Islamist group in one country, such as the Muslim Brotherhood in Egypt, may use strictly nonviolent means to achieve its ends, while a similar group in another country, such as the Muslim Brotherhood in Palestine, may use violent means. In addition, even within the same country, certain groups that use violence, such as Hamas, also run charities. Finally, the degree to which moderate and radical networks may or may not be connected to each other also poses a challenge for any definitional distinction between moderate and radical Islamism. Despite these difficulties, I use a distinction based on support for the use of violent or nonviolent means to achieve goals. While both moderate and radical Islamism share the same loosely defined ultimate goal of a society and state governed by Islamic law, radical Islamists are willing to, and do, use violence as a means to achieve their ends.[52] Moderate Islamists, on the other hand, while certainly not unified, reject the use of violence. While this definition implies that an individual can be moderate in one area and radical in another, when discussing Islamic social institutions, I am clearly referring to nonviolent Islamism.

Islamic social institutions thus stand solidly within moderate Islamism. Central to the project of moderate Islamists is the reorganization of society and the establishment of alternative institutions to that of the secular state —institutions based on Islamic values and laws. We therefore find, in addition to religious institutions such as private mosques and political institutions such as national parties, syndicate and university parties and an interrelated network of day care centers, schools, hospitals, charities, facilities for the mentally disabled, detoxification centers, banks, manufacturing businesses, and medical clinics such as the one I visited in Cairo. Within this network of institutions bound by social, institutional, and political ties, solidarity, and identity, ISIs are an attempt to apply the Islamist ideal specifically to the economic or socioeconomic realm. The degree to which there is indeed an Islamic framework within ISIs is one of the topics I investigate in this book.

THE NEW MIDDLE-CLASS ISLAMISTS

It is somewhat ironic that the social groups to whom moderate Islamism most appealed were those increasingly marginalized by the growth of the state—the state that to a large extent had been responsible for their creation. It has been the middle classes that have engaged in the attempt to reorganize society along new institutional lines. During the 1920s and 1930s, at the time of Hassan al-Banna (founder of the Muslim Brotherhood in Egypt), for example, the Brotherhood appealed to primarily urban groups that had lost status because of British control and the impact of Western industrial economies, such as artisans and small-scale manufacturers, as well as groups that had been created by these same forces only to have their upward mobility halted during the Depression—petty bureaucrats, school-teachers, and modern-sector labor.[53] Richard Mitchell's study of the early Brotherhood notes that the Brotherhood was dominated by emergent self-conscious middle-class urban Muslims.[54] The archetypical Muslim Brother was thus probably urban, middle class, literate only in Arabic, politically aware, strongly nationalistic, pious, and had uncertain career prospects.

Today, urban support for the Brotherhood continues to attract the middle classes, but increasingly it draws middle-class professionals, such as doctors, lawyers, and engineers—the new middle class—those who have found that despite their advanced educations (thanks to the state), opportunities for advancement remain largely closed and in the hands of the dominant elites.[55] In the rural areas there is evidence that a heavy proportion of secondary-school teachers are members of the Society.[56] While the Muslim Brotherhood does not constitute all of moderate Islamism, the general profile in the literature of moderate Islamists is therefore one of upwardly mobile, educated, middle-class professionals. In both Yemen and Jordan, for example, in which there are legal Islamic political parties (Hizb al-Islah and the Islamic Action Front (IAF), respectively), and consequently detailed data on party members, an examination of the membership lists is quite telling. The composition of the members of the IAF's founding committee reveals that a disproportionately high number of members are white-collar professionals. Of the 353 founding members of the IAF (1992), 37.7 percent were professionals (this figure excludes businesspeople and salaried employees). This includes twenty-four university professors, twenty-six physicians, twenty-two engineers, sixteen pharmacists, twenty-five lawyers, seventeen managers, and three journalists.[57] In Yemen, Hizb al-Islah presents a similar picture. The Islah Party in Yemen is best understood as a coalition of (northern-based) conservatives who have historically supported the ruling republican regime since it came to power after the 1962 revolution and who share conservative social objectives. Included in this group are prominent tribal leaders and businessmen and several different religious groups that include the Muslim Brotherhood, a pro-Saudi Wahhabi group, and several prominent ideologues with modest personal followings. A 1993 survey conducted among 190 of 196 of Islah's electoral candidates showed that eighty-one had university degrees. The majority of these degrees were bachelor's degrees (sixty), predominantly in the fields of legal and religious studies (thirty-one) or education (twenty-four). Those who did not have a university education were predominantly from the tribal stream of the Party.[58] The Islamists within the Party were precisely those middle-class professionals discussed above.[59]

Both Islah and the IAF thus represent, using Marion Boulby's words, the hopes of an emergent professional class for political power.[60] The upward mobility of Islamists, who come from modest backgrounds, derives from their education, usually in the technical or professional sphere, which sets them apart from their family origins. To a large extent, however, this education has not translated into economic affluence.[61] While the "typical" Islamist has gained dramatically in education, prestige, and social status, his/her career ambitions are generally frustrated by both the economic conditions in his/her respective country and by the stranglehold of established, generally Westernized, elites over key economic and political sectors. While the education of Islamists has certainly allowed them to improve their economic standing above that of their parents, it has not necessarily fulfilled their expectations.

In this vein, scholars repeatedly refer to Islamists as deriving from an alienated class or a class caught in between. Mustapha al-Sayyid, for example, states that "those who carry out . . . activities in mosques . . . are not traditional . . . shaykhs, . . . but young professionals who received their education in the country's Western-type universities and who are alienated for a variety of reasons from the country's social and political system."[62] Indeed, in the case of Egypt, Malcolm Kerr noted as early as 1965 that the radical or oppositional potential of the educated strata could be attributed to the gap between high expectations and limited economic opportunities.[63] This alienation is experienced in the social, economic, and political realms. In Jordan, Islamists seek a better school system than the public system, yet they cannot afford the Western-based private school system available to the country's political elites. In Egypt, Islamist doctors struggling to make ends meet have turned the doctors' syndicate into an effective tool for providing its members with material goods, such as refrigerators, at reduced rates. In Yemen, educated young women from families that are economically vulnerable, who find that their education is not sufficient for job opportunities elsewhere and who are constricted by social norms that disapprove of women traveling about in mixed circles, find jobs as teachers in the Islamic charities. ISIs therefore represent not just an institutional challenge to the secular state but a challenge by the new middle class for political power.

ISIS AND THE STATE

The politically potent message ISIs signify simply by existing is not lost on the states of the region. Nor is the fact that ISIs alleviate the economic burden of the states. Given the inability of Middle Eastern states without oil wealth to address the needs of their populations, the growth of ISIs is not surprising—both as a solution to underemployment or unemployment among educated professionals (such as doctors in need of extra income) and as a solution to address the needs of the poor. From the perspective of Middle Eastern states, the growth of NGOs, while encouraged, is largely unwelcome. States warily support NGOs, and particularly ISIs, because they satisfy the poor and lower middle classes and limit the number of those who seek help from the overburdened states.[64] In all three case studies in the book, ISIs are the most successful grassroots initiatives helping the poor and the middle classes today. Furthermore, in the context of decreasing state services and Islamist opposition, Middle Eastern states can neither deny their citizenries alternative sources of social services nor appear to be non-Islamic or, worse, anti-Islamic, by prohibiting specifically Islamic social institutions. In fact, secular states in the region have attempted to undercut the Islamist movement by attempting to appropriate Islam and Islamic symbolism for themselves. As a means of legitimizing the state and undermining the Islamist movement, for example, states in the region have sponsored their own Islamic institutions, such as Islamic Cultural Centers in Jordan.

The result is a conflicting approach toward NGOs, particularly ISIs. On the one hand, Middle Eastern governments seek to curb NGO activities because of the political and symbolic threat they pose to secular states. NGOs must overcome various bureaucratic hurdles in order to register and are regularly monitored and controlled. Cases of closure by the authorities (without the right of appeal in the courts) are not unheard of. On the other hand, despite government rhetoric and even legislation designed to control and monitor NGOs (particularly ISIs), ISIs exist, indeed flourish, with the aid and encouragement of government and state. This support can be financial or legislative. Islamic social institutions benefit from subsidies; government-sponsored training, advice, and joint ventures; and/or legislation that privileges them uniquely. State support can also be expressed by a lack of enforcement—a selective exemption from the bureaucratic controls and regulations applied to other NGOs.

Middle Eastern states are aware that what is at stake is the secular state and the dominant powers that uphold it. Between Islamic social institutions and the state, therefore, there is a symbolic struggle contesting the very boundaries between public and private, between secular and religious, and over the figures and nature of authority and the right to rule (and even over basic Islamic concepts).[65] Within this context, social activities conducted in the name of Islam become politically charged—even if those working within them may not attribute political significance to their activities. Social welfare activities (regardless of the intent of those providing them) become part of a larger conscious and unconscious effort to transform tradition as well as a symbolic political act suggesting dissatisfaction with state institutions. ISIs are therefore central to understanding political change in Egypt, Jordan, and Yemen. They lie at the heart of the contest between secular and religious forces in the region.

WHY EGYPT, JORDAN, AND YEMEN?

Within this broadly shared historical and political context, the choice of Egypt, Jordan, and Yemen as case studies for this book was based on a variety of methodological and practical criteria. Most important, the data from these three countries offered an excellent opportunity to examine different types and structures of Islamic social institutions and thus allowed me to question whether or not the horizontal ties I had witnessed differed according to different institutional type, structure, and targeted patron. The three case studies further differ in the degree to which they have institutional (formal) as opposed to social (informal) ties to the other Islamic social institutions, in particular the Islamic political parties, in their respective networks. Within Egypt, the majority of Islamic medical clinics belong to individual or independent associations registered in one location or community, and have largely only social ties to other associations. Due to the restrictive nature of Law 32, which regulates associational life in Egypt, only a very limited number of Islamic associations are nationally registered with a mother association and branches. In contrast to Egypt, nationally registered associations are permitted in both Yemen and Jordan, and in both cases the largest nationally registered associations are Islamic associations—the Charitable Society for Social Welfare (also known as the Islah Charitable Society) and the Islamic Center Charity Society (ICCS), respectively. Both the Islah Charitable Society and the ICCS differ from ISIs in Egypt in that they are not only structurally large institutions, with branches throughout their respective countries, but they both have openly close and legal ties to Islamic political parties. The Islah Charitable Society has financial and social ties to the Islah Party, although it technically does not belong to it. In Jordan, the ICCS was established by the Muslim Brotherhood, which also helped establish, and now dominates, the Islamic Action Front. Both associations, furthermore, run a significant number of nonprofit activities as part of their charity activities. In addition to the services they offer for the poor—food, clothing, and aid distribution; schooling for orphans; and medical care—they have established private commercial schools and hospitals. This phenomenon is far more advanced in Jordan, where a greater percentage of the ICCS's activities are essentially commercial enterprises charging relatively expensive user fees. The three case studies enabled me to examine the role of horizontal networks in independent Islamic social institutions and national Islamic social institutions (or "chains"), charity and non-profit Islamic social institutions activities, and Islamic social institutions offering services such as medical care and those offering financial and material aid.

SOCIAL MOVEMENT THEORY:
NETWORKS, PARTICIPATION, AND IDENTITY

I use social movement theory as an aid in understanding ISIs. An underlying question of the book is whether or not ISIs are exceptional or unique; in other words, if they behave as social movement organizations elsewhere. I argue that ISIs do in fact act as social movement organizations globally and confirm the literature on social movement theory. The research on social movements overwhelmingly supports the fact that social movements largely consist of multiple organizations bound together by institutional and social ties. The social networks in which social movement organizations are embedded are generally homogeneous in nature, reflecting a specific social category. In the case of ISIs, this social category is the educated middle class. According to social movement theory, it is through social networks that individuals come to participate in the activities of social movement organizations. Finally, social networks are essential to the negotiation and renegotiation of movement identity. Indeed, social movement theory is most helpful in illuminating the formation of solidarity and consensus that often occurs in ISIs and the middle-class networks that develop around the ISI activities and their mission. In these regards, the study of ISIs confirms (and is enlightened by) research on social movements globally. However, the case study of ISIs challenges the prevailing view within resource mobilization theory that these rewards and benefits play a strictly positive role. The very success of a social movement organization in providing these benefits can undermine a movement when the instrumental needs of the organization and/or movement override the goals of the social movement organization or become the goals in and of themselves.

According to resource mobilization theory, social movements are a large complex set of collective events oriented toward some general social change goal.[66] Social movement organizations constitute the essential institutional backbone of social movements or, as Bert Klandermans states, the "structural vehicles of the social construction of protest."[67] In other words, a social movement organization is the "carrier organization of social movement aims."[68] Social movement organizations do not operate in isolation from one another. Resource mobilization theory conceptualizes a web of linkages or interactions connecting social movement organizations to the broader social movement. Broadly speaking, linkages between social movement organizations can be found at two levels—between organizations and between individuals. At the organizational level, linkage networks develop between a social movement organization and any other organization that provides periodic donations, makes occasional statements, or has one or more of its leaders working as board members of the social movement organization.[69] Individual linkages are established by the multiple and overlapping affiliations of members as well as between social movement organizations and the general public. As is the case with interorganizational linkages, "individual" linkages or social networks, depending on their strength (the degree of resource transfer) and breadth (the extensiveness of linkages), can provide a social movement organization with a membership base, legitimacy, money, prestige, information, and power.[70] If we apply this to Islamic activism, Islamic medical clinics as social movement organizations become independent institutions with their own distinct aims and strategies: they have connections (usually through common friends) to other Islamic institutions such as day care centers or schools, they actively apply Islam to the public sphere, and they consciously or unconsciously engage in a larger symbolic political protest against the ruling secular state in support of the implementation of an Islamic state based on Islamic law, *shariʿa*. Organizational linkages exist between Jordan's ICCS and the Muslim Brotherhood which founded it and between Yemen's Islah Charitable Society and the Islah Party which donates to the Charity. Individual or personal linkages (social networks) are what connect a doctor in an Islamic medical clinic to his/her friend who works in another medical clinic or Islamic day care. They are the linkages allowing a female student at an Islamic university in Sanaʿa to meet a friend who works at the Islah Charitable Society at an informal weekly Qurʾanic study group in another friend's home.

Within this conceptualization, resource mobilization theorists generally theorize that social networks play their most significant role in terms of movement participation and/or recruitment. Informal groups of people—social groups—provide the rudiments of organization for a movement, such as communication, that are needed to translate talk into action.[71] Social ties are good for conveying information about alternative options—political, social, economic—between socially related actors.[72] This form of communication helps members overcome a feeling of powerlessness and the belief that they are individually unable to change societal conditions. As Doug McAdam explains, when individuals lack contact with each other, they are less likely to attribute social problems to the system and more likely simply to chalk them up to personal attributions. Without communication along social ties, there is a greater chance that individuals will feel that a problem is their own and not a systemic problem that affects numerous individuals and that can be changed. Ferree and Miller note that the chance of attributing a problem to a system appears to be greatest among extremely homogeneous people who are in intense regular contact with each other. In the words of McAdam, "cognitive liberation" is most likely to occur among those with homogenous personal social ties. Furthermore, people who are integrated into interpersonal networks are more likely to perceive a greater chance of a positive outcome from social action than those who are not and, as a result, are more likely to get involved.[73] Social networks thus pull participants into action.

The importance of social networks in participation in a social movement is certainly supported by McAdam's famous study of the 1964 Mississippi Freedom Summer project. McAdam notes that volunteers in the project had more prior ties to other project volunteers than those who withdrew from the project. More to the point, he found that while weak (or no) social ties had little impact on whether or not an individual became a participant in the project, strong interpersonal ties with prior members had a significant influence. Having a close friend who was a participant had a far greater influence on participation than having a friend of a friend. The reverse also held true; the withdrawal of a close friend from the project also increased the chance of withdrawal.[74]

Similarly, in his study of mobilization for the environmental movement in the United States, James Kitts notes the positive relationship between recruitment and in-group ties. His findings confirm that members are more likely to share the level of involvement of others who are located nearby in their field of social relations.[75] Examining the data from ten different studies of social movements, David Snow, Louis Zurcher, and Sheldon Eckland-Olson also argue that the results are clear—social networks constitute the primary source of recruits for movements. Data concerning the Nichiren Shoshu religious movement reveals that public proselytizing efforts are not very productive. Out of forty forays studied, only two were successful and resulted in recruits to the movement. The vast majority of Nichiren Shoshu recruits were the result of preexisting, extramovement interpersonal ties. More than three-quarters of the sample of Nichiren Shoshu members stated that they were recruited into the movement by relatives, friends, or acquaintances.[76] Similarly, when Mormons proselytize from door to door without the aid of social ties, the success rate is only 0.1 percent. However, if a Mormon friend or relative provides his home as the place where missionary contact occurs, the odds of success reach 50 percent.[77]

In their study of religious sects and cults, Rodney Stark and William Bainbridge also found "overwhelming support for the crucial role played by social networks in the formation and growth of such groups."[78] In their study of the Moonies, the early followers of Reverend Sun Myung Moon, they found that when interpersonal bonds did not develop, newcomers failed to join. Recruitment to the movement predominantly occurred through preexisting social networks. In fact, they note that

the great majority of members of the cult at that time had been mutually linked by long-standing relationships prior to any contact with Moon's movement. In fact, once Moon's missionary had made her first American convert, all subsequent members were drawn from this first recruit's immediate social network until the group uprooted itself from Eugene, Oregon, and moved to San Francisco. In San Francisco it was unable to grow for a considerable time because its members were strangers lacking social ties to potential new recruits. Indeed, some new recruits continued to come out of the original Eugene network. Only when the cult found ways to connect with other newcomers to San Francisco and develop serious relationships with them did recruitment resume.[79]

Other research on the Church of the Sun confirms these results, as does the case of the Jesus Movement and a study on Mennonites; in each case, interpersonal bonds strongly influenced retention of orthodox tenets of the sect. Stark and Bainbridge furthermore cite an interesting example of a radical religious group that retreated into underground shelters in order to survive Armageddon. While eventually the group leader had a new revelation and the entire group left the shelters en masse, studies on the group members reveal that the majority of "early defectors" were those members with no close relatives in the group. Of the sixty adult members in the shelter, forty-five were members of an extended kinship structure linking them to the three leaders of the group. Seventy-five percent of the group formed a single social network based on kinship, and nearly all the other members were longtime friends of those in the kinship network. Of those who left the shelter early, two-thirds had no close relatives in the group. As Stark and Bainbridge state, for those who had to abandon their families and faith to leave the group defection was rare, but for those without familial ties to the group defection was the rule. So strong is the evidence of the influence of interpersonal ties upon recruitment to social movements that Stark and Bainbridge argue that all faiths, including conventional religions, rest on the influences of networks. They point to studies on Episcopalianism, Methodism, and the charismatic movement among American Roman Catholics. Among evangelical Protestants, "born-again" students are very likely to have "born-again" friends.[80]

Indeed, the Mormons are well aware of the importance of social ties to successful recruiting. In their study of Mormon recruiting strategies in the United States, Stark and Bainbridge note that Mormon missionaries are exhorted to use their existing social networks to create new friendships as part of their effort to gain new recruits. Mormon recognition of the importance of social bonds for successful recruitment is evidenced by the fact that activists are advised to give personal testimony to their faith only after a strong friendship bond is created. Of the thirteen-step set of instructions for recruitment (published in a widely read Mormon magazine), activists are repeatedly admonished to refrain from discussing religion until completion of ten prior steps aimed at developing tighter social relations.[81]

Research on recruitment patterns from social movements around the world thus strongly indicates that "individuals are drawn into participation not by the force of the ideas or even the individual attitudes but as the result of their embeddedness in associational networks that render them 'structurally available' for protest activity."[82] Networks, particularly social networks, make people available for recruitment, make them more inclined to join (particularly if many friends and family members are already members), and make them the targets of recruitment. Due to both push and pull factors, people are structurally predisposed to join social movement organizations.[83] Interpersonal ties encourage the extension of an invitation to participate and they ease the uncertainties one experiences when joining a new group.[84] Social bonds also help potential joiners overcome various perceived costs of joining a social movement.[85] Indeed, John Lofland and Rodney Stark's study of the followers of the Moonies found that "persons were sometimes drawn by their attachment to group members to move into the Moonie commune while still openly expressing rejection of the Moon ideology.... Rather than being drawn to the group because of the appeal of its ideology, people were drawn to the ideology because of their ties to the group—final conversion was coming to accept the opinions of one's friends." In their words, "blood is thicker than attitudes."[86]

These findings are confirmed in Egypt, Jordan, and Yemen. In all three ISIs, we see the important role of social networks as conduits of donations and of ISI participation or involvement. ISIs find their employees and volunteers through social networks—through the friend of a friend of a friend of a.... In Cairo's Islamic medical clinics only a limited number of the largest and wealthiest clinics have formal hiring procedures. The majority of clinics neither advertises for nor interviews prospective employees. In Jordan, the director of an ICCS center will contact his friends, both in Jordan and abroad, for donations. And in Yemen, women in the Islah Charitable Society find, through word of mouth, a seamstress who is willing to sew clothing for the poor for little or no financial compensation. In all cases, individuals were coaxed and encouraged to become volunteers and employees (social movement participants) because of their social ties, their friends. As social movement theorists argue, the stronger the tie, the stronger the influence.[87] Individuals are drawn into participation by the encouragement of their friends or the desire not to be left out and lose friends.[88] While prior attitudes or predispositions or goals are not irrelevant, they are not enough to account for those who participate in a movement.[89] Interpersonal bonds come first and then ideology, not the reverse.[90]

According to social movement theory, the impact of this recruitment process itself is that social movements tend to be homogeneous in nature. The constituency of social movement organizations and social movements, regardless of type, most often follows specific lines of social categorization—for example, race, gender, religion, or class. As Bert Klandermans states, "as a rule, the set of individuals interacting in one's social networks—especially one's friendship networks—is relatively homogenous and composed of people not too different from oneself."[91]

Bert Klandermans and Dirk Oegema's study of the Hague peace demonstrations in 1983 strongly indicates that people are not only more likely to join a movement if approached by people they know, but that this results in social homogeneity. In the case of the Hague peace demonstrations, participants in the movement tended to be highly educated, left-leaning young professionals. This was not because highly educated individuals were more sensitive to political or economic developments, but because these individuals were more connected with the social networks engaged in recruitment. The authors found that people who were not reached by the peace movement were generally on the right side of the political spectrum. Social networks tended to remain on the left, thus not reaching the "right side" of the political spectrum. Stated differently, the composition of the peace platform reproduced itself in the composition of the group reached by the mobilization attempts.[92]

So prevalent is this tendency that, in order to reflect the socially homogeneous nature of social movements, Charles Tilly utilizes the word "cat-net" (an amalgam of category and network) to signify a social category with a collective identity.[93] While direct mailings, posters, and the like can be successful in recruiting new members from the mobilization potential (people most likely to share the same views as social movement organization members because of similar lifestyle preferences or social category) to a social movement,[94] face-to-face interaction with a trusted individual from one's social network is the most successful way to ensure participation.

Furthermore, social movement theory is strongly supported by the empirical evidence that horizontal and not vertical ties are being developed in Islamic social institutions. In fact, the literature on social movements argues that even when large-scale coalitions are formed between different networks and social movement organizations and a movement indeed becomes more heterogeneous, the primary solidarity of most actors remains with the homogenous social networks within which their identity was forged. While a social movement may eventually encompass different streams and in doing so potentially becomes not only significantly larger but more heterogeneous in nature, it often remains vulnerable to these fault lines between different streams. In their examination of the ecology movement in Milan, for example, Mario Diani and Giovanni Lodi state that the interconnections between the three currents within the movement should not be taken as a sign of increasing integration. Each of the streams maintains a distinct cultural and political approach to ecology issues.[95] Along similar lines, Ben Schennick's study of the peace movement in the Netherlands in the 1980s demonstrates the potential fragility of heterogeneous movements. When the Interchurch Peace Council (the social movement organization representing the Dutch peace movement throughout the 1960s and 1970s) announced its decision to depart from its strategy of abstaining from political action in 1977, it was not able to produce consensus in the churches and to mobilize a clear majority of church members to participate in protest activities. Despite its growth in numbers, the change in strategy brought the divisions between churches to light. More important, it also brought into the open the differences between church members and the new nonchurch (predominantly left-wing) members in the movement.[96]

The theoretical literature also is generally unanimous regarding cross-class recruitment and alliances between the middle classes and the poor. Cross-class alliances are weak and short-lived. Looking specifically at the interclass alliance that formed the pro-democracy movement in the 1970s in Brazil, Maria Alves notes that the alliance was not able to sustain itself.[97] She argues that working-class interests were consistently and systematically bypassed by the middle-class membership. Specific working-class interests were pushed aside in order to maintain a united program and front. Eventually, according to Alves, as the movement became more successful, drawing more and more (predominantly poor and working-class) people to the streets, the sheer vastness of the movement frightened the middle classes—almost as much as it frightened the military they opposed. Afraid of losing hegemonic control over the interclass alliance, the middle classes entered negotiations with the military supporting the indirect election of the president by the electoral college against which it had previously fought. In essence, it abandoned the working class and concentrated on its own needs.

Similarly, in their exhaustive historical comparative examination of democratization of advanced capitalist countries in Latin America, Central America, and the Caribbean, Dietrich Rueschemeyer, Evelyn Stephens, and John Stephens also note the difficulty, indeed fragility, of interclass alliances. Looking in particular at the middle classes, they argue that the attitudes of the middle classes toward the working classes (their natural allies in the struggle against the landed upper classes and the political power they possess) was not consistent. Alliances depended on the needs for and possibilities of an alliance with the working classes: if the middle classes "started feeling threatened by popular pressures under a democratic regime, they turned to support the imposition of an authoritarian alternative."[98]

Participation in social movement activities thus occurs along homogeneous networks, and this tends to reproduce the homogeneity of a movement. Furthermore, the networks of class-based movements are largely horizontal. According to social movement theory, we would expect and do find that the social networks within and connecting ISIs are predominantly horizontal, binding middle-class members with each other. While there is a formal vertical relationship between the middle class and the poor, such as that between a doctor and a patient, these ties are weak and are not part of the social networks in which ISIs are embedded.

Robert Putnam's study of regional governments in Italy is highly instructive in this regard.[99] At the core of Putnam's thesis is the argument that social capital, such as trust, norms of reciprocity, and networks of civic engagement, are central to the success of successful cooperation and organization (including social organization such as democracy).[100] Most important, he argues that horizontal networks—such as those that I argue connect and underlie ISIs—are far more successful than vertical networks (those linking unequal agents in asymmetric relations of hierarchy and dependence) at sustaining the social trust and cooperation necessary for an organization. This is, in part, because the threat of exploitation undermines the development of trust in vertical networks.[101]

Obviously, as Putnam states, almost all networks are mixes of the horizontal and the vertical: "Even bowling teams have captains, while prison guards occasionally fraternize with inmates."[102] Nevertheless, as he states, the basic contrast between web-like and "maypole-like" networks is reasonably clear. Within ISIs, vertical networks do exist, not only between the clients (the poor) and the patrons (the doctors, for example), but also between the employees in the ISIs (the doctors, for example) and the directors. Horizontal networks, I argue, dominate.

Furthermore, horizontal networks, such as the middle-class networks in which ISIs are embedded, are highly conducive to the development of social capital—trust, solidarity, and identity—that underlie an organization and social movement. In fact, social movement theory has demonstrated that much of what goes on within social networks is the formation of consensus. In the words of Bert Klandermans, people tend to validate information by comparing their interpretations of grievances with significant others, particularly like-minded individuals.[103] "Grievance frames" are thus formed in close social networks, as are collective identities; expectations of social solidarity, loyalty, and trust are developed. Rather than simply sustaining the organization, activists use networks to create what Alberto Melucci calls "networks of meaning"—communities that accept, internalize, and promote a particular set of values.[104] All of these elements are vital to a successful social movement. Steven Pfaff notes that despite the riskiness of the endeavor, the East German revolution was facilitated and made possible by the creation of collective identities and social solidarities that arose in private spheres of trusted friends and associates. Especially in repressive regimes, where open public discourse is eliminated, small personalistic groups based on informal ties and loyalty are key to providing the only avenues for genuine participation. Furthermore, Pfaff argues, this suggests that instead of viewing identities as constructed privately and prior to participation, identity should be seen as a "dynamic construct drawn from collective narratives."[105] Identity formation is an ongoing process of negotiation and renegotiation that occurs during the entire life cycle of a movement.[106]

Within ISIs, we find that the women volunteering for the Islah Charitable Society in Yemen form a web-like network with other middle-class women in Qurʾanic study groups, in the Islah Party, or at other Islamist institutions such as the Islamic universities or schools. Through their activities, Islamist women in the Charity engage large and different social networks of women, bringing non-Islamists in contact with Islamist networks and worldviews. Depending on a woman's degree of involvement in the Charity, new bonds of friendship may develop between women as they work together to achieve a goal, whether it is sewing clothing or donating books.

As a result, girls and women may slowly enter new Islamist networks that encompass many aspects of life—networks that eventually may lead them to withdraw from their previous childhood friends. New circles of women who are gradually developing a common activist understanding of *daʿwa* and are engaged in *daʿwa* (whether it be for the Islah Society, the Islah Party, or themselves) are created. This potential reconfiguration of social circles or clusters thus both breaks down and builds upon existing social networks to create new clusters or subgroups bound by an activist understanding of Islam and a commitment to *daʿwa* activities. These women do not experience an epiphany in which they undergo a radical change and identify themselves as Islamists; rather, what were once perceived as simple acts of religiously inspired charity gradually become forms of activism, of *daʿwa*. Gradually, and often unconsciously, an increasingly greater sphere of activism is perceived as part of religious practice. This transformation in perception has an impact upon women's sense of community and may inform their self-identity. As the literature indicates, it is a logical outcome of SMO/ISI participation. In the terminology of social movement theory, these women slowly become engaged in a process of negotiating and renegotiating a collective identity—an Islamist collective identity based on *daʿwa*. Within these new social groups and networks, the Islamist identity and ideology is reinforced through deed and through word.

The breakdown and creation of new social circles that I witnessed in Yemen confirms the dominant view within the social movement theory literature. Although members of a protest organization may have joined because of a preexisting social tie to an activist, they are also introduced to new social networks and may form new social relations while participating in collective protest. The prevailing view within the literature is that once a member becomes part of a movement, new social ties matter more than old ones.[107] New bonds are created (and presumably old ones are reinforced) along a new common identity, common sense of solidarity, and common vision. These newly created bonds and networks become the fabric of the social movement.

SOCIAL MOVEMENT THEORY,
SELECTIVE INCENTIVES, AND BENEFITS

According to the social movement literature, participation in social move-ment organizations such as ISIs and the horizontal social networks in which they are embedded is to a large extent facilitated by the benefits that social movement organizations provide their participants. In the case of ISIs, these benefits include well-paying jobs, flexible work schedules, and private schools for their children. According to the literature, benefits, or "selective incentives," play a positive role. The study of ISIs, however, indicates that this is not always the case.

Debra Friedman and Doug McAdam confirm that networks draw indi-viduals into collective action by providing incentives and rewards—both nonmaterial and material. Refusing to respond to the call of network part-ners means the potential loss of all benefits provided by that tie.[108] These benefits may be social, such as friendship or social honor, or material, such as jobs.[109] The encouragement of important others to participate is in itself a social incentive.[110] McAdam refers to the myriad of interpersonal rewards that ongoing participation in a group or informal association provides as the "structures of solidarity incentives."[111] Rodney Stark and William Bain-bridge, citing the example of Protestant groups in predominantly Catholic Guatemala City, note that prior to joining, members had had especially weak social ties compared to their neighbors who remained Catholic. The act of joining Protestant groups thus provided gratifying relationships, and through them the members acquired and maintained Protestant beliefs. The two authors point out that the Ananda cult similarly provides its mem-bers with companionship unavailable in the larger society.[112] Regarding his study of the Moonies, Stark observes

> remarkable improvements in the ability of some members to manage inter-personal relations. They came to the group suffering greatly from low self-es-teem and lack of confidence that disrupted their interactions with others. . . . Forging strong affective ties to other group members quite noticeably raised the self-esteem of new recruits. . . . Moreover, direct rewards available to cult and sect members are not limited to affection. Groups such as the Hare Krishnas and the Moonies offer specific material inducements—they clothe, feed, and shelter adherents. Indeed, they offer them a career that, at least within the group, enjoys considerable prestige. . . . Furthermore, there is considerable scope for ambition. . . . Some members can rise to positions of considerable status and power. Bainbridge found that the original core mem-bers of The Power lived in considerable luxury and exercised a great deal of authority over newer members (including sexual access).[113]

Indeed, ISIs are not the only groups to provide incentives to their participants. Many groups, aware of the seduction of incentives, consciously provide various forms of rewards. Stark and Bainbridge note that the Mormons' thirteen-step instructional program for recruiting new members reveals a strong priority on "showering tangible rewards upon potential new members."[114] And Snow, Zurcher, and Eckland-Olson observe that both the Moonies and the Nichiren Shoshu strategically go about "the business of 'luring' and 'securing' recruits." Both of their respective recruitment processes are organized to gradually "sell" potential members the benefits of participation and thereby provide them with reasons for joining and remaining members of the respective movements.[115]

So important are selective incentives that Mancur Olson argues that, other than coercion, there is really no other way to get collective action going.[116] Selective incentives may be positive or negative—they can punish a member for reneging or reward or induce one to participate. Only such an incentive, Olson argues, will stimulate a rational individual to act in a group-oriented way as opposed to pursuing individual interests. The incentives must be selective, in that they by and large are reserved for those in the group and not for outsiders. Olson concurs with other theorists that these incentives may be economic or they may be less tangible and include prestige, friendship, and social status. Olson does not discuss any negative side effects with regard to selective incentives—they play a necessary and positive role.

The case study of ISIs, however, challenges the prevailing view within resource mobilization theory that these rewards and benefits play a strictly positive role. In the case of ISIs we see that the provision of benefits by a social movement organization, such as well-paying jobs with flexible work schedules, can both help and hinder the organization and perhaps even the movement. While there is no doubt that various benefits have been pivotal to middle-class participation in ISIs, the very provision of benefits is creating a tension between the stated aims or goals of ISIs and the needs of the Islamist movement. While Islamists establish ISIs in order to address the needs of the poor, the requirements of ISIs (their need for a pool of educated doctors, for example) and the needs of the Islamist movement to expand its membership base by providing benefits for the middle class mean that ISIs do not necessarily prioritize the needs of the poor over those of the middle class. While the ICCS in Jordan loudly boasts of its efforts to alleviate poverty in Jordan, its most prominent "charity" activity is that of the Islamic Hospital—a relatively expensive hospital that is inaccessible to Jordan's poor.[117] In Egypt, the best Islamic clinics are located in the more affluent areas of Cairo—where the holders and donors of money are located. In Yemen, the Islah Charitable Society in Hodeidah offers day camp for children during the summer at exorbitant rates. This tendency has not gone unnoticed by the general public, including the middle class. The mere fact that in Jordan the Islamic Hospital is commonly referred to as the "Criminal Hospital"—a reference to its high fees—is telling evidence of the negative side effects offering benefits can have.

However, few social movement theorists view any possible negative repercussion from the benefits social movement organizations have to offer. Hanspeter Kriesi briefly states that to the extent that the provision of selective incentives becomes an end in itself, the social movement organization has turned into a business enterprise.[118] He does not provide any empirical evidence, however. Frances Fox Piven and Richard Cloward have written in an in-depth manner on the deleterious effect of benefits and rewards. In their study of poor people's movements, they argue that "organization can hurt organizing." They argue that formal organization is detrimental to poor people's movements, such as the civil rights movement, because as they formalize, they become vulnerable to internal oligarchy and stasis and to external integration with and co-optation by the elites they are lobbying for changes. Organizational demands (and temptations) soon supersede the needs of the membership. Within this larger argument, the authors discuss the specific concerns of this book, the provision of benefits to members. One example they cite is that of the welfare rights movement in the United States. Established by middle-class activists, the movement offered poor, relatively powerless people various leadership positions. However, these positions soon became a source of intense preoccupation and competition. As they state:

> Considering the hard and dreary lives which most welfare recipients had previously led, the rewards of prestige and organizational influence which accrued to those who could win and hold office were enormous. An equally enormous investment in the politics of leadership naturally followed. These circumstances constrained the expansion of membership, for the leaders came to have an investment in membership stasis.[119]

Once a leader got into power, he/she tended to focus on cultivating and strengthening their ties with the group that brought them to power and not on increasing the movement's membership.[120] However, Piven and Cloward deal predominantly with the issue of organizational form and only tangentially with the issue of benefits and rewards.

The case study of ISIs strongly indicates that the strategy of luring and securing movement participants through the provision of various benefits can have a negative effect upon a movement. The case studies do not dispute the fact that benefits can and do aid the expansion of a social movement organization's participants; however, when the provision of benefits themselves comes at the expense of the stated goals of the organization, the long-term impact upon the movement can be detrimental. Particularly in the case of social movement organizations in which the goal of the organization is to serve a different audience than that of the membership of the movement, the provision of benefits to the movement's membership runs the risk of overriding or sacrificing the goals of the social movement organization. The very success of an organization at providing benefits to lure and secure movement members (or, ironically, to operationalize the goal of the social movement organization) can undermine a movement when they override the goals of the social movement organization or become the goals themselves.

PULLING IT ALL TOGETHER: ISLAMIST NETWORKS AND THE NEW MIDDLE CLASS IN EGYPT, JORDAN, AND YEMEN

Based on the three case studies of Egypt, Jordan, and Yemen, I argue that Islamic social institutions are run by and for the middle class—specifically members of the educated middle class whose career ambitions rest on their secular, largely professional educations. Because of the operational and instrumental needs of Islamic social institutions and of the Islamist movement of which they are part, we consistently find that the needs of the poor are sacrificed. This is the result of the operating demands of the Islamic social institutions as well as of strategic decisions to cater to and thereby strengthen the largely middle-class membership of the movement. In the course of attending both to the operating imperatives of Islamic social institutions and to the interests of the middle class, strong middle-class social ties and networks are forged and reinforced. Islamic social institutions thus are embedded in middle-class social networks. As participants engage in ISI activities, a strong sense of teamwork, trust, and solidarity develops and new social networks are created. By bringing social networks, Islamist and non-Islamist, together in the provision of charity, ISIs facilitate the introduction of an activist or Islamist worldview to new social circles. However, I argue that while this gradual accumulation of social capital is the basis of a social movement, it is not a social revolution.[121] The case study of Islamic social institutions indicates that moderate Islamism seeks more to coexist and compete with the dominant institutions and social arrangements than to dramatically alter them. Most important, I argue that the strategy of catering to middle-class needs undermines the movement in the long term.

Each of the three ISIs under examination owes its existence and viability to its ability to attract educated middle-class donors, volunteers, and employees. The means by which the respective ISIs do so is their utilization of and dependence upon middle-class social networks—those who have time, money, and skills to offer. The heart and soul of ISI funding is through individual appeals—largely verbal, sometimes written—to neighbors, fellow workers, and friends. Quite simply, for an ISI to succeed, it needs an active and well-connected director or board of directors. Directors of ICCS branch centers energetically write, telephone, and visit their friends both within Jordan and abroad for regular donations. In Yemen, volunteers for the Islah Charitable Society approach friends for donations at the end of Qur'anic study group sessions. In Cairo, founders of an Islamic medical clinic encourage neighboring community members to donate cement, iron pillars, and windows, and electrical wiring in the building of the clinic. In this sense, the overlapping networks between the home, mosque, workplace, other ISIs, clubs, and even friends living abroad make the establishment and continuation of an ISI possible. These same middle-class networks provide necessary contacts in the bureaucracy to facilitate the legal registration of the ISI. Without connections within the government—friends, former army mates, or schoolmates—ISIs would not be able to expedite the frustrating bureaucratic quagmire necessary to register an NGO and ensure a successful outcome. Middle-class networks are also the most important source of volunteers and "skilled" labor. The case study of Islamic medical clinics in Cairo reveals that the vast majority of clinics hire their doctors and nurses by word of mouth—without advertising, targeted recruiting, or interviewing. Through conversations among friends, clinic directors learn of the brother of a friend of a friend who is a doctor and is looking for extra income or experience in the evenings.

Beyond appeals to friends, ISIs must be able to attract doctors and nurses to their organizations on a professional level. ISIs must be able to meet middle-class needs that are not being met (or are being insufficiently addressed) elsewhere. When possible, ISIs thus engage in strategic decisions concerning hiring and adopt strategies of providing incentives for a middle-class doctor to work in an Islamic clinic as opposed to elsewhere (or in addition to elsewhere). They must lure and secure employees and volunteers by offering various benefits or selective incentives.[122] In Egypt, where the underemployment rate among doctors is extremely high, this is less problematic. The high underemployment rate means that positions in Islamic clinics can be highly sought after, particularly by interns and junior doctors. Islamic clinics can sometimes offer these doctors experience, income, and, a potential client base should they open their own private practices. Where underemployment among doctors is not such a problem, ISIs are often more strategic. In the case of Jordan, doctors are lured to Islamic clinics and hospitals by flexible work schedules and the prospect of working on some of the finest equipment in the country. ISIs associated with the ICCS regularly adopt a strategy of purchasing limited pieces of sophisticated, specialized, and, as a result, expensive medical equipment as opposed to more numerous pieces of lower-quality equipment. While this strategy has a certain symbolic appeal in terms of demonstrating (or boasting of) the viability and/or superiority of the Islamic alternative, it is also strategically chosen with the desires of Jordanian doctors in mind. Professionally it makes sense to work in an ISI. In this way, ISIs are assured a secure supply of an educated labor force. By addressing the economic, professional, and other needs of middle-class professionals, ISIs assure their own viability and sustainability.

Thus, the founding and running of ISIs involves middle-class contacts and ties on a one-time and ongoing basis. It involves loosely and tightly knit networks of people who donate time, energy, skills, and money on a regular or irregular basis and branch out to include hundreds of people who may in fact have never visited the ISI in question. These networks include both Islamists and non-Islamists.

In this regard, the operational needs of an ISI largely dictate that ISIs cater to the middle class, specifically the educated middle class (e.g., doctors and interns) and, as a result, become embedded in middle-class networks. ISIs need doctors, nurses, and teachers in order to provide their services to the poor. They furthermore need those with resources—or material—to donate. However, the expansion or embeddedness of middle-class networks is also due to the demands of the Islamist movement itself. Doctors, lawyers, engineers, and university students make up the bulk of the support of the Islamist movement. In the context of states that cannot provide adequate economic and other opportunities for their citizenries, the movement seeks to provide for the needs and demands of its membership. There is thus a push from within the movement itself to establish private schools and hospitals that cater strictly to middle-class needs. The ICCS in Jordan runs both private (and expensive) institutions, such as the Islamic Hospital, and welfare institutions, such as those that provide free lessons to orphans on the Qur'an, all in the name of charity. This push is further fueled by the ideological endeavor of creating alternative institutions—the belief in activist *da'wa*. The expansion of ISIs to include private enterprises further enlarges the middle-class web in which ISIs are situated.

The result is that ISIs can be divided into two types: Islamic commercial institutions (ICIs) and Islamic welfare institutions. Islamic welfare institutions (IWIs) are those ISIs catering to the welfare of the poor. They provide financial aid to orphans and reduced-price medical services to the poor, for example. ICIs are those ISIs that are mostly private commercial (albeit nonprofit) institutions that cater, as evidenced by their relatively high fees, to the middle class—the movement's membership. One ISI, such as Jordan's ICCS, can have both IWIs and ICIs.

ISIs are thus embedded in ever-overlapping social networks largely comprising educated middle-class professionals. As are social movements elsewhere, these networks are not exclusively composed of the educated middle class, but they are overwhelmingly homogenous in nature. The head of an Islamic women's charity and a member of an Islamic political party may attend the same Qur'anic study group. The former may also attend classes at a commercial Islamic university where she encourages friends to also participate in the study group. She may ask her tailor to sew school uniforms at cost for orphan children at Ramadan or she may organize a book sale at the state university in order to raise money for her charity. Similarly, she may ask for donations at the closing of the Qur'anic study group. Alternatively, the director of an Islamic school may also be the founder of an Islamic marriage society that aids the poor by providing inexpensive wedding services and may also be active in an Islamic political party. His/her daughter may be on the student council at state university representing the Islamic List and write in the student newspaper. At each one of these institutions, she/he will overlap with other social networks, including Islamist networks, of the same socioeconomic level. In this manner, the middle-class nature of ISIs and their associated networks reproduces and reinforces itself as the social networks expand. Like-minded people generally associate with one another and prefer to share opinions with each other.

Those who work in ISIs are not all Islamists. Neither does one automatically become an Islamist by working in or contributing to an ISI. Volunteers, employees, and directors of ISIs have numerous and varied reasons for working in an ISI. Indeed, part of the success of ISIs lies in their flexibility. The networks that sustain ISIs include those who may only donate once per year on the occasion of Ramadan, those who are simply looking for an extra income, supporters of a variety of different (including non-Islamic) political parties, those wanting to fulfill a largely personal Muslim obligation, and more committed Islamists. Many volunteers and employees do not view their activities in ISIs in any political light. Working or volunteering in an ISI does not mean one becomes a committed Islamist.

In stating this, I am making a distinction between different levels of movement support within an ISI. A participant in an ISI—a volunteer or an employee—may or may not identify with the ideology or goals of the ISI or the Islamist movement. This becomes more evident when we examine the numerous employees (as opposed to volunteers) in ISIs. Particularly given the economic situations in Egypt, Jordan, and Yemen in which jobs, even for professionals, are not available or secure, we cannot assume that employees work in ISIs because they identify with their ideology and/or goals. They may simply be seeking a job.

I therefore am making a distinction within this book between members and nonmember participants. A nonmember participant is a person who works within an ISI, a doctor, for example, and in this sense is a participant but one who does not necessarily identify with the Islamist movement. A donor or volunteer who sees his/her act as one of simple charity is also a nonmember participant. A member, on the other hand, is one who actively regards his/her activities within the ISIs as part of his/her identity as an Islamist, as an act of *da'wa,* and as an important component in the Islamist movement. In this case, a director, for example, would be far more integrated into the middle-class social networks that link his ISI with other Islamist institutions. It would be relatively rare to find a director of an ISI who is a nonmember participant; the same cannot be said of the employees. In some instances, depending on the tightness of fit between the goals of the social movement organization and the goals of the social movement, this distinction may not apply. However, in the case of ISIs—where the goal is to provide for the poor—and the Islamist movement—where the goal is to expand its middle-class membership base—the "fit" is not always tight.[123] Participants in ISIs may identify with one or the other goal, with both, or with neither. There is a difference between a doctor who comes in the evenings to work in an Islamic clinic for extra income, does not pray on a regular basis, does not socialize with fellow workers, and simply returns home at the end of the evening, and the doctor who socializes with the members of the board of directors, may have another family member working in the clinic, prays at the community mosque, and is friends with numerous community members who drop by the clinic for social chats. Time constraints, religious conviction, political persuasion, and personality all influence the degree of identification with movement goals and integration in activist social networks.

However, donating to, volunteering for, or working in ISIs gradually creates a sense of teamwork and middle-class networks of trust and solidarity. Indeed, it is this sense of teamwork, family-like relations, and solidarity that marks ISIs and largely sets them apart from other NGOs. What makes ISIs "Islamic" is less the implementation of Islamic rules and procedures than this invisible process of building social capital. The Islamic nature of ISIs is thus not necessarily apparent to outsiders—those outside the associated middle-class networks. This sense of solidarity and commitment is reinforced by the benefits the middle class receives—jobs or better working conditions, higher incomes, educational and health services, a sense of purpose and self-confidence, leadership roles, and friendships. Furthermore, by bringing different social networks together in the provision of charity, ISIs facilitate the creation of new social networks and the introduction of Islamist networks and worldviews to non-Islamists. In doing so, ISIs indirectly contribute to the potential diffusion of Islamist worldviews and the breakdown and rebuilding of social networks with an activist understanding of Islam.

THE POOR

ISIs can be conceptualized as being situated within two networks of horizontal linkages—those of the directors and middle-class professionals who run the ISIs and benefit from their welfare and commercial institutions and their related networks—and those of the poor—the clients of Islamic welfare institutions. This book argues that ISIs do not forge strong vertical ties between the two. Indeed, this is entirely in keeping with the experiences of social movements elsewhere. This is not to state that the poor do not benefit or that those who work in the Islamic welfare institutions do not care about the poor but that to a large extent, due to operational and strategic reasons, there are more benefits for the middle class and the poor are not integrated into the middle-class social networks that are the backbone of ISIs and ultimately of the Islamist movement. The poor are neglected or, more accurately, alienated from the Islamist social and political vision. Furthermore, while the poor receive numerous benefits from ISIs, it is doubtful that their experiences within ISIs provide the same sense of shared meaning. As members of different social networks, the poor are not participants in (and are largely not privy to) the trust and solidarity building among the middle class that works in and benefits from ISIs.

In all three countries, there is a large diversity of the types of ISIs and a disparity in the quantity and quality of services they offer. While the middle class benefits from the better Islamic welfare institutions and the five-star services offered in private commercial institutions, those services targeted explicitly for the poor are often of inferior quality and are inconsistent on a year-to-year basis. In Cairo the quantity and quality of ISIs differ dramatically in accordance with the socioeconomic milieu of the surrounding neighborhood. The most successful Islamic medical clinics in terms of available services and sustainability are simply not in the poorer areas of Cairo. Rather, these areas are dominated by clinics that have one doctor, have few or no supplies or equipment, are often inconsistent in their operational hours, and teeter on the verge of closure. In Jordan, the jewel in the ICCS's crown is the Islamic Hospital in Amman—a nonprofit hospital that charges rates the poor cannot afford even with the subsidies offered by the hospital's Fund for the Sick and Poor. None of the profits from the hospital are directed toward other branches of the ICCS, such as those dealing explicitly with the poor. Indeed, the commercialization of many of the ICCS's "charity" services led one prominent Jordanian Islamist to complain to me that the Muslim Brotherhood had abandoned the poor.

The analysis of the three case studies of Egypt, Jordan, and Yemen furthermore highlights that there is nothing uniquely Islamic about ISIs. The experiences of the poor in ISIs are similar to their experiences in other social institutions or NGOs. Indeed, the poor reach out for any help they can receive, including services offered by nonreligious NGOs and by the government. ISIs are important and necessary providers of a technical and charitable service. However, in terms of a "demonstration effect" (whether or not ISIs demonstrate that Islamic medical facilities are superior to government medical facilities), the poor are not necessarily exposed to "superior" Islamic medical services that demonstrate the illegitimacy of public services and confirm the viability, efficacy, or preferability of an Islamic state. ISIs are "Islamic" solely in the sense that they perform charity work for the poor, not in terms of their organizational structure, regulations, or functions. Stated differently, they are Islamic in the hearts and minds of those who provide the services or in the sentiment or attitude with which they are run.[124] Very few, if any, ISIs differ in their operational procedures from private, philanthropic, or other social welfare associations. In this regard, they do not provide a model for or alternative to the state.

ISIs are often one of several options the poor regularly frequent for services. Indeed, ISIs complement the services of the government and other secular NGOs; they do not replace them. In Jordan, for example, many of the ICCS centers dealing specifically with the poor have "social workers" on staff. One of their duties is to ensure that the recipients of monthly subsidies are not receiving monthly allowances from other charity sources and thereby raising their combined (undeclared) "income" to a level that technically excludes them from charity programs.[125] The poor take advantage of whatever means is available—regardless of political ideology.

Finally, while the poor are not nameless clients in ISIs, they are also not members of the executive decision-making bodies of ISIs or of their general assemblies.[126] It goes without saying that they cannot afford the schools and other commercial services of which the middle class can take advantage. Furthermore, more informal social gatherings among the middle class, such as Qur'anic study groups, also generally exclude the poor as they are not part of middle-class social circles and generally do not have the time to engage in such leisure activities. They thus have little access to middle-class social networks.

What emerges is a picture that is very different for the poor and the middle class. More to the point, the economic benefits and the meaning, solidarity, and satisfaction that may be experienced by the middle class in ISIs is not being expanded to the lower classes. The Islamization or recruitment of the poor appears to be neither the intent nor the result of ISIs. Indeed, Asef Bayat's examination of the Islamist movement in Egypt confirms that Islamic social welfare organizations are not places for Islamist political activism among the poor.[127] ISIs appear to be run by middle-class Islamists for their middle-class supporters and voting constituency.

MIDDLE-CLASS BENEFITS

ISIs offer both services the middle class demands and jobs the middle class needs. The middle class is employed in ISIs, often in good-paying positions as doctors, and benefits from private schools and hospitals for themselves and their families—all in the name of charity. This is both due to the operational requirements of ISIs and due to the movement's desire to cater to its membership and increase that membership. I argue, however, that contrary to the prevailing literature on social movement theory, the catering of ISIs to middle-class needs, often at the expense of the poor, may in fact be detrimental to the movement. It may be backfiring among potential middle-class members—the potential recipients of those very benefits.

The three case studies thus indicate that when the provisions of benefits to prospective members and members supersedes the goals of the organization, this can have a deleterious effect upon the movement. This tendency is most pronounced in Jordan, where there are strong indications that the tension between the needs of the movement—to address the demands of the middle-class membership by offering benefits—and the stated goals of the ISI—to help the poor—has resulted in a perceived sense of hypocrisy among Jordanians that undermines the movement and its recruitment potential. Quite simply, ISIs are seen as betraying their values, and this reflects negatively upon the movement.

My argument—that benefits under these conditions can hurt a movement—provides a contribution to the literature on social movements in which the prevailing view is that benefits can only help secure membership expansion. In the context of states that cannot adequately provide for the various needs of the educated middle class, including jobs, the provision of these needs takes an extremely important role in the movement. In addition, ISIs need middle-class participants in order to fulfill their goal of providing for the poor. The result is that the provision of middle-class benefits can come to dominate ISIs—at the expense of the poor. When this occurs, the fit between the goals of the movement and that of the social movement organization begins to break down or loosen—to the detriment of both.

THE CHAPTERS IN THIS BOOK

This book is divided into five chapters, including this introduction and the conclusion. Chapters 2, 3, and 4 examine the case studies of Egypt, Jordan, and Yemen. Each chapter begins with the political, economic, and social context of ISIs in their respective countries and proceeds to a microexamination of the establishment, services, directors, employees, volunteers, and clients of the ISI under examination and its associated networks. Each chapter focuses on a different, although commonly shared, aspect of ISIs. In Chapter 2, I examine charitable medical clinics in Cairo and the manner in which they are created, funded, staffed, and maintained. I argue that the operational needs of the clinics dictate that they cater to the middle class and that, furthermore, the poor do not receive the same services as the middle class, are not part of middle-class social networks, and, as a result, are not participants in the sense of teamwork and mission within ISIs. Indeed, there is very little that is "Islamic" about Islamic clinics in Cairo. Chapter 3 examines the ICCS in Jordan and particularly the commercial institutions it runs, such as private schools and hospitals. I argue that the ICCS prioritizes the needs of the middle class over those of the poor by focusing the majority of its efforts in these commercial institutions. This occurs, however, all in the name of charity. Chapter 4 takes an in-depth look at the Women's Sector of the Islah Charitable Society in Yemen and the networking that occurs in the provision of charity and the dynamics within those networks. In Chapter 5, the conclusion, I delve more deeply into the overall argument of the book, particularly into the long-term implications of my findings. I argue that the study of ISIs indicates that the moderate Islamist movement is indeed quite moderate and that its own strategies may hurt its ability to expand its membership among the middle class. While all three case studies support the overall argument of this book, I felt it would be more interesting and informative to focus on different elements of the book's argument in each chapter. I hope I have presented both an in-depth and well-rounded analysis of ISIs and their significance in the Middle East.

TWO

Islamic Medical Clinics in Cairo: The Operational Imperatives of ISIs and the Role of Middle-Class Networks

As with most researchers and journalists in Egypt, the Mustafa Mahmoud medical clinic was the first clinic in which I conducted interviews. Situated in a commanding position on a major thoroughfare in the wealthy Cairene district of Mohandessin, the Mustafa Mahmoud clinic is one of the largest, most impressive, and most famous Islamic clinics in the country. The clinic is a multistoried building attached to a popular mosque, the Mustafa Mahmoud mosque. During Ramadan, thousands of worshipers can be seen surrounding the mosque and in the streets, blocking all traffic, conducting prayers. The Mustafa Mahmoud Association was founded by Dr. Mustafa Mahmoud himself, a former Communist and now Islamist, who earned his fame through his popular television show, *Faith and Science.* The doctor's fame is an important reason behind the large amount of donations that flow, often from the Gulf countries, into the clinic and enable it to offer an impressive array of services and equipment and to hire some of the finest doctors in the country. Depending on the time of day, the clinic can be a crowded, even chaotic place, with patients (many of whom have flown in from throughout the Arab world) spilling outside to a waiting room of benches under a permanent form of canopy or roof. Indeed, approximately 8,000 families receive various types of financial aid and medical services annually.[1] Approximately 200 doctors and 200 nurses and clerks work inside the medical complex. While many of the examination rooms are extremely small, the Association provides physical exams, blood testing, urinalysis, diagnosis, kidney dialysis, appendectomies, heart treatment, dentistry, and psychological treatment.[2] The complex also houses various administrative offices (including that of Mustafa Mahmoud) as well as a tiny Islamic library and geological museum. On the whole, however, as is the case with most Islamic clinics, the complex is very plain with little in the way of adornment on the walls other than lists of the various doctors and treatments available.

In this first visit to the clinic, I interviewed the administrative director with the goal of determining what exactly made the clinic, indeed the entire complex, including the hospital, Islamic. Before the interview even began, an army officer burst into the office and began shouting at the director in front of all those waiting. His outrage was caused by the fact that the clinic had no female gynecologist for his wife to visit; if she wanted to see a female gynecologist she would have to go elsewhere. The officer found it simply unacceptable that a medical establishment that claimed to be Islamic would not have a female gynecologist on staff. The director calmly explained that this was due to a lack of available female gynecologists. The officer stormed out of the office unassuaged. I never found out if the officer's wife went to a different Islamic clinic or perhaps to a government hospital. I did, however, feel as if one of my questions had at least been partially answered.

The degree to which Islamic clinics are indeed Islamic is one of the issues that lies at the heart of the larger question of whether vertical or horizontal ties dominate Islamic clinics. The scholarly literature depicts Islamic associations, including their clinics, as fronts for the proselytization of the poor to Islamism. Even if this is not done directly, the mere successful provision of services is seen by many scholars as propaganda which increases the number of adherents—particularly among the poor—to the Islamist movement both in the streets and at the ballot box.[3] The concern that ISIs, in this case Islamic clinics, are arenas for the recruitment of the poor appears to be based on one or more of the following three implicit assumptions: 1) the poor are integrated into the general assemblies of the clinics or the associated networks involved in their establishment and ongoing management; 2) Islamic clinics are providing quality facilities or services for the poor; and 3) there is something uniquely Islamic about Islamic clinics. These three assumptions encapsulate the concern that the poor will become politicized either through contact with Islamist doctors and clinic directors or through a "demonstration effect"—the demonstration of superior Islamic medical services or an effective Islamic model in action.

The case study of Islamic clinics in Cairo demonstrates that the successful registering, building, equipping, and staffing of the clinics, particularly in the context of (often arbitrary) state control, requires extensive middle-class ties—often at the expense of vertical ties to the poor. Not possessing the sorts of useful contacts and/or resources clinic directors seek, the poor are excluded from the social networks that are pivotal to the establishment and management of the clinics. They are furthermore not in the general assemblies or on the boards of directors of the clinics. The relationship of the poor to the middle class in the clinics is strictly one of doctor/patient. Because of economic factors, however, doctors working in Islamic clinics cannot be assumed to be Islamists. As a result, the poor are neither part of the middle-class networks that make Islamic clinics possible nor are they necessarily in contact with middle-class Islamists. The weakness of vertical ties within the clinics is further reflected in the discrepancy in the quantity and quality of services offered in Islamic clinics located in the more affluent areas of Cairo and those in the poorer or *sha'abi* (popular) neighborhoods. Lacking sufficient middle-class contacts and, as a result, the connections to ensure registration, materials to build the clinic, and the funds with which to pay doctors and buy equipment, clinics in the poorer areas, where the need is greatest, are the least able to provide medical care. Teetering on the verge of closure, clinics in poorer areas of Cairo have too few—and often unreliable—doctors, no equipment beyond a chair or bench, and the most basic of services. The finest examples of Islamic clinics are located where the middle classes are located, not where the poor dominate. In terms of the organization or running of the clinics, be it the segregation of the sexes or veiling of female employees, there is nothing concretely or uniquely Islamic about Islamic medical clinics. In most clinics, there is little in the way of a "demonstration effect." In sum, despite some notable exceptions, for the majority of the poor, Islamic medical clinics are just one of the numerous, largely inadequate options to which they must resort in an attempt to address their health care needs.

This chapter is an in-depth examination of the context in which and the processes by which Islamic clinics must register, establish, and maintain themselves, and demonstrates the necessary and important role middle-class networks play in these processes. I use the term private voluntary organization (PVO) in this chapter, and not NGO as I do in the other chapters in this book. In contrast to the interchangeable use of the two terms which dominates the literature on the Middle East, the literature on Egypt makes a distinction between the two and treats PVOs as a subcategory of NGOs. In the Egyptian context, the term PVO excludes professional syndicates and unions in which membership is mandatory by law in Egypt. Data on Egyptian PVOs, as opposed to NGOs, is thus more reflective of processes and phenomena occurring in ISIs.

HEALTH CARE, COLONIALISM, AND THE RISE OF PVOS IN EGYPT

PVOs in Egypt first arose at the end of the nineteenth century as a response both to the socioeconomic problems associated with the development of industrial urban society and to the perceived interference by foreigners in the political, social, and cultural affairs of the country.[4] While there can be no doubting the genuine religious feelings in Egyptians that led to the establishment of associations to aid the poor, PVOs are historically closely associated with a larger anti-colonial struggle. Private voluntary health clinics are no exception, for the issues of poor health conditions and colonial rule were closely related. Under British occupation, the budget of Egypt's School of Medicine at Qasr al-Aini was cut back in accordance with British plans to eliminate Egypt's debt and reduce government spending. The British restricted the number of entrants and the availability of services, and, although they gave more European doctors permission to practice in Egypt, they did not allow Egyptian students at Qasr al-Aini to specialize. The British effectively reduced the number and the quality of Egyptian doctors, the positions available to them, and, as a result, the quantity and quality of doctors and services for the Egyptian public.[5] Indeed, adequate medical facilities existed only in European neighborhoods in Cairo and Alexandria.[6]

It is not surprising, therefore, that public health came to be seen as a political issue in the struggle against British colonial rulers and, after the Revolution of 1919, against the pro-British monarchy. In the 1940s, a series of epidemics

> caused a massive mobilization in which King Faruq; majority and minority political parties; elite women volunteers; Islamic, nationalist, and communist groups; British authorities; experts from the Rockefeller Foundation and other international agencies; and, of course, the people in the infected regions took part. The contenders for power in Egypt sought to win public goodwill not only through their efforts in the public health wars but also through their support for public health reform.[7]

Triggered by the anti-colonial struggle, the origins of today's PVOs in Egypt are therefore also rooted in the historical competition between different intellectual and political currents over Egypt's national identity.[8] Each created grassroots associations to deal with societal needs, such as health care, and competed against each other both for resources and supporters. The Muslim Brotherhood, the Communists, the Wafd Party, and the Young Egypt Party (Misr al-Fatat), as well as smaller and less well-known religious and charity groups, all offered a variety of social welfare services. There were also numerous individual philanthropic efforts. All of these groups competed for the means with which to conduct or offer their activities and for the patrons to use them.

The establishment of ISIs in particular was furthermore provoked by an additional, but related, factor: the presence of foreign Christian missionaries. Christian missionarism in Egypt began in 1815. Seeking converts, Christian missions established schools and charity associations throughout the country.[9] The Muslim Brotherhood and other Islamist groups soon came to perceive them as a source of alien national and religious values and as a major agent of Western cultural imperialism. Missionarism, they felt, was an attack on Islam. These nationalistic fears were fueled by cases of religious conversion. Even today, the highest concentration of Islamic clinics can be found in areas with large numbers of Christians and Christian clinics.

HEALTH CARE IN EGYPT TODAY

Given its historical political significance, as well as the alarming state of health of most Egyptians, health care continued to be an important aspect of state policy after the Free Officers rose to power with the 1952 revolution. Under the new presidency of Jamal Abdul Nasser, health care became a top priority; it soon became a hallmark of Nasser's regime and one of the pillars of state legitimacy. The government immediately sought both to improve the education of doctors and to establish a network of free medical centers throughout the country. This included the expansion of older facilities, the establishment of new ones, and the nationalization of various private philanthropic societies and foundations. As early as 1956, the state exercised a near monopoly of health care.

Presidents Anwar Sadat (1970–1981) and Hosni Mubarak (1981–) inherited this legacy. They also inherited a health care network that was inadequately supplied and staffed. Under both Nasser and Sadat, planning for health care was irregular and late and budgets were revised from one year to the next.[10] On paper, Nasser established one of the most integrated health infrastructures in the Third World, with a rural health care unit at a maximum distance of three kilometers from each village.[11] In reality, even today, the number of rural health care units remains below the target of 2,500.[12]

When Mubarak first came to power, health care received a more significant place in the budget than it had under Sadat.[13] As of the mid-1990s, the Ministry of Health offered three levels of health services: 1) a network of rural and urban units offering basic health services, including preventative health care and health orientation; 2) 211 general and central hospitals, 188 specialized hospitals, and 582 rural units (with beds) offering government medical services; and 3) twenty-five university hospitals administered by the Ministry of Education and eight teaching hospitals and eight specialized institutions run by the Ministry of Health. In 1994, there were 66,931 hospital beds in Egypt, 59.2 percent provided by level-two hospitals and 19.3 percent by level-three hospitals.[14] A 1995 survey found that in terms of quantity, the provision of public health care in Egypt is relatively comprehensive—in total, the Ministry of Health had 3,700 primary, secondary, and tertiary health care facilities.[15]

However, given the small percentage of the budget devoted to health care in the 1970s, inflation, the percentage of the budget which goes to state-employed doctors' salaries (as opposed to the maintenance of equipment and new investment), and inequalities in the geographical distribution of the state's medical expenditures, the budgetary prioritization of health care has had little positive impact on the services available to Egyptians.[16] Public facilities suffer from old and used equipment, poor hygiene conditions, a shortage of medicine, and a lack of technical and, especially, nursing staff. Doctors are unreliable and unmotivated because of their relatively poor salaries and the frustrating bureaucratic red tape with which they must deal on a regular basis.[17] Despite examples to the contrary, the poor reputation of the government services drives patients to seek other alternatives.[18] A. K. Nandakumar, Mukesh Chawla, and Maryam Khan found that 49.7 percent of Egyptians seeking outpatient health care go to private facilities; only 21.2 percent go to the facilities offered by the Ministry of Health and 18.8 percent go to other forms of government or subsidized health care.[19]

This trend has been accelerated under Egypt's present Economic Reform and Structural Adjustment Program (ERSAP). In an effort to reduce its crushing debt, Egypt agreed to ERSAP with the International Monetary Fund (IMF) and the World Bank in 1991. Egypt thus embarked upon an economic reform program based on macroeconomic stabilization and the structural transformation of the economy. The aim of the program is to reorient Egypt's state-directed economy, which was largely established under Nasser, toward market forces, the private sector, and external trade.[20]

While there has been remarkable macroeconomic improvement under the present economic restructuring program,[21] the same cannot be said of the micro level. In fact, quite the opposite is true. Microlevel conditions have never been so bad: wages and salaries have fallen; average per-capita yearly incomes have fallen; prices on foodstuffs, transportation, rents, gasoline, and electricity have risen as subsidies have been removed; and the incidence of malnutrition has risen (after steadily falling from the early 1950s to the late 1980s).[22] According to the UN's Human Poverty Index, 32.3 percent of the population is living in poverty.[23] The Egyptian Planning Institute estimated that in 1995–1996, the rate of poverty in Egypt was as high as 48 percent of the total population; the percentage of people living in absolute poverty reached 33 percent.[24]

At the grassroots level, the elimination of subsidies and social programs and the shifting of public service expenses to the private sector under

ERSAP's privatization program are having a twofold impact. The first is a decrease in wages and an increase in unemployment. The Graduates Program, according to which university graduates received automatic employment in the state, was recently eliminated. This translates quite simply into poor and middle-class Egyptians having even less to spend.

The second is the need for Egyptians to find better social welfare services outside the state. In this regard, ERSAP is having its greatest impact in the areas of health and education which traditionally have been heavily funded. In the area of health care,

> [Figures] show a downward trend in the Ministry of Health's medi-care expenditures in relation to the State budget and the Gross Domestic Product (GDP): from 2.3% [and] 1.21% in 1981 to 1.9% and only 0.6% in 1993/94. Hence, government hospitals suffered a shortage in resources which led to neglecting renovations [and] maintenance and a sharp drop in medical facilities, causing widespread dissatisfaction with the offered services.[25]

Despite a 33 percent increase in outpatient facilities in government hospitals, there was a 23 percent drop in outpatients from 1982–1993 and a drop in bed occupancy in government hospitals from 60 to 45 percent during the same time period. The number of beds provided by the Ministry of Health dropped from fourteen to slightly less than twelve beds per 10,000 persons from 1984 to 1994.[26] Furthermore, statistics from the World Bank show that the population per physician increased from 732 in 1980–1985 to 1,316 in 1989–1994.[27]

In addition to the Ministry of Health, certain ministries also have their own network of health care. The Ministry of Education owns and controls twenty-one hospitals and education institutions. The Ministry of the Interior, the Ministry of Defense, and the Ministry of Transportation also have centers of health care and hospitals reserved for their personnel. Several of the professional syndicates also have their own insurance programs. Each of these health care centers, however, caters to a specific and limited type of patron.

In the gap left by the state in the provision of medical care, a variety of private and semiprivate options have arisen. The semisubsidized alternatives include the government's social insurance program (the Health Insurance Organization) that covers employees in the formal sector and school-children.[28] However, the criteria for beneficiaries, based upon job type and salary revenue, exclude independent workers, workers in the informal sector, and seasonal or irregular workers from coverage. In addition, the highest concentration of beneficiaries is limited to Alexandria and the most health centers are concentrated in Alexandria, Cairo, and Giza. Finally, these facilities also suffer from a lack of adequate financing and equipment.[29]

Within the private sector, Egypt possesses a wide variety of doctors in private practice; private pharmacies, clinics, and polyclinics; and private-investment hospitals.[30] The majority of these facilities, however, are targeted for Egypt's small affluent class. In the private-investment hospitals a room can cost hundreds of dollars per day. Their fees are so high that they often operate below capacity. Even if more Egyptians could afford their services, the reputations of some of the investment hospitals were marred in the 1980s by managerial and ethical irregularities. The result is that they do not even meet the health care needs of the rich; investment hospitals have not proven to be an adequate substitute for the curative trips abroad that the affluent take.[31] Private hospitals have therefore not solved the problem of the lack of good and affordable medical care for Egyptian patients. For the vast majority of Egyptians there remains only one alternative: the secular and religious voluntary medical clinics. Among the most popular of these are the mosque-based Islamic medical clinics.

ISLAMIC MEDICAL CLINICS:
THEIR NUMBER, SIZE, AND FACILITIES

All Egyptian PVOs must register with the Ministry of Social Affairs (MOSA), which delineates fourteen categories of activities: community development associations (CDAs); social assistance; religious, scientific, and cultural services; maternity and child care; family welfare; special-categories and handicapped welfare; old-age welfare; friendship among peoples; family planning; social protection; management and administration; prison inmates' welfare; literacy; and multiple activities. MOSA makes a further distinction between "welfare private voluntary organizations"— those working in the field of welfare (categories two to fourteen)—and CDAs. CDAs differ from welfare private voluntary organizations (welfare PVOs) in that they are working in the broader field of community development, providing a village or urban neighborhood with the basic social services. They therefore carry out more activities than other PVOs. For the sake of clarity, the thirteen welfare PVO categories can be broken down into four basic fields of activity: health, education, infrastructure (such as water and sewage systems), and credit for income generation and microenterprise.[32]

The majority of PVOs are individual or independent associations registered in one single location or community, but there are also nationally registered PVOs. These are "chains" of associations that belong to one "mother" association. In 1990, MOSA estimated the number of community PVOs at 12,832 and the number of national PVOs at 160.[33] Of these 12,832 PVOs, 74.5 percent (9,556) were estimated to be welfare PVOs, including Islamic PVOs. The majority of PVOs are located in urban areas, with the largest number in Cairo (3,453).[34]

While there is no precise data, MOSA estimates that the PVO membership in 1992 was approximately 3 million. Based on the documented increase in membership (up from 2 million in 1990), it can only be assumed that the number has risen significantly since 1992. The number of beneficiaries in 1992 was estimated as 5.5 million Egyptian citizens. While the average number of beneficiaries per activity is approximately 3,000, there is tremendous variation between PVOs. For example, two out of forty PVOs in Saad Eddin Ibrahim's in-depth study did not engage in any activity, while five had more than ten major activities. Not including the two which were defunct, twelve of the forty PVOs (30 percent) each served fewer than 300 members of their respective communities, while two served as many as 10,000 or more each.[35]

Precise data is difficult to find regarding the number of Islamic PVOs or ISIs.[36] In 1974, MOSA reclassified all religious PVOs into one category together with cultural and scientific PVOs. MOSA furthermore created the category of "multiple type," under which a religious PVO providing health or educational services could be categorized. In 1991, the number of "religious, cultural and scientific" PVOs reached 2,457, representing approximately 26 percent of all welfare PVOs. However, multiple-type PVOs, of which many are religious, amounted to 3,316 (35 percent). In 1991, therefore, religious PVOs could have comprised up to 50 percent of all welfare PVOs. Amani Kandil estimated the percentage of Islamic PVOs at 43 percent in 1991.[37] The largest number of Islamic PVOs are concentrated in the cities of Upper Egypt, where 56.8 percent and 44.3 percent of all Islamic PVOs are located in the cities of Menia and Assyut, respectively.[38] Cairo houses 21.8 percent, and Alexandria, 33.3 percent, of Islamic PVOs.[39]

Islamic social institutions may include projects such as day care centers, schooling, adult literacy classes, secondhand clothing shops, classes to upgrade skills, wedding and funeral services, and medical clinics. In 1987, Soheir Morsy estimated the number of Islamic medical clinics at one to two thousand nationwide and between 300 and 350 in Cairo.[40] While there is no precise data concerning the number of beneficiaries of Islamic clinics, a study by the United States Agency for International Development (USAID) estimates that health services provided by PVOs reached approximately 14 million people in 1992. While many of these services are provided by large, modern hospitals, "a considerable volume of such services is provided by dispensaries attached to mosques."[41]

The majority of ISIs are independent initiatives, located in one community; however, there are nationally registered ISIs. Examples of Islamic "chains" include Al-Jamʿiyat Ansar al-Sunna (The Society of Sunna Advocates) and Al-Jamʿiya al-Sharʿiya li al-ʿAmilim bi al-Kitab wa al-Sunna al-Muhammadiya (The Lawful/Religious Association for Those Who Behave According to the Book and the Muhammadan Sunna). Al-Jamʿiya al-Sharʿiya is the largest nationally registered ISI and has a branch in each of the nation's twenty-six governorates and 123 branches in Cairo.[42] The various branches host medical centers as well as day care centers, orphanages, schools, and libraries.[43]

Between ISIs there is very little or no coordination or cooperation. ISIs generally operate autonomously from another even if they are branches in the same chain, such as Al-Jamʿiya al-Sharʿiya.[44] One of the branches of the Al-Jamʿiya al-Sharʿiya chain I visited is located beside a mosque in the oldest district of Cairo (the original city of Cairo). It houses a medical and dental clinic, has a staff of twenty-six doctors and five nurses, and offers numerous medical specializations, including dermatology. While the branch directors do meet on a regular basis, the branches are financially independent. The branch I visited received funding from a variety of sources, including the embassy of the Netherlands and the Ministry of Social Affairs. As the director explained to me, he runs his branch as he sees fit, while the main headquarters offers "spiritual" advice and dictates certain regulations. The various projects even within one ISI are often run very independently, so that if one service, such as the medical clinic, fails, it will not be financially rescued by the profits from another service, such as day care.

Islamic medical clinics vary greatly in terms of their size and facilities. Located in or beside mosques, they range from those with one doctor (and are little more then a dispensary) to those with 200 doctors and 200 nurses. The larger, more sophisticated Islamic clinics, of which there are a handful in the city (including the Mustafa Mahmoud medical complex discussed above), often offer surgery, cardiology, ophthalmology, gynecology, dentistry, X-ray facilities, and laboratories for research. Medium-sized clinics, with ten to twenty-five doctors, may focus on a specialized service such as physiotherapy. The Religious Association of Imam Abu al-Azm provides an excellent example. It is located in a multistoried building on a busy commercial street in the older district of Sayyida Zeinab (near the mosque of the same name). The Association was founded in 1952 by the imam himself and was funded by the sale of approximately seventy books he wrote. Today, there are thirteen doctors and four nurses, several of whom are the founder's descendants. The Religious Association is, in this sense, a family business. It is a very popular clinic with several specialties, including pediatrics, gynecology, gastroenterology, dentistry, ophthalmology, otolaryngology, and orthopedics. The clinic has an X-ray machine and performs simple outpatient operations (those that require little or no anesthesia, such as tonsillectomies). In addition to the clinic, the Association also has a day care center and a working mothers' program (together with the government, the Association helps place poor women in homes as cleaners), and it boasts one of the country's very few alcohol detoxification centers. The majority of Islamic clinics, however, have neither the staff nor the facilities of Mustafa Mahmoud or the Religious Association of Imam Abu al-Azm. Rather, they are very simple facilities with one doctor and nurse attending to the basic needs of their clients and housing perhaps only an examination table and scales with which to weigh babies.

STATE CONTROL OF PVOS:
LAW 32 AND THE REGISTRATION
AND ESTABLISHMENT OF PVOS

As stated above, Islamic clinics must register with the Ministry of Social Affairs. Established in 1939, MOSA's official function is to encourage individual efforts in the social domain. Its goals include collaborating with associations and encouraging, orienting, financially aiding, and coordinating them and raising their standard of social work.[45] However, in practice, MOSA appears to focus on regulating and monitoring the associations.

The primary instrument by which MOSA regulates or controls PVOs is through Law 32, issued in 1964.[46] Under Law 32, MOSA is given wide powers of discretion to rule on the right of an association to exist. The authorization of an association is based on such vague criteria as the extent to which the association's activities are "consistent with the requirements of society" (Article 12). Similarly, the grounds for dissolving an association include the "violation of public order or morality" and "undermining the security of the republic or the government's republican form" (Article 2).[47]

MOSA is able to dissolve an association without asking a court to carry out its orders. While associations may appeal, it is only to an administrative authority within MOSA and they can do so only if their applications are rejected, not if they are dissolved.[48] MOSA can oppose any candidate for the administration council of an association. It can nominate up to 50 percent of a council's representatives from MOSA for an unlimited time period, and it can dissolve councils and nominate new ones.[49]

Registering an association as stipulated by MOSA is quite onerous and entails a minimum of ten bureaucratic steps, public notarization of all founders' signatures, a written by-law, and the approval of over three ministerial bodies, including the Ministry of Interior's General Security Department.[50] The entire procedure is frustrating, time-consuming, and without guarantees.

Once registered, PVOs labor under a variety of other restrictions. Saad Eddin Ibrahim's 1994 study of the impact of Law 32 on Egypt's PVOs and private foundations finds six categories of constraints which MOSA imposes upon PVOs: administrative, geographic, substantive (activities), financial, organizational, and technical.[51] Law 32 imposes stringent requirements in terms of its record-keeping and inspection of PVOs. These constraints include limitations on membership, fund-raising, beneficiaries, and the scope of activities.

In terms of fund-raising, Law 32 prohibits receiving money from a foreigner and/or a foreign organization without the prior permission of MOSA. It does not permit PVOs to collect donations from the public or organize shows, bazaars, sporting events, or any other fund-raising activities except by permission of MOSA. A maximum of two requests for fund-raising campaigns may be granted.[52] Law 32 also places restrictions on investments.

Another way MOSA controls PVOs is through the designation of certain PVOs as acting in the "public interest." PVOs which reach a certain size and level of effectiveness may be placed by MOSA in this category and, as a result, receive certain privileges and funding. A high concentration of MOSA's financial aid goes to these public-interest PVOs.[53] Assigning this status is an effective means of control, as these PVOs generally become mere extensions of the state, implementing MOSA's own projects. In their 1994 study, Amani Kandil and Sarah Ben Nefissa estimated that there were 330 PVOs registered as public interest, and of these 128 were Islamic PVOs.[54]

Violating the provisions of Law 32 can result in penalties and a prison term for up to six months. Activist PVOs which have incurred the displeasure of the authorities have also been prosecuted under a wide range of legislation which limits freedom of expression in Egypt and have been detained under the emergency legislation. Hence, the ability of Law 32 to inhibit the development of PVOs cannot be overestimated.[55]

As if the requirements of Law 32 were not onerous and arbitrary enough, MOSA is not the only ministry to exert control over PVOs. Depending on the services they offer, PVOs may have to register and comply with the regulations of the Ministries of Education, Culture, or, in the case of clinics, Health. In addition, associations with clinics must register their medical clinic with the doctors' syndicate. However, the syndicate has no real control or regulative power over the clinics.

The restrictions and regulations imposed by MOSA and other ministries are problematic enough to force some PVOs to operate illegally or to register under a different legal form. A study carried out by the Ibn Khaldoun Center for Development Studies in 1993 found that there were on average seven informal (illegal) grassroots initiatives for every formally reg-istered PVO.[56] Recognizing that the Egyptian bureaucracy is massive and slow, activists, whether they be upper-class liberal-oriented women estab-lishing an English-speaking day care center or Islamists offering adult liter-acy classes, open illegal PVOs and hope that their activities will be over-looked. Many of the smaller Islamic clinics in particular are not registered. Even those clinics that are registered with MOSA are often missing other types of registration—for example, the necessary permission to expand their facilities.[57]

The restrictiveness of Law 32 can be attributed to a variety of factors, including a broader state policy to curb and eliminate Islamist militancy. The 1990s were Egypt's bloodiest decade since the turn of the century. What had started out as a series of sporadic acts carried out by a group of small radical Islamist groups in the 1970s evolved into a widespread low-level insurgency against the Egyptian state by the 1980s and 1990s.[58] In the hopes of bringing down the Egyptian government by isolating Hosni Mubarak's regime internationally and depriving it of much-needed hard foreign currency, Islamic militants extended their use of violence to include attacks on foreign tourists and Egyptian Christians, and numerous assassi-nation attempts on public figures (including a number of attacks upon Mubarak's life). Certain parts of the country—rural provincial cities pre-dominantly in the south and urban shantytowns in Cairo—were in a near state of war as Islamists and Egyptian security forces fought each other in the streets.

In an effort to crush the militants, beginning in the early 1990s, the government adopted a more confrontational approach to Islamic activism than had been practiced during President Mubarak's first decade in power. Rather than attempting to draw moderate elements, such as the Muslim Brotherhood, into its fold and marginalize the radical elements, the govern-ment increasingly began to make no distinction between moderate and rad-ical forms of Islamic activism. Moderate Islamic activists, however, are integral to civil society through their activities in syndicates, clubs, associa-tions, and PVOs. Over approximately the last twenty years Islamists, pre-dominantly the Muslim Brotherhood, have run in most of the country's professional syndicate elections. Until the 1990s, despite the interference of previous governments in the elections and workings of the syndicates, under Mubarak the professional union elections had come to be considered the only free elections in Egypt and therefore had become an important stronghold in the battle for greater democracy. In fact, since the mid-1980s, Islamic Lists have repeatedly won elections in the syndicates of doctors, en-gineers, pharmacists, and lawyers (as well as in university student councils and sporting clubs).[59] As a consequence of the shift in government policy toward Islamist militancy, however, civil society as a whole has been under legislative assault from the government. In 1993, the government declared the creation of a new professional syndicate law, the Law for Democratic Guarantees in Professional Syndicates (Law 100 for 1993). Based upon the rationale that the Brothers are winning the elections only because an active minority of supporters are participating in the elections, the law requires a quorum of voters for the results to be considered legal. If after several rounds of elections the quorum is not met, the syndicate will be run by an appointed council made up of the oldest members of the syndicate and will be presided over by a judge. When Islamists proved they could still win the elections under the new law, the government invoked various pretexts to postpone elections in syndicates dominated by Islamists.[60] In 1994, the government also enacted legislation to terminate village mayoral elections and university elections—where moderate Islamists had been winning more often.[61] For example, now academic deans in Egypt's universities and mayors are appointed, which has ended twenty years of popular voting. The government has also moved to interfere in elections. In the forty-eight hours prior to the 1995 national elections, hundreds of Islamic activists were arrested. Many of those arrested, including thirty-seven women, were poll watchers registered with the Brotherhood.[62]

Representatives from the entire political spectrum have spoken out against Law 32 as detrimental to political pluralism and democracy in Egypt.[63] Law 32 stands in contradiction to the 1971 Constitution, which guarantees the right of association, as well as the International Covenant on Civil and Political Rights (1982), which Egypt ratified.[64] These criticisms, as well as the continuation of Islamic violence, led the government to review the effectiveness of Law 32 and the premise that the control of PVOs is necessary to curb militant Islamic unrest.[65] In late 1997, under a new minister of social affairs, Mervay al-Talawy, the government set up a committee to draft a new law regulating PVO activities. This committee was composed of approximately thirty legal experts, activists in civil society, and intellectuals.[66]

In 1999, Law 32 was officially nullified and replaced by Law 153. However, Law 153 was dismissed by the Supreme Constitutional Court in June 2000 on the grounds that it was adopted unconstitutionally. While human rights groups had lobbied for years to replace Law 32, Law 153 came as an unpleasant surprise when it continued to give MOSA wide-ranging powers to interfere in PVO affairs and when it was made law without presentation to Parliament (as required by Article 195 of the Constitution).[67] Human rights activists thus found themselves protesting the new law. While Law 153 has been successfully defeated, this meant the de facto return to Law 32 and a return to square one for human rights activists.

It is within this challenging political, economic, and social context that Islamic medical clinics are established. To become registered and established, they face tremendous bureaucratic and regulatory hurdles designed to curb their numbers. As is the case with other PVOs, Islamic medical clinics furthermore use all means at their disposal to facilitate and accelerate the registration process, including the cultivation of contacts within the bureaucracy through social networks. The instrumental needs of Islamic clinics means that they must cultivate ties and networks with the middle class, those who possess the necessary contacts and resources, and not with the poor.

MIDDLE-CLASS NETWORKS
AND THE REGISTERING OF A CLINIC

Islamic clinics, like all PVOs, are confronted from the outset with major bureaucratic and economic obstacles. They need both government approval in order to register and establish a clinic and the resources to build the facilities, buy the equipment, and hire the staff. Clinic founders use their neighborhood, job, mosque, army, family, and other connections to overcome these two basic obstacles. The success or failure of an Islamic medical clinic rests on the informal (usually social) networks it creates both within the relevant ministries and in its surrounding communities. Contacts within the ministry can accelerate the registration process and ensure its approval. A friend in MOSA can reduce the waiting time for a license by as much as a year. These same networks aid in fund-raising and procuring resources for the construction, equipping, and staffing of clinics. Founders and directors of successful clinics are thus engaged in a continual process of enlisting the assistance of people within the community who have the time, skills, means, or connections to help facilitate the registration and the physical building or expansion of the clinic. It is by and large the middle-class members of these neighbors who have such time, contacts, or resources. Without middle-class ties, Islamic clinics struggle to be viable.

In most cases, the idea of establishing a clinic originates from the neighborhood; community members approach the mosque about establishing a clinic or approach an association about building another clinic in a different location.[68] An already established association may also decide to expand its services and add a clinic to the premises. In the limited number of cases of larger chains, such as Al-Jamʿiya al-Sharʿiya, the Association's headquarters may itself identify a location in the city and establish a "trophy clinic"— one that is designed to be highly prominent and a shining symbol of the Association and the Islamist movement. Typically, Al-Jamʿiya al-Sharʿiya chooses locations that are easily accessible and carry a high profile as noteworthy and particularly "marketable" for its trophy clinics.[69]

The majority of clinics, however, are founded by people from the neighborhood—the local middle class with the resources of extra time and money. They are largely motivated by a genuine Islamic sense of charity and, to a degree, by a sense of competition with other nearby mosques that may already have a clinic. Not wanting their mosque or community to be found lacking, people in the neighborhood who have in one sense or another "made it" approach the mosque about forming an association that would manage a clinic and perhaps, in the future, other services such as a day care center.[70] As the nation's structural adjustment program negatively affects more and more of them, members of Egypt's middle class also have established clinics as a way to provide affordable health care for themselves and their families.

The most viable PVOs are active in the field of social welfare, predominantly in the areas of health and child care, family planning, or medical centers attached to mosques. In all of the cases studied by Ibrahim, leadership proved to be the most decisive factor in the success of any initiative. He asserts that the leader must possess three essential and necessary qualities: integrity, rhetorical skills for the mobilization of the community, and organizational skills. He notes that since the success of any grassroots initiative lies in the ability of its leaders to raise funds, a person must be respected and held in high esteem by the community that it targets.[71] Most leaders are educated and professionally skilled and/or command a high degree of respect from their respective communities.

An examination of the membership of PVOs in Ibrahim's case studies reveals that the educational level of the membership of the PVOs is markedly higher than Egypt's general population: "Those among them [who have] some formal education, and hence are at least literate, constituted over 85.0%, compared to Egypt's literacy rate of about 50.0% (for those above 10 years of age)." With respect to occupational background of the membership, he found that "state civil servants and public sector employees constituted about 75.0%, while those in the private sector (including farmers) were the remaining 25.0%. These figures contrast [with] Egypt's manpower distribution in which state and public sector employees make up about 31.0% (or about 4.0% of 13 million)."[72]

Ibrahim's study further indicates that the potential success of a PVO is augmented by the sheer number of its members. The founding members of a PVO can be as few as two people or as many as several hundred. However, a larger number of founders has several implications for the continued viability and dynamics of a PVO. Quite simply, it "provides a larger pool from which to draw leadership and volunteers." Founders attract like-minded individuals to participate in development projects which then include more members of society as facilitators or as beneficiaries. The larger the original pool of founders, the larger the possible number of members, employees, volunteers, and donors. Furthermore, the greater the number of founders, the greater the number of new leaders who are able to take over when the original leaders become fatigued.[73]

However, as the present study demonstrates, the ability to recruit members, volunteers, employees, and donors is more than a simple numbers game. Founders seek specific characteristics in their members. They are looking for people who can help the associations, not just through their ability to pay the yearly fees but also through their ability to donate resources, including useful (and often necessary) contacts. For example, once they make the decision to register a clinic, founders face the bureaucratic quagmire of regulations and forms. Without some form of personal direct access to the powerful MOSA, the entire process may easily take a year or longer.[74] As Diane Singerman states, most PVOs,

> whether religious or secular, can only operate in the present political and economic environment through support from the community and the patronage and acquiescence of political elites. The high degree of government control and supervision of any organized association . . . necessitates that the leaders of the NGO maintain amicable relations with various bureaucracies and political leaders. Even if a group has the financial resources to establish an organization that provides needed services, it must still first obtain various government clearances.[75]

Research by the World Bank confirms that Egypt's most successful associations usually have either connections in MOSA, powerful people on their boards of directors, or MOSA employees on their boards of administration. Of Egypt's largest PVOs, which constitute 5 percent of all PVOs, "one-half . . . are social service associations with close historical ties to government (usually the Ministry of Social Affairs) and directed by former (retired) senior ministry officials with government-seconded staff."[76] While MOSA officials temporarily assigned to PVOs have been known to interfere and place obstacles before associations (most notably by demanding various forms of income and payment for attending meetings), most seconded officials have proven to be highly useful to associations, helping them work through government regulations and bureaucracy.[77]

Islamic clinics are no different.[78] ISIs rely on the development of horizontal linkages with state employees, which are based on prior ties of kinship or acquaintance, mutual economic interest, or shared ideological commitments.[79] A good example is provided by the Religious Association of Imam Abu al-Azm, in which the director is also a retired police general with numerous connections within the government. In addition, several ministers are members of the association. In an interview with the author, the director stated:

> The Association of Imam Abu al-Azm is not to be toyed with. I'm a general in the police, graduated in 1954, and the Minister of the Interior was in the same graduating class as me and we also have support of four governors: Port Said, Mansura, Asyut, and El Minya. The governor of El Minya was a bunkmate.

A large degree of an association's success depends on the members' ability to get around impediments through informal arrangements and social networks which incorporate state officials.[80] Furthermore, each time an association wants to expand its premises or add a new service, it must register with MOSA. Bureaucratic connections are thus needed throughout the life of a PVO. Networking efforts do not stop after an initial connection has been made because relevant bureaucrats with whom good relations have been established may get transferred to a different ministry or may simply sever connections with the clinic due to overuse of the connection.[81]

NETWORKS: THE BUILDING AND FINANCING OF A CLINIC

Once they are registered, ISIs must raise the resources to build and equip the clinic and staff it. It is through social networks that these resources are most easily accessed. It is the ability of clinics to develop useful middle-class networks that to a large extent also explains the yearly variations in the amounts of revenue a clinic obtains (and, as a consequence, the annual variations in the services it offers). Law 32 permits seven possible ways for PVOs to obtain revenues: members' subscriptions, fees for services rendered, *waqf* revenues, income from lottery sales and exhibitions, donations from indigenous sources (money, materials, and skills), assistance from foreign donors (with MOSA's permission), and Egyptian government aid (including tax and customs exemptions). In his 1994 study of forty PVOs, Ibrahim found that for 37 percent of PVOs, the single leading source of revenues was returns from activities. Governmental aid was the main source of revenue for 20 percent of PVOs in his study, donations were the main source for 18 percent, other private Egyptian organizations were the main source for 20 percent, and registration fees were the main source for 5 percent. The single most important source of revenue for the majority of clinics therefore is returns from activities and donations from nongovernmental sources in Egypt. In fact, dues and donations were the only sources of revenue for 46 percent of the PVOs Ibrahim sampled.[82]

Approximately 35 percent of PVOs were able to receive some form of additional funding from the Egyptian government, primarily MOSA. The amount of funding PVOs receive from the government varies greatly, with public-interest PVOs—those PVOs largely implementing MOSA's own projects rather than their own—who receive the majority of MOSA funding. A further 25 percent of Ibrahim's sample obtained as much as 50 percent of their total annual revenues from foreign donors—predominantly American and European.[83] Finally, annual membership (subscription) fees, financial returns from the sale of goods produced on site, and funding from lotteries or festivals are minimal.

A World Bank study on PVO revenues reveals very similar results to those of Ibrahim. However, the World Bank study notes that while (secular) social welfare PVOs, religious welfare PVOs, and CDAs all primarily rely on their own resources for most of their income—activity fees, private donations, and other sources—there are some significant differences.[84] Religious welfare PVOs, the study argues, are far more independent of state aid and other grants than secular social welfare PVOs and, in particular, CDAs. Activity fees make up approximately 52 percent, donations account for 34 percent, and state and foreign aid contribute 9 percent of the total revenues of religious welfare PVOs. In contrast, in secular social welfare PVOs, activity fees represent approximately 22 percent of revenue, donations 24 percent, and state and foreign aid approximately 20 percent. Finally, the percentage of activity fees, donations, and state and foreign aid of total revenues of CDAs is approximately 31, 15, and 34 percent, respectively.[85] Religious welfare PVOs, of which Islamic welfare PVOs are the majority, are the most successful at raising funds and donations locally.[86]

Islamic clinics confirm these general trends—activity or user fees make up the bulk of the incomes of Islamic medical clinics. Most clinics charge between 2 and 5 LE (Egyptian pounds) per visit. Some charge as little as 1 LE and a few as much as 7 LE; these fees are still significantly lower than the fees private doctors charge. Some of the larger wealthier clinics have programs for waiving or reducing fees for the very poor. In some of the less affluent clinics, fees may be waived on an ad hoc basis, depending on the generosity of the individual doctor. The sheer number of patients is what brings substantial finances into the clinic.

As in the case of all religious PVOs, the most important source of clinic funding, beyond activity fees, is private donations. The ability of ISIs to raise donations is aided by the fact that Islamic PVOs receive certain fundraising privileges not granted to other PVOs. Article 17 of the by-laws of Presidential Decree 932 of 1966 gives religious PVOs the right to collect donations in places of worship without prior permission from MOSA, a privilege denied to other PVOs under Law 32.[87] Article 18 requires all other PVOs to apply for such permission to collect money at least sixty days in advance, and Article 19 limits the number of such permits to two each year.

However, much like the networks that help with registration, the success of ISIs in attracting donations (and, indirectly, in attracting patients) relies on the middle-class networks in which they are located—the informal, often social, networks they have created in the community and the ministries. ISIs reach out to neighboring communities to marshal their resources. Alternatively, they seek useful community contacts or networks to reach beyond the immediate community to other prospective donors who have the necessary resources. In the case of larger and/or older clinics with more extensive and established networks, the associations are able to appeal farther afield for donations. Some of these clinics are able to ask for donations from wealthy former members of the neighborhood who have moved to more affluent areas of the city or who have migrated to the Gulf. The Mustafa Mahmoud clinic has been highly successful at raising donations from the Gulf countries. Mustafa Mahmoud's personal fame and vast networks throughout the Arab world enable him to regularly appeal to the religious community at large in Egypt and abroad for donations to the clinic.

Other clinics use more domestic connections to approach companies for donations. One clinic in a wealthier district of Cairo approached a contact in a branch of the Bank of Alexandria and convinced the Bank not to distribute its annual New Year's promotional gifts, such as free calendars, but instead to donate the money to the clinic. It is no coincidence that this clinic had a retired police general with numerous connections to prominent people on its board.

As for the large number of small clinics tucked away in some of Cairo's poorest neighborhoods, donations usually come from local sources close to home.[88] Members of the association and the surrounding community donate everything from cement, iron pillars, windows, electrical wiring, and money to physical labor to facilitate the building of the clinic. Community members who own small businesses donate some of their inventory, other community members manually help with the building of the clinic, and still others approach friends who may have building equipment or a truck for transporting materials. However, these sorts of community efforts are dependent upon members who are themselves not poor. They are largely reflective of Cairo's many mixed-use neighborhoods. Many poorer neighborhoods have neither these resources nor contacts to people who have these resources.

NETWORKS AND THE HIRING OF DOCTORS

Networks not only provide the bureaucratic and economic means to exist, they also often produce the actual doctors and nurses who work in the clinics. While the image of a PVO brings to mind a purely volunteer organization, PVOs, including Islamic clinics, may have a volunteer and/or a paid staff. In fact, Saad Eddin Ibrahim's study indicates that a high percentage of Egyptian PVOs rely entirely on paid staff or rely only partially on volunteers. In his study of thirty-five PVOs for which data was available, Ibrahim found that only 40 percent relied on volunteers extensively. Twenty-five percent relied on volunteers on an occasional basis. Thirty-five percent did not use or rely on volunteers; the projects they initiated and administered depended instead on full-time or part-time paid employees.[89] This percentage rose to 65 percent in the specific case of "religious, scientific and cultural" PVOs.

Most Islamic clinics similarly rely on a paid medical staff. The process of hiring this staff is dependent on the types of contacts a clinic's membership has. In the majority of cases, doctors are hired through a friend (or the friend of a friend of a . . .) in informal processes.[90] Only the largest and wealthiest of clinics, such as the Mustafa Mahmoud clinic, have a formal hiring procedure by which they attempt to get the best doctors possible. Mustafa Mahmoud also approaches the better students in medical school. It successfully recruits Egypt's brightest graduates precisely because it can offer good salaries and top-quality equipment.[91] In smaller clinics, where facilities and pay are lacking, this simply isn't feasible or possible. Most clinics are content with any doctor they can get—although they would prefer the best they can get. Because they pay little money, they are in no position to be choosy. Clinics are thus dependent upon the goodwill of doctors and use their networks to locate doctors (or interns) who are willing to work in the evenings at the clinics.

The fact that Islamic clinics are successful in getting any form of cheap medical help is to a large extent due to the fact that they alleviate the problems of underemployment and unemployment among Egyptian doctors. Despite the fact that there are thousands of untreated Egyptians, Egyptian doctors are driving taxis because the government is unable to provide sufficient medical facilities in which they can practice.[92] The doctors themselves usually cannot afford to open their own practices.[93] In fact, only 25 percent of Egyptian doctors are in private practice.[94] In addition to the expense of equipment and supplies, rental rates in the central areas of cities and towns are too high for the majority of doctors. Furthermore, the number of private clinics in existence is already too great in relation to the size of the population that is able to afford such services.[95] Doctors who open clinics in the cheaper peripheral areas of towns and in newly created towns find that they must compete with each other and with religious clinics that specifically cater to those who cannot afford services. Many of these private clinics are forced to implement a sliding-fee scale and must charge little or no money to the poor if they want to gain a patient base.

The majority of doctors are employed by the Ministry of Health, where salaries are woefully inadequate. In 1996, doctors were earning as little as 120 to 150 LE per month in state-run hospitals and clinics.[96] And in 1995, newly graduated doctors were earning only 80 to 90 LE per month, which is insufficient to live at a decent standard.[97] This is compared to the doctors in private hospitals, whose salaries can reach up to 5,000 LE per month.[98] In a 1988 survey, two-thirds of Egyptian doctors stated that their salaries were not enough to cover their living costs.[99] It is for these reasons that doctors are forced to seek part-time evening employment.[100]

Indeed, Sylvia Chiffoleau notes what she calls the "bi-polarization" of the medical profession. Between the 1960s and 1995, the number of Egyptian doctors exploded to 100,500.[101] However, of these, only 8 percent have private practices with "solvent" patients. On the other end of the spectrum, approximately 75 percent are working in a Ministry of Health facility, 70 percent are under 40 years of age, and two-thirds, unable to afford the costs of a car, furniture, or property generally required to get married, are single.[102]

For the clear majority of doctors, work within the clinics is driven mainly (but not solely) by the need for a supplementary income or medical experience and/or the opportunity to build one's own clientele for a future private clinic.[103] As one doctor working in the Islamic Medical Society (Al-Jamʿiya al-Tibbiya al-Islamiya) bluntly stated to Sullivan: "We come for the extra income."[104] This is confirmed in my own interviews. When I asked physicians and nurses why they chose to work at an Islamic clinic, none mentioned any religious reason other than charity or helping the poor. A small number of responses included the good medical experience they would be receiving, and others explained that it was simply a way to earn a living. Some stated it was because of proximity to home or the fact that they had begun working at the clinic while still in training and consequently decided to continue working there upon graduation. When specifically asked if Islam had influenced their decision to work in the clinics, the majority of doctors and nurses stated that it was not important that the clinic was an Islamic one. A substantial minority stated that it was important that the clinic be an Islamic clinic, but in each case they explained this position in terms of aiding the poor, which is not exclusive to Islamic clinics.

The typical doctor is thus motivated to work in an Islamic clinic for economic and, to a lesser extent, charitable reasons. He or she has two jobs—

one during the day for the Ministry of Health and one at the Islamic clinic in the evening.[105] It is furthermore through his/her personal ties and social networks that he/she is able to obtain an evening position (usually without any interview—formal or informal) in the Islamic clinics, where he/she generally works from 7 P.M. to 10 P.M.

Despite the low pay and high rate of underemployment among doctors, Islamic clinics often struggle to obtain and maintain good medical staff. Most clinics do not engage in long-term budgetary planning. This is reflected negatively in the hiring procedure of doctors, the rate of pay of doctors, and the equipment that is available to doctors. Purchases are relatively ad hoc and depend on the amount of donations received on a monthly basis. (In some clinics, fees may similarly change from month to month.) Many clinics post a long list of available services and specialties that may not be adequately provided. Smaller clinics in particular may claim to have dentistry and laboratories, but there is in fact no dentist's chair and nothing but a sink in the "laboratory." Perhaps the doctor is capable of these services in terms of his/her training, but the necessary facilities in order for him/her to practice do not exist. Ultimately, these conditions often result in a doctor's lack of loyalty to the clinic. Many doctors hop from one clinic to another until they find one with which they are satisfied. Others show up less and less frequently as they concentrate on building up their own private practices. Some may secretly demand an extra fee from patients.[106] Others may simply be unreliable—without a strong financial incentive, doctors show up for work at the clinic only when they have no other pressing concerns.

Ultimately, this means that social networks are pivotal in locating and keeping a doctor. Doctors who live in the neighborhood or have a strong loyalty to the friends (or family) who hired them have a far greater chance of being reliable and committed to the clinic. In the Religious Association of Imam Abu al-Azm, I found that at least three doctors of the clinic's thirteen are related to each other, as well as to the director quoted above. Clinics that are not able to attract doctors with high salaries or up-to-date equipment must rely on these sorts of connections and loyalty. Without finances with which to pay doctors (as in the case of larger clinics such as Mustafa Mahmoud) or board members with connections, smaller basic clinics in the poorer areas of the city struggle to locate and maintain doctors.

HORIZONTAL VERSUS VERTICAL TIES IN THE ESTABLISHMENT AND RUNNING OF ISLAMIC CLINICS

The bureaucratic and financial circumstances under which PVOs in Egypt operate mean that social networks are crucial. For a clinic to be successful, directors and members of the boards of directors must have connections to finances, materials, and skills—or useful government contacts. The operational needs of Islamic clinics thus foster the development and maintenance of horizontal, specifically middle-class, ties as opposed to vertical ties to the poor who less commonly have these sorts of resources and connections. What this means is that we generally do not find the poor in general assemblies, the boards of directors, or in the social networks that are crucial to the ongoing success of Islamic clinics. Yet it is precisely here, in the assemblies and boards of directors, that the poor would have direct access to or integration in the networks of solidarity and teamwork that make the clinics Islamic.

Ibrahim's study confirms that the leadership and core organization of PVOs in Egypt is "almost exclusively dominated by the members of the middle class."[107] He furthermore argues that, as a result, PVO participation assumes an elite-mass character (i.e., PVOs are elitist in terms of composition and character), with little enthusiasm on the part of the middle class to seek the active participation of those at the grassroots of society. The poor are largely excluded from PVO activity except as mere recipients of benefits.[108] While development workers have indicated that this phenomenon is partially due to the hierarchical structure of Egyptian society, integrating the poor into the membership of PVOs, including clinics, simply has no useful value in the financing, building, and staffing of PVOs, and hence is not pursued.[109]

Technically, membership in the association of an Islamic clinic is open to anybody provided they can afford a small fee (and pay regularly). Yet, as in other PVOs, membership in the associations also tends to be limited to the relatively wealthier, more educated members of the neighborhood.[110] My interviews in Islamic clinics confirm that although fees are required for membership in the associations, the major obstacle to greater participation of the poor does not appear to be the fee but rather a lack of encouragement. In only one rare exception did I find a board of directors with an express policy of ensuring that poorer members of the surrounding neighborhood, including one illiterate member, are present on the board. In the vast majority of cases, boards of directors tend to be very homogeneous. Members on boards of directors actively try to cultivate useful ties with various patrons and bring them onto the board so that they will have a greater personal stake in the success of the clinic. In this way, ties are made stronger and more enduring.

This is not to deny the existence of highly mixed neighborhoods, class-wise, throughout Cairo or the fact that vertical ties do exist within Islamic clinics. The integration of clinics (particularly the smaller clinics) into their respective neighborhoods is often well established. During interviews, I observed numerous scenes in which association members and others from the neighborhood gathered in the office of the medical director or the association director to discuss the clinic and general events. In the course of these discussions, community concerns are also raised. Patients and people from the neighborhood may and do come to make suggestions about the clinic. In all the clinics, the medical directors are easily found and approached because they are present each evening working in their capacity as doctors. Many of my own interviews became group affairs, as people from the neighborhood, even *shayookh* (pl.; sing. *shaykh*) from neighboring mosques (which have their own "rival" clinics), dropped by and participated in the discussions with the doctors and directors. One particularly memorable interview ended at 1:00 A.M. with the entire group of us eating *kushari* (a popular rice dish) in the director's office! Although as a rule, clinics become more formalized the larger they become, even in the larger clinics, such as Mustafa Mahmoud, patients and their families have relatively easy access to various directors and, if certain situations arise, even to Dr. Mustafa Mahmoud himself. The predominance of horizontal ties does not mean the exclusion of vertical ties. However, while open avenues to the neighborhood do exist, the informal social visits I witnessed were overwhelmingly (but not solely) by middle-class neighborhood friends.

Thus, the primary contact the poor have with Islamic clinics and their networks is strictly as patients. Yet clinics located in poorer areas struggle to maintain a consistent staff, which hinders the development of vertical ties. Many clinics lose patients because doctors are not always available. Furthermore, as clinics attempt to locate and maintain medical staff, they can even find themselves in the position of hiring doctors who may in fact be unsympathetic to (or at least not supportive of) the Islamist movement.

In my interviews, when I questioned doctors about their voting habits in both the doctors' syndicate and the national elections, their responses revealed a wide diversity of political sympathies. In terms of the doctors' syndicate elections, responses included both the Islamic List and the National Democratic Party (NDP, the party of the president). Doctors voted in national elections for the NDP and Labour Party/Islamic List as well as for the leftist Tajammuʿ Party and the nationalist Wafd Party. In fact, I interviewed one doctor (he requested the interview be at home and not at the clinic) who had a large poster of Che Guevara in his waiting room! Some doctors specifically requested that they be interviewed at home so that they could talk freely and critically of their associations and even of Islamism. When I asked doctors what the phrase "Islam is the solution" meant to them, one responded by saying: "When they explain the slogan, then I will be able to give an opinion." Another doctor exclaimed to me: "Empty people say that; unfortunately those are the words of empty people. It is a slogan some parties need, just slogans repeated by some parties with no objectives." While there are exceptions, doctors working in Islamic clinics do not as a rule participate in fostering an exchange (or fostering the perception of an exchange) of medical services for political support.

Thus, the data simply does not support the assumption that the poor are integrated into the general assemblies or their associated networks involved in the establishment and ongoing management of Islamic clinics. The poor are mere recipients of services.

NETWORKS AND THE LOCATION AND QUALITY OF CLINICS

The pivotal role informal social networks play in the registering, building, funding, equipping, and staffing of an Islamic clinic has an enormous impact upon the quantity and quality of services a clinic can offer. Clinics vary according to their success at forging useful networks. Ultimately, those clinics with either few founders and/or founders with limited connections to resources suffer. It is not surprising that clinics in poorer neighborhoods, those neighborhoods with fewer members of the middle class or fewer members with access to useful connections, are commonly small in size and inadequate in terms of services. Ultimately, this means that the poor have very different experiences in the Islamic clinics located near their homes than the residents of affluent neighborhoods such as Ma'adi, Mohandessin, or Heliopolis have in theirs.

Based on their sources of wealth, size, and facilities, clinics can be divided into roughly three categories. Loosely estimated, 15 percent of the clinics are larger clinics that are well staffed and well equipped. These clinics often compete with any Western facility in terms of staff and facilities and attract patients from all over Cairo, Egypt, and even the Arab world. They may have as many as 200 doctors and receive numerous sources of domestic and international funding. Many of them receive funding from the Gulf; others receive "public relations" donations from the Bank of Alexandria or perhaps the Suez Canal Bank. This type of large donation is dependent upon connections—knowing someone in the bank.

Approximately 35 percent of the clinics are medium sized, with perhaps twenty doctors. Many of these medium-sized clinics have one particular specialty, such as physiotherapy, with which they are able to attract patients from all over the city. People travel to these clinics for a specific service as opposed to being drawn by its overall reputation, as is the case with the larger clinics. These clinics rely on domestic sources of funding and have extensive networks that facilitate their success. As in the case of the Religious Association of Imam Abu al-Azm, many of these medium-sized clinics are family-run businesses; the grandfather established the clinic and his sons and daughters work in it as doctors and directors. The majority of chains of clinics are usually in these first two categories of clinics. Al-Jamʿiya al-Sharʿiya, for example, concentrates on moneymaking clinics—those in wealthier areas, which are less politically sensitive and in which they can draw upon a more affluent patient base. Many of these trophy clinics are attached to the city's most prominent and wealthy mosques.

The largest category, roughly 50 percent of the clinics, is one-room, one-doctor clinics with little or no equipment, funds, or medicine. They are furthermore without substantial or useful networks. Most are close to extinction and serve the immediate neighborhood—usually the poorest neighborhoods in Cairo.[111] My research informally estimates that as much as 70 percent of these smaller clinics are barely getting by.[112] Without networks, clinics are simply not able to marshal the resources they need to survive. This problem is exacerbated by the fact that some of the poorer areas are overcrowded with inadequate clinics, resulting in competition and duplication of the same few services. Furthermore, government and international assistance tends to go to larger and more successful associations. Government aid correlates with the ability of a PVO to provide services that the government deems necessary rather than those which meet the financial needs of the PVOs; hence this category of aid is primarily directed to CDAs.[113] International assistance is biased toward larger PVOs, those with a greater capacity for identifying and implementing projects. In this scenario, the increasing number of urban poor are most hurt. Smaller clinics in poorer areas are caught in a vicious cycle of few or no influential board members with helpful connections in the government, a lack of trained personnel, an increasing number of patrons without the means to pay even a minimal fee, limited or no state or foreign aid, and, ultimately, limited effectiveness.

A small clinic in the poor Cairene neighborhood of Boulaq provides an excellent example. The clinic is located in a tiny residential alley of low-storied apartment buildings teeming with people. The neighborhood is extremely poor. The clinic—essentially two rooms—is located on the second floor of a small building and is relatively unnoticeable as it has no sign. Only one full-time doctor, one occasional doctor, and one full-time nurse work in it. The lack of equipment and supplies is readily apparent. The clinic has a small number of cotton swabs and tongue depressors. It also has "used" medicine (medicine that previous patients did not finish) available to give to the poor. The clinic is far from sanitary. It receives few patients. One elderly woman lacked the means to buy a wheelchair, and her grandson and doctor had to carry her upstairs on a chair. The clinic's financial problems are typical of the vicious circle faced by the many of the smaller clinics—

without supplies, equipment, financially solvent patients, or high salaries, they have difficulty keeping doctors. The clinic's greatest challenge has been finding a doctor who is consistent in his/her hours. Because of his studies, the present doctor is irregular in the hours and days he keeps. Without a consistent medical staff, patients do not gain the necessary trust and find other medical options if they can.

Unlike the cases of the ICCS in Jordan and the CSSW in Yemen, Islamic clinics in Cairo do not have any specific criteria by which they screen the poor. Technically, anyone from any socioeconomic bracket may go to a clinic and receive services. However, given the level of services and facilities, in practice, the smallest clinics in the *sha'abi* areas cater strictly to the poor. In medium-sized and larger clinics, which are often located in more affluent areas, we find the poor but we also increasingly find military officers, university professors, and other members of the middle class who struggle to make ends meet. Since the introduction of ERSAP in 1991, real wages in the public industrial sector have dropped. Other public-sector wages have remained steady, but, as Mitchell states, "could be maintained only because the salaries remain below a living wage." A schoolteacher or other educated public-sector employee takes home less than $2 US per day.[114] This, not the poor, is increasingly the clientele that seeks the services of Cairo's larger and medium-sized (and better-equipped) Islamic clinics.

ISLAMIC CLINICS?

The assumption that there is something uniquely Islamic about Islamic clinics cannot be supported—there is little that is unique or specifically Islamic about Islamic medical clinics. The difference between Islamic clinics and other clinics may lie in the spirit of teamwork with which services are provided; however, there is little demonstration of superior Islamic medical services or an effective Islamic model in action. While the middle class may be privy to this important sense of teamwork and solidarity as directors, donors, or employees, the poor experience little that makes Islamic clinics significantly different from the numerous other (inadequate) medical options that are available to them. The Islamic nature of Islamic clinics does not indirectly foster vertical ties.

What would make an Islamic clinic Islamic? From the perspective of the patients, an Islamic clinic must have much more than a reference to Islam in its name. At a very minimum, patients generally expect to find a higher degree of personal attention, care, charity, and honesty in Islamic clinics. My interviews reveal that while most patients do not explicitly articulate the fact that they expect an Islamic clinic to provide some sort of model that follows Islamic precepts, they generally assume that there will be some degree of segregation between the sexes. Female patients (and their husbands) assume that they will find female gynecologists.[115] Many Egyptians expect all females working in Islamic associations to be dressed modestly and veiled. Many also expect that staff in the clinics will observe all prayers.[116]

Certainly one can find Islamic clinics that are strenuously attempting to fulfill these criteria. Al-Jamʿiya al-Tibbiya al-Islamiya, the Islamic Medical Society, is one chain (it has sixteen branches) that attempts to do so. First established in 1977, the Society clearly sees the education of young doctors to be practicing Muslims as part of its mission. The Society has very strict regulations concerning attire, prayers, and segregation. Some clinics conduct weekly Friday seminars and, in the case of the Religious Association of Abu al-Azm, doctors are encouraged, but not obliged, to present papers dealing specifically with Islam and medicine. Yet on the whole, Islamic clinics do not follow any particular Islamic rules.

Although many clinics do not open their doors until after evening prayers, in those that do open before prayers, the majority do not close for prayers and the doctors do not stop working. Doctors and nurses are generally not given any specific guidelines concerning Islamic modes of conduct and behavior they must follow while working at the clinic. Only a limited number of clinics require that female doctors and nurses be veiled. When seeking doctors and nurses, the boards of directors of these clinics generally do not explicitly specify that females be covered; rather, through word of mouth, applicants are made aware of the atmosphere and expectations of each clinic. Female doctors who do not don the veil would not be inclined to apply for work in these clinics. One clinic in the district of Zaytoon requires (through example) that its female employees veil and attempts to enforce segregation of the sexes. All the nurses in this clinic wear a head-covering and face-covering (*niqab*) that leaves only their eyes exposed. However, it was also at this clinic where I interviewed a doctor who was decidedly secular and who, when interviewed upon his request at his private practice, strenuously objected to the Islamist movement.

Female doctors work in all fields of medicine within the clinics, treating both men and women. A high percentage of female doctors are gynecologists and/or pediatricians; however, this does not mean that Islamic clinics do not have male gynecologists (as evidenced by the example described above at the Mustafa Mahmoud medical complex). Even if a clinic has a female gynecologist listed on staff, it does not mean a patient will be able to see her. Because many female doctors have numerous household responsibilities, women doctors have a fairly high rate of absenteeism. Many female doctors work on a drop-in or ad hoc basis only. If the female doctor is not there (providing the clinic has more than one doctor), the patient must go to a male gynecologist. There is little or no segregation in the clinics.

I found no real Islamic model being followed in Islamic clinics, one that would make Islamic clinics significantly different from other medical options and would indirectly foster some sort of vertical loyalty, political or otherwise. Islamic clinics are one of many similar options available to Egyptians. Islamic clinics have not supplanted or dominated other medical options for the poor; they are simply one of several medical options they regularly consult. In my interviews, some former patients expressed their preference for private clinics or a different Islamic clinic.

Recently published data on Egyptians' utilization of outpatient facilities clearly supports my contention that Islamic clinics are just one of numerous medical options that are consulted. A survey of 50,661 people found that 44 percent of the respondents reported an illness within the two-week period prior to the survey and, of these, 21 percent sought treatment. Of those seeking treatment: 21.2 percent went to Ministry of Health services; 10.4 percent went to other ministries' facilities; and 8.4 percent went to the semipublic social insurance facilities (Health Insurance Organization and Curative Care Organizations). Alternatively, 49.7 percent went to private physicians (private practice), 6.3 percent to mosque clinics, 3 percent to pharmacies, and 1 percent to other types of services. Most important, the survey found that the level of income played a relatively insignificant role in the choice of medical facility. The poor, just as their affluent counterparts do, visit a variety of medical options, and they prefer to (and do) visit fee-for-service private providers. By relying just as heavily as the rich on private medical care, the poor pay disproportionately more for health services than the rich.[117]

A study of Mashiet Nasser, a lower-income settlement in Cairo, similarly notes that its residents have a choice of government facilities (including a hospital with more than seventy doctors), a plethora of private practices, private polyclinics, and Muslim, Christian and secular PVOs. The study's authors note that families take their sick children to private clinics, health centers, and hospitals within Manshiet Nasser and all over the city of Cairo. Of these visits to professional medical sources, on average 66 percent are to physicians (42 percent to physicians inside the settlement and 14 percent to those outside), 24 percent of the visits are to a hospital, and 10 percent are to a health center or pharmacist.[118] These visits, however, are not mutually exclusive. Nor are professional sources the only ones consulted; many traditional forms of medicine are also consulted.

These findings are further supported by various ethnographic studies. Evelyn Early's research on *baladi* culture (the culture of rural people) in Cairo found that poor patients consult several specialists in their search for the most authoritative opinion.[119] She notes that on behalf of her children, a mother may fill more than one prescription and administer all, assuming the more medicine, the better. She sees no contradiction in combining medical and nonmedical cures; she make take her child to the clinic and proceed from there to a shaykh to obtain an amulet.[120]

Limited-income women, Early states, visit a "panoply of clinics to locate an inexpensive cure, judge the care at each and strategize methods to extract better service."[121]

Early tells how one Muslim mother took her sick daughter to a woman in the neighborhood, who rubbed goat's milk on her chest and forehead. She then proceeded to a Christian woman who lived in her father-in-law's building, who pierced a doll and then pinned a plastic cross on the girl's chest. When the girl was still sick one week later, the mother took her to another woman in the neighborhood, who rubbed mother's breast milk and oil on the girl's chest. Two days later, she made a paper doll for her, pierced it, and burned it and made a cross on her forehead with the ashes. The next day, the child's health worsening, the mother took her to the Ministry of Health mothers' clinic. However, visitations by children of her daughter's age group were designated for a different day. The mother then went straight to the government's maternity hospital and, after paying the standard fee and slipping some money to the nurse orderly, she was seen immediately. The mother bought the prescribed medicine from the outside pharmacy.[122]

Similarly, Nayra Atiya writes of the housekeeper named Suda who took her mother to three doctors in one day. The first two doctors were neighbors in their apartment building and she visited them in their homes. The third doctor was in the Embaba district of Cairo. When she saw no improvements in her mother's condition, she took her to the hospital. When the mother objected to the prescribed medicine, a friend took the two of them to a woman she knew in Boulaq, another part of the city. She recommended a ritual involving the slaughtering of various barnyard animals. Before doing this, the daughter consulted another wise woman living along the Nile, a *shaykha*. She too recommended a ritual involving the slaughtering of chickens. She paid one more visit to this *shaykha,* and "took [her] mother to the doctor after that."[123]

In general, these studies indicate that the poor seek medical options that are good, affordable, and familiar in the sense that there is some sort of firsthand or secondhand knowledge of the caregiver. Hence, Suda first visited the two doctors living in her building—both because she knew them and because visiting them at home ensured a cheaper bill, if there were one at all. My interviews with patients and former patients of Islamic clinics confirm that patients judge Islamic clinics on the type of treatment they receive and, in particular, the reliability of the doctor and the care he or she gives. Whereas middle-class patients are drawn to the larger clinics by the facilities and equipment, patients go to medium-sized and small-sized clinics out of loyalty to a doctor. The problem is that in smaller clinics, doctors are often unreliable. Certainly in at least one clinic, the nurse complained to me that it was due to the absenteeism of the doctor that the clinic was failing. (Absenteeism, interestingly enough, is also one of the biggest problems in the government hospitals.) In smaller, poorer-paying clinics, doctors are simply less committed to their jobs and this can be reflected in less punctuality and reliability on the part of the doctors and a less caring environment in the clinics in general.

It would seem therefore that from the perspective of the poor, Islamic clinics can be one more inadequate medical option among many that include free government services, private clinics, non-Islamic benevolent societies, and perhaps even nonmedical options (in the Western sense of biomedicine), such as *shaykhat* and other forms of folk medicine. There does not appear to be anything uniquely Islamic about Islamic clinics, nor do their services appear to be the only options available. There are superb Islamic clinics, offering top-notch medical services. However, these clinics may not be geographically or financially accessible to the poor. Poor patients may in fact find a relatively adequate solution closer to home.

THE EXPERIENCES OF THE MIDDLE CLASS: TEAMWORK AND SOLIDARITY

The abovementioned survey on the utilization of outpatient facilities in Egypt reports that there is little difference in usage between levels of income. Yet the experience of the middle class in Islamic clinics is different than that of the poor. Furthermore, while the poor may experience little that is Islamic in Islamic clinics, this is not necessarily the case for the middle class.

The fact that most Islamic clinics are not implementing or enforcing Islamic codes of conduct, such as prayers or segregation, does not mean that the directors and doctors in the clinics do not perceive a difference between Islamic clinics and other clinics. In fact, they do. For example, when I asked doctors, directors, and nurses if they felt that the clinic in which they were working was Islamic, the majority said yes.[124] As their justification, they cited issues such as reasonable prices, charity, low wages, serving the district, helping poor Muslims, and the fact that the clinics are maintained on donations. Other doctors mentioned the cooperation, solidarity, and family-like relations, including patience, tolerance, consensus, and consultation, among the doctors of the clinic. Some of those interviewed mentioned that participants within Islamic clinics follow an Islamic code of behavior such as observing prayers, wearing Islamic dress, wearing the veil, conducting same-sex examinations of patients, and upholding of Islamic morals. Finally, a significant minority felt there was no difference at all between clinics; they felt that an Islamic clinic was the same as any other clinic.

When asked if they felt that any Islamic principles were being followed in the clinics in which they were working, most stated that Islamic principles were reflected in the fact that the clinic charged low fees or gave low pay, that the goal of clinic was not material success, or that the clinic helped the poor or was a form of social work. Others gave moral or behavioral reasons such as sympathy, hospitality, honesty, mercy, and performing one's job as best one can. Others stated that the doctors in the clinic were "like a family" and that the operations of the clinic were based on cooperation and consultation. Some pointed to the observance of prayers while others said that no Islamic principles were present in their respective clinics.

Finally, when I asked about the difference between an Islamic clinic and a nonreligious clinic (private or public), doctors, directors, and nurses predominantly responded with charity reasons, such as reduced fees. A significant number also mentioned the good attitude of the doctors, the fact that the clinics reflect the views of Muslim doctors, the fact that decisions are made based on consultation and consensus, the family-like relations among staff members, teamwork and solidarity within the clinic, and the good relations between the doctors and the patients. Some stated that there was no difference at all.

A number of dominant themes thus emerge: Islamic clinics are Islamic due to their spirit of charity, their family-like relations, and the cooperative, consensual manner in which decisions within the clinics are made. Those who work in the clinics, therefore, perceive Islamic clinics to be defined by a positive environment and a strong sense of teamwork created by a common mission to help the poor. This sense of teamwork and solidarity is further enforced by the perceived Islamic values being encouraged in the clinics, such as tolerance and a decision-making process that is rooted in the Islamic concept of *shura,* or consultation. As one doctor in an Islamic clinic in the poor district of Olali in Cairo stated to me:

> Islamic clinics must be different in management, in the administration. However, sometimes you find Islamic clinics far from being Islamic, with no connection or tie to Islam. The difference between these clinics and a truly Islamic clinic is substantial. An Islamic clinic has a goal and an origin and is not based upon persons. They are different in the aspects of *shura:* organization or *tanzim,* commitment and devotion, and observing God in doing one's work. All these characteristics and attributes entail a good connection with God, or commitment.

Based on the values of *shura,* this same doctor clearly stated that his clinic was indeed Islamic, even though the commitment to the observance of Islam, such as prayers, particularly among the nurses, was weak.

These intangible values and attitudes, this development of networks of teamwork, trust, and solidarity is exclusive to the middle-class networks of those who work in and are associated with Islamic clinics. What makes Islamic clinics Islamic is thus not necessarily identifiable to the outsider— those outside these middle-class networks. What makes them Islamic is in fact the invisible process of the building of social capital.

While a number of respondents did note that their clinics upheld Islamic codes of conduct, such as prayer and segregation, most of these doctors were in fact working in clinics in which this was not the case. It must be kept in mind that doctors sometimes answered in theoretical terms, not in terms of the reality. In one instance a doctor clearly laid out the Islamic principles underlying an Islamic clinic. He stressed the fact that in an Islamic clinic only a female doctor examines female patients. He also felt that the clinic he worked for was Islamic. When I asked what type of doctor he was, he replied that he was a gynecologist!

The fact that some respondents clearly stated that there was nothing Islamic about their clinic, or at least no difference between it and any other, indicates that the building of teamwork and solidarity is not consistent across all clinics. I came across cases in which there was friction between the medical staff and the administrative staff. In one case the doctors' syndicate was asked to step in and make recommendations. Clinics may have doctors working in them who are unsupportive or unsympathetic to the Islamist movement. In this sense they are nonmember participants—participants in an ISI but not members of the networks of teamwork and solidarity and, potentially, according to social movement theory, the negotiation and renegotiation of identity. In the case of Egypt, where many doctors seek work in Islamic clinics simply for extra income, these networks of shared meaning may at times be limited to (or stronger in) those associated with the directors and donors whose participation is not driven strictly by economic need. What is important, however, is less these exceptions but more the fact that these processes, when they occur, are along horizontal lines and not along vertical ones that include the poor.

CONCLUSIONS

The success of Islamic clinics lies in the state's failure. They provide an intermediate form of care between the expensive "investment medical care" and the government's inadequate services. From the perspective of the patients, they pay less than in private hospitals and clinics and do not suffer the lineups and rudeness of doctors the government employs. The popularity of the clinics is due to the generally courteous treatment patients receive and their convenient locations. Patients' disgruntlement with other forms of health care is matched by the problem of unemployment and underemployment among doctors. Without the availability of doctors, there simply could not be so many Islamic clinics.

The Egyptian state also plays a far more direct role in the lives, and success, of Islamic clinics. The Ministry of Social Affairs regulates the registration, building, expansion, and fund-raising of Islamic clinics through Law 32. Islamic clinics are highly dependent upon the state for the permission they need in order to be able to establish themselves and provide their services. Islamic clinics are further tied to the state and its goodwill in that Islamic clinics, more so than any other type of PVO, receive various other state-granted privileges, such as greater freedoms to fund-raise. As compared to other PVOs, a very high percentage of Islamic clinics are also designated as public-interest clinics and as such receive additional privileges. Finally, Islamic clinics are also dependent upon, if not invested in, the state: a high percentage of the founders and directors are in fact civil servants and, most important, the majority of doctors are dependent upon their daytime jobs in public hospitals for their primary form of income. The vast majority of clinics simply cannot supplant the role of the state as the medical profession's main employer. To a large extent, therefore, Islamic clinics may chafe under onerous state regulations, but they also benefit from the state. In this sense, Islamic clinics have little cause to demand a dramatic overhaul of state practices.

Within this context, the key ingredient to making these clinics work is the members of the boards of directors and their ongoing efforts to create and integrate into a myriad of social networks. Throughout Cairo, hundreds of community-based Islamic associations are engaged in a process of widening and deepening social networks in order to facilitate the provision of health care to the city's poor and middle classes. The clinics are generally founded by the local middle class which forms the core of the clinics' boards of directors. The ongoing creation and maintenance of networks by the directors to ensure the survival of the clinics creates overlapping nodes where doctors, directors, nurses, volunteers, mosque-goers, neighbors, family, army buddies, university classmates, civil servants, shopkeepers, business-owners, and migrants meet and meet again. These networks or circles are generally of the middle class—those people who are able to aid the clinic in order to obtain and maintain a license, find doctors, buy equipment, speed up a building permit to expand the facilities, or protect the clinic from onerous government interference.

In the course of developing the reciprocal relations that are at the core of the clinics' networks, the clinics themselves become intertwined in numerous other uncoordinated networks that overlap in activities, memberships, and friendships. Clinics and their boards of directors thus become one of many nodes or meeting places in ever-widening and overlapping middle-class circles of reciprocity and exchange. These networks encompass a variety of people—donors, employees, and volunteers—with different degrees of commitment and involvement in the clinics. They also include both Islamists and non-Islamists. Even within the clinics themselves we can find doctors who would not classify themselves as Islamists and may in fact be unsympathetic to the Islamist movement. While Egypt does suffer a high rate of unemployment and underemployment among its doctors, Islamic clinics are not the solution to the problem. The majority of clinics offer little pay and relatively poor conditions in terms of the availability of equipment and facilities within which to work. Doctors thus may hop from one clinic to another in order to find a better working environment or they may simply use clinics while building up client bases for their own private practices. They may also be unreliable in the days and hours they keep while they study for exams or have other pressing issues to which to attend. While this is far less of a problem in the larger clinics, such as the Mustafa Mahmoud clinic, smaller clinics are often forced to hire whomever they can. The networks in which Islamic clinics are embedded, therefore, include both nonmember participants and members—those who participate in the clinics but who do not necessarily identify with the Islamist movement and those who actively see their activities within the ISIs as part of a team or mission and potentially as an act of *da'wa* and part of their identity as an Islamist.

It is within these middle-class networks that this sense of shared commitment, teamwork, solidarity and, potentially, identity is developed. While in no way can it be assumed that all who work in Islamic clinics are Islamists, it is out of the networks of directors, doctors, and donors that networks of shared meaning are created. It is this sense of teamwork and solidarity in providing health care in the name of Islam that makes the clinics Islamic, not their rules or regulations or their practice of medicine. Outwardly, Islamic clinics are no different from any other medical provider. Few stop for prayers or enforce dress codes. However, inwardly, in the attitudes of the providers of health care, and most specifically, of those members in the networks of shared meaning, we find an important perceived difference.

These networks, however, do not extend to the poor. As a whole, the poor are not integrated into the reinforcing social networks of middle-class directors, doctors, and donors; they are not part of the networks of shared meaning. The poor do not have the resources that they can contribute to the clinics, nor are they socially part of the middle-class networks that are created and maintained in the everyday functioning of the clinics. Indeed, they are generally not even in the general assemblies or on the boards of directors of the clinics.[125]

The experiences of the poor in Islamic clinics furthermore differ from those of members of the middle class. On the whole, Islamic clinics located in the poorer areas do not provide the same services as those located in more affluent areas of the city that can attract donors and doctors by offering them large salaries or beneficial medical experiences in terms of equipment and facilities. Without the necessary contacts and networks with which to establish and run a viable clinic, clinics in poorer areas are markedly inferior to those in more affluent communities with wealthier donors and useful contacts. Within smaller clinics the greatest complaints of patients concern the punctuality and reliability of the doctors. Clinics without consistent and regular staff have problems keeping people; quite naturally, patients want to see the same doctor on a consistent basis. Absenteeism is particularly a problem in the smaller clinics. While in the larger clinics the patients would have another doctor to go to, this is not the case in the smaller, poorer clinics. Patients are extremely grateful for the health care they receive; however, they complain about misdiagnoses, the need for additional services, and the extra payments some doctors demand. Patients and nurses report that behind closed doors some underpaid doctors have been known to resort to charging a second fee, encouraging patients to visit them in their private clinic, or stating that the patient needs extra services available only in his/her private clinic.

While these complaints are not exclusive to the smaller poorer clinics, punctuality and reliability are less of a problem in the larger and medium-sized clinics.[126] In larger clinics, doctors are more committed to their jobs because of better pay, better equipment, and the opportunity to obtain more experience. In many of the medium-sized family-run clinics, doctors are also more committed, as is a doctor whose family lives in the neighborhood. If in either of these types of clinics a doctor misses days from work, the patient can always see another doctor. This is not the case in smaller clinics, where doctors are less committed and there is no other doctor working at the clinic. On the whole, the quality of care patients received in clinics located in the *sha'abi* areas of Cairo is debatable. It certainly is not comparable to Islamic services offered elsewhere. In this context, Islamic clinics become one of many sources—including other PVOs (religious, secular, domestic, and international), the government, political parties, local patrons, neighborhood self-help associations, and families and friends—that the poor rely upon but do not necessarily participate in.[127]

It would appear that the primary beneficiary of Islamic medical clinics is the middle class, through the better-quality services Islamic clinics offer in more affluent districts, and not the poor. Middle-class doctors receive various benefits from ISIs. Interns and doctors benefit from an extra salary, necessary experience, and, occasionally, the opportunity to build a private clientele. As most doctors work without a contract (and most clinics would have to struggle to find a better replacement), they are additionally able to create highly flexible work schedules to their advantage. Doctors working in Cairo's "five star" clinics, such as the Mustafa Mahmoud medical complex (where loyalty is ensured by the top-quality working conditions), furthermore participate in a worthwhile and exciting team endeavor to improve the health of Egyptians by offering services many government hospitals cannot offer.

Without a doubt, Cairo's Islamic clinics cater to a broad or diverse class base—perhaps more so than ISIs in Jordan and Yemen. One sees a broad spectrum of patients in the clinics, from the poorest of the poor to various segments of the middle classes. Cairo's massive size, relatively poor infrastructure, traffic congestion, and shortage of affordable housing and the mixed economic and residential usage of its neighborhoods mean that people of all classes populate even the wealthiest of areas. Those serving the middle class and the rich as housecleaners or doormen try to live in or as close as possible to the area. For example, the poor have built homes on some of the rooftops of apartment buildings in one of Cairo's historically more affluent areas, Zamalek. The mixed neighborhoods, the lack of adequate state medical facilities and the fact that the clinics do not employ any criteria by which they screen or select patients to "qualify" for treatment all mean that Islamic clinics are not exclusive to any one class. However, there are marked differences between affluent areas, such as Ma'adi, and historically poor areas, such as Boulaq. And it is in the areas in which the middle class dominates that one finds Islamic clinics with the best facilities, services, and doctors. The poorer the neighborhood, the smaller and less extensive the services and facilities and the more the clinic exclusively treats the poor.

One will also find directors who are of the middle classes but not necessarily of the new petit bourgeois. They are part of the local elite who want to do something for their community. Some of them are leading figures in the neighborhood mosque; others are local merchants. An examination of the various boards of directors, however, indicates that the educated middle class dominates—and it is this educated middle class, and particularly the clinics' doctors, who benefit tremendously from the jobs and services being provided by Islamic clinics. While exceptions can quite naturally be found, Islamic clinics are run by and for the middle class.

Within Cairo's Islamic clinics, therefore, we see that it is the horizontal networks, predominantly those of the middle class, that are being created and strengthened, rather than vertical networks. The poor are not being politicized through integration into the general assemblies and boards of directors or through their associated networks or through the demonstration of quality services and facilities or through an Islamic model or mode of operation. The poor are not only clients (as opposed to members), they are also subjects of relatively little religious propaganda. (To a certain extent, this is due to state prohibitions.) With the exception of the largest clinics, clinics are devoid of any pamphlets concerning Islam; most clinics are fairly bare, "adorned" strictly with information concerning the services and procedures within the clinics. The Mustafa Mahmoud complex is decorated with photographs and busts of Mustafa Mahmoud himself. Poor patients who are not part of middle-class social networks have their greatest contact strictly with doctors. Yet many doctors regard their employment in the clinics simply as a form of salary augmentation. They are, in this regard, nonmember participants. It would seem that generally doctors working in Islamic clinics cannot be assumed to be strong links in creating vertical networks.

While Islamic clinics do not outwardly differ from other forms of health care, patients, and presumably prospective patients, do judge Islamic clinics differently than other health care providers, including both the state and other PVOs. There is no doubt that patients are grateful for the relatively cheap services of the clinics. As structural adjustment progresses, the gap between the cost of visitations to private clinics and Islamic clinics is increasing. A medical doctor in a private clinic who is also a full university professor can easily charge 100 LE or more. As one cynical patient stated to me, it is better to pay 2 LE in an Islamic clinic and be ignored by a doctor than to pay 50 LE to be ignored by a more expensive doctor elsewhere. While complaints by patients are relatively few, Islamic clinics appear to be judged more harshly than their non-Islamic counterparts. With the label "Islamic" comes certain expectations. At Islamic clinics, ones that are assumed to be working for the poor in the name of Islam and clinics that are located in neighborhood mosques, community members and patients generally expect the fees to be very low and clinics to be community oriented. Despite examination fees of only 2 LE, some former patients complained to me that the fees were too high and that the clinics had become too commercial. As one stated: "I'd like to know what they do with the donations they receive. The fee has become expensive and they have become commercial." Another complained: "Since the founder died the fees have increased a lot, so I prefer to go to a private clinic instead of the hospital here." Similarly, "The people in charge of the clinic do not try to enlighten the community in terms of sanitary issues. They work like government officials, just sitting in their offices. . . . They work like a government party." As will be seen to a far greater degree in the case of Jordan, at issue is a tension or conflict between expectations of what an Islamic clinic should be—whether it should be free or cheap—and the reality of relatively expensive fees.

The operational needs of Islamic clinics to a large extent dictate the forging, reforging, and strengthening of horizontal ties as opposed to vertical ties. Larger Islamic associations, those that have chains of branch clinics have also established "trophy clinics." These are not endeavors initiated from within local communities but clinics that are established by an administrative decision in the association's headquarters. They are located in areas of high prominence, thus ensuring that they have tremendous symbolic value. The existence of trophy clinics leads one to believe that the prioritization of the middle class is not entirely due to the operational needs of the clinics.

THREE

The Islamic Center Charity Society in Jordan: The Benefits to the Middle Class

---

Located in the arid flat outskirts of the northern city of Mafraq is a regional branch of the Islamic Center Charity Society (ICCS), Jordan's largest ISI. I drove to Mafraq from Amman on a glorious sunny day and spent an extremely pleasant afternoon with the director of an active and caring group of teachers, other employees, and volunteers. As was apparent during the drive, the governorate of Mafraq is sparsely populated with predominantly Transjordanians (those who lived in Jordan prior to the arrival of Palestinian refugees) and Bedouins, and it is also the country's poorest region. The center, however, is quite large; it has ninety employees and houses a kindergarten, a boys' and girls' junior school (grades one to six), a senior school for boys (grades seven to ten), and a center for orphans and the needy.[1] The center, including its administrative offices and schools, consists of several buildings surrounding a courtyard that is used as a playground. There is also a very small agricultural project where food is grown for orphans.[2] Seven school buses bring well over 1,000 pupils and students to school each day; the largest number of students (672) attend the junior school. The center financially assists thirty-five orphans, fifty-five needy families, and a limited number of university students on a regular basis.[3] Several hundred needy individuals receive financial or material aid on an irregular basis. However, while the school fees are subsidized by donations and are kept down as much as possible, they remain quite high. The kindergarten fees are 120 Jordanian dinar (JD) per year plus 55 JD per year for transportation; this fee rises to 160 JD per year plus 75 JD for transportation for students in grade ten.[4] Despite the surrounding poverty and the fact that some orphans do attend the school for free, the school is a private one and remains, as the director stated to me, a middle-class school.[5]

While there can be no doubt that the Islamic Center Charity Society serves large numbers of poor and does an invaluable service, its school in

Mafraq is indicative of all its schools and many of its other projects, particularly its hospitals, in that it largely serves the middle class and not the poor. Indeed, the middle class benefits both in terms of services and employment. The nonprofit commercial services established by the ICCS, such as its private elementary and secondary schools, offer the middle class—which is disgruntled with the state educational system that is viewed as too Western, is unable to afford the private schools of the "velvet circles," and is alienated by the Western curricula of the private schools—an alternative curriculum, one that promises greater religious content and a high-quality education.[6] At the same time, these same institutions provide jobs to Jordan's educated middle-class professionals. These include such positions as doctors, nurses, pharmacists, dentists, teachers, and principals, to name just a few. The profits that accrue from these private ventures are directed back into the schools and hospitals and not toward charity activities.[7] They go toward improving middle-class services and working conditions. While these nonprofit commercial facilities and services are embedded within the ICCS network of activities, they serve a different audience than the audience for the ICCS's charity activities. They demonstrate the degree to which ISIs are run not only by the middle class but for the middle class.

As in the case in Egypt, in Jordan we see that the various ICCS centers or projects are initiated both from the bottom up—they are grassroots initiatives in which members of a local community approach the ICCS headquarters about establishing a project—and from the top down—as in the case of Cairo's "trophy clinics." The ICCS's "five star" institutions—nonprofit commercial institutions such as the Islamic Hospital in Amman—are established by a decision made by the ICCS executive committee. As in Egypt, the middle-class bias within the ICCS is partly a result of the operational demands of ISIs; they need skilled middle-class employees and they need donors. However, in the case of Jordan, we more clearly see an intentional strategy to target the middle class by providing it with employment and services. The ICCS executive's decision to target the middle class arises both from pressure within the movement—the pressure of its middle-class membership to have its needs met—and from the need to enhance its membership by recruiting the middle class. These "five star" institutions are also a result of a conscious decision by the ICCS to build powerful symbols of the Islamist alternative to the state. They are a concrete expression of Islamist identity. However, there are indications that this strategy has not come without a price. Not only has it created debate within the Brotherhood circles, but there are indications of a growing sense among the middle class that the ICCS, and by extension the Brotherhood, is betraying its values.

THE MUSLIM BROTHERHOOD IN JORDAN

In 1999, King Abdullah came to the Jordanian throne following his father's forty-six years of rule and his great-grandfather's tenure under British mandate beginning in the 1920s. Since that time, the monarchy has endured a series of challenges to its stability, most notably two massive waves of Palestinians, the first in 1948 with the creation of Israel and the second in 1967 with Israel's victory over the West Bank. Today, approximately 60 percent of Jordan's population is Palestinian. Jordan's monarchy has remained strong due in no small part to the loyalty of East Bank Jordanians, that mix of tribes whose forefathers, like the Hashemite family, hailed from the Arabian peninsula in the nineteenth and early twentieth centuries. This loyalty has historically been secured through economic favoritism. The linchpin to the monarchy's—and Jordan's—stability, therefore, has been what Laurie Brand calls "budget security"—the state leadership's drive to ensure the financial flows necessary for its survival.[8] This has translated into the securing of funds to ensure the privileged position of Transjordanians economically, socially, and politically. Transjordanians, or East Bankers, have thus traditionally dominated the civil service and the military in Jordan.

The Muslim Brotherhood, which was officially established in the 1940s but has roots reaching back into the 1930s, has existed almost as long as the state. Although the Brotherhood has had its conflicts with the successive regimes, it has benefited enormously from its privileged position as the sole legal nongovernmental (and quasi-political) social organization in Jordan, particularly when democratic multiparty politics were suspended in 1957 and during the period of martial law that lasted from 1967 until 1989, when democratic elections were reintroduced. The size of the Brotherhood, in terms of its activities, financial budget, membership, and political influence, has expanded substantially under this protective umbrella, and the ICCS is but one wing of the Brotherhood. While the Brotherhood was founded by largely Transjordanian merchants, since the late 1940s and particularly the early 1950s, its leadership and membership have been dominated by middle-class professionals and professionals in the making, and, increasingly, by Palestinian middle-class professionals. The history of the Brotherhood largely reflects the desire of an emergent professional class for political power.[9] This middle-class bias has an ongoing and important impact on the political success of the Brotherhood under the banner of the Islamic Action Front (IAF) and on the success of the ICCS.

The Jordanian branch of the Muslim Brotherhood (MB) was established in 1945 by Abdul Latif Abu Qura.[10] Abu Qura, a wealthy merchant from Salt, first came into contact with members of the Egyptian Brotherhood when he visited Palestine in the late 1930s.[11] In 1944, he was reintroduced to the writings of Hassan al-Banna through the Brotherhood publication *Al-Ikhwan al-Muslimun*. Impressed by al-Banna's call for a *jihad* (holy struggle or striving) against colonialism and Zionism, Abu Qura wrote al-Banna and asked to visit him in Egypt. He did so later that same year and upon his return to Jordan, al-Banna sent two Egyptian Brethren to help him establish Jordan's first branch of the Brotherhood.

Under the patronage of King Abdullah, the Brotherhood obtained legal status as a charitable society in Jordan in January 1945.[12] As in Egypt, the Jordanian Brotherhood heavily emphasized education in Islamic principles, *da'wa*. Indeed, most of its activities took place in primary and particularly secondary schools. It was strongly focused on *jihad* in Palestine, and in 1947 Abu Qura took 100 men to fight in Palestine. King Abdullah had several reasons for supporting the Brotherhood. As Marion Boulby states, by legalizing the Brotherhood, he hoped to prevent it from becoming violent, as it was in Egypt. In addition, his patronage of the Brotherhood would indirectly buttress his own Islamic legitimacy based on his descent from the tribe of Prophet Mohammed. Finally, the growth of the Brotherhood could potentially offset the rise of pan-Arab nationalism which was on the rise throughout the Arab world and which was a direct threat to the monarchies of the region. Having embraced the Brotherhood, the monarchy was able to keep a close eye on it, particularly on its policies with regard to Palestine. The Brotherhood, in return, remained largely apolitical because of Abu Qura's loyalty to the monarchy, his pragmatism, and the relatively uneducated and unpoliticized nature of Jordanian society at the time.[13]

After the 1948 War and the massive influx of Palestinian refugees into Jordan, the Brotherhood rapidly evolved from a loosely knit coalition of merchants into a political organization that could compete with secular political parties under the leadership of a growing class of professionals. The arrival of a more educated Palestinian population that rapidly became active in the country's pan-Arabist political parties galvanized Transjordan's small but growing new generation of professionals (that was slowly emerging as a result of urbanization and of the establishment of educational facilities throughout Jordan in the 1950s) into action. The Brotherhood thus became dominated by the first generation of the professional or new middle class in Jordan. This was the first generation in Jordan that sought "to advance itself though their professional skills and talents rather than through the use of wealth and personal connections," and pursued its livelihood through salaries, technical fees, scholarships, and professional activities. These were thus often the first generation of men in their families to be literate and, most important, to "discover their best friends at school or in a political movement, not among kin. They [were] the first to trust strangers on grounds of competence or shared ideology." Thus, the Muslim Brothers began to share a certain common profile. As Boulby states, they were young, usually in their twenties; had attained some degree of postsecondary education; were professionals or professionals in the making; and generally came from landowning East Bank families who had profited from the expansion of commercial activities during World War II. Most of the Brethren met while at school in Jordan or abroad. (This profile has changed relatively little over time. MB deputies in Jordan's first democratic elections in 1989 reflected the same social profile as the movement's leadership in the 1950s—the majority were well-educated professionals and academics, many of whom possessed postgraduate degrees from Western countries.)[14]

Under this new leadership, the Brotherhood continued to stress nonviolence, moderation, reformism, and cooperation with the regime. However, its program became far more comprehensive and political, calling for the implementation of *shari'a* and the establishment of an Islamic order. In keeping with its professional-class perspective, it also continued to stress education as a means by which a more Islamically oriented generation would come to power. To a large extent, the ideological foundations of the Brotherhood today have strayed little from the core values of this early period.[15]

In 1953, the Brotherhood's status was legally changed to that of a "'general and comprehensive Islamic committee' allowing it to spread its call and be, de facto, politically active."[16] As a charitable society, the Brotherhood was able to survive the 1957 ban on political parties and the imposition of martial law.[17] It founded its first school in the 1950s, and the number of schools continues to expand today. With the opening of Jordan's first university in 1962, the University of Jordan, the Brotherhood also extended its activities into postsecondary education. Its activities continued to grow, and in 1963, the Brotherhood officially established the ICCS to deal specifically with its charity activities. By the 1980s it politically dominated the student councils of all university campuses in Jordan—at the expense of leftist groups on campuses.[18] In 1979, the Brotherhood opened its own college, the Islamic College in Zarqa. At the same time, it also made significant gains—indeed, victories—in the majority of the country's professional associations (many of the Brothers had gained their experience on university student councils), where they ended the traditional monopoly of the nationalists and leftists. In the absence of national elections, many of the professional associations, such as the Engineers' Association, became highly politicized as the Brotherhood used the associations as pulpits from which to vocalize their message. As in Egypt, the associations were seen as one of the country's few bellwethers by which to test the political sentiments of the population.

Much of the Brotherhood's success can be attributed to its protected status as a charity organization in return for its political support of the monarchy. While the Brotherhood has criticized various policies, it has by and large refrained from criticizing the political structure or the legitimacy of the monarchy itself. It has operated aboveground and has never espoused violence. Prior to the reintroduction of elections in 1989, Brotherhood leaders were often further rewarded for their loyalty and cooperation with inclusion in various governments, particularly the Ministry of Education and the Awqaf.[19] For example, the loyalty of the Brotherhood during the 1970–1971 Civil War was rewarded by the king, who made Izhaq Farhan the Minister of Education for five consecutive cabinets, from October 1970 to November 1974.[20] He was minister of Awqaf in 1972 for approximately one year.[21]

While the relationship between the state and the Brotherhood has not always been a smooth and easy one, for all intents and purposes, the monarchy's policy of cooptation has succeeded.[22] The Brotherhood's long history as a charity organization has provided it with invaluable experience and, more important, the opportunity and time to build an extensive network of voluntary and charity institutions with enormous resources and capabilities. Today, the Brotherhood has at its disposal an estimated 200 million JD in resources. This makes MB a major competitor of all major social organizations, including the General Union of Voluntary Societies, the Queen Alia Fund for Voluntary Social Work, and the Noor al-Hussein Foundation.[23]

The historical, organizational, and institutional advantage the Muslim Brotherhood holds served it well in Jordan's first parliamentary elections in 1989.[24] Political parties were still banned in 1989 and candidates, including the Muslim Brothers, ran as individuals or independents, albeit with clear ideological positions. Muslim Brotherhood candidates won twenty-two seats which, combined with approximately ten independent Islamists who had won seats, created a Muslim Brotherhood–dominated Islamist bloc that controlled 40 percent of the assembly.[25] Several factors worked in the Brothers' favor in 1989, not the least important of which was the fact that having acted as Jordan's sole quasi political organizations for decades, it had the structure, the organization, the skills, and the contacts with the population that other candidates did not have.[26] Furthermore, the Brothers capitalized on the fact that the PLO did not run in the Palestinian camps.[27] The strong Brotherhood position in defense of the liberation of all of Palestine earned it votes throughout the camps.[28]

The candidates ran on a platform that largely focused on Jordan's economic problems and corruption. Economically, the 1989 platform called for the protection of private property, reduction of government debt, lowering of inflation, cutting government spending, measures to boost investment confidence, the redistribution of wealth through tax reform, the protection of infant industries, a virtual ban on imports, national self-sufficiency even in sectors where Jordan does not enjoy a comparative advantage, and the elimination of usury. Socially, the Brotherhood condemned moral corruption—alcohol, gambling, drugs, dance halls, bawdiness, and the use of makeup. Finally, the platform called for greater democratic freedoms in Jordan, including freedom of expression, movement, and worship.[29]

Six months after what can only be called the landslide victory of the Brothers in 1989, the Brotherhood was involved in in-depth negotiations with other prominent independent Islamists to form an umbrella political party (albeit one dominated by MB). In 1992, the Islamic Action Front was the first political party to apply for authorization after the introduction of the new Political Parties Law that legalized political parties. The IAF received its license in December of the same year.[30]

In the 1993 elections, the Islamists, some of whom continued to run as independents, managed to hold on to their approximate share of total votes (15.6 percent in 1989 and 16.0 percent in 1993) but experienced a dramatic decrease in the number of seats, down from thirty-two to twenty-two seats (the newly created IAF won sixteen of the twenty-two).[31] The Islamists lost approximately one-third of their seats. To a large extent, the loss of seats can be directly attributed to the new electoral law, dubbed the one person, one vote law.[32] While under the old system, voters could cast as many ballots as there were seats in his/her constituency (a practice called the multiple transferable vote), the new law—still enforced today—gives each voter one vote (the limited single nontransferable vote), regardless of the number of seats in his/her district (which could vary from two to nine). The new law had a dramatic effect because it forced voters to choose between competing loyalties, such as choosing between a tribal/familial candidate and a candidate for a particular party (conservative, leftist, Islamist, nationalist, and so on). In a country where tribal loyalties remain strong and where most social, economic, and political objectives are achieved through traditional patronage and kinship relations, political parties found themselves at a distinct disadvantage.[33]

Although the IAF decided against a boycott in reaction against the law in 1993, its consultative council did decide to boycott the 1997 elections in protest over both the one person, one vote system and the severe restrictions on press freedoms introduced in the months preceding the elections.[34] Two Brothers who refused to abide by the boycott and four other Islamists (out of a total of thirty-two Islamists) won seats.[35] The IAF decided not to participate in the elections and lost all access to and influence in Parliament.

Indeed, it lost its most important public platform from which to express its views.

When one examines voter behavior in the 1993 elections, it becomes clear that the IAF's power base is concentrated in the central parts of the country, predominantly in Amman and Zarqa, and in Palestinian refugee camps (particularly in Baqa'a camp). Amman, Zarqa and Baqa'a alone constituted 49.8 percent of the total votes cast for the IAF in the 1993 elections.[36] In 1997, the dominance of urban areas in the central part of the country, Amman in particular, repeated itself.[37]

It is no coincidence that Jordan's middle class lives predominantly in Amman. Indeed, the IAF seats in Amman are in middle-class constituencies.[38] The Islamists won their seats in constituencies in Amman that are dominated by middle-class Palestinians—the educated middle class that is most excluded from the economic wealth and opportunities provided by the state.[39] While there are numerous well-known East Bankers in the Brotherhood, the Brotherhood is dominated by Palestinians. Palestinians have historically been excluded from professions within the public sector, including government hospitals; as a result, they generally dominate the private entrepreneurial sector.

In his class analysis of the city of Amman, Musa Shteiwi finds four distinct classes in Amman: the upper class, the middle class (which is subdivided into the traditional middle class and the new middle class), the working class, and the dispossessed class. In 1991, he states, 31.3 percent of Amman's population was middle class. Of these, 15.3 percent were professionals of all kinds, 9.3 percent were semiprofessionals, and 6.7 percent were clerks. Ninety percent of the professionals were salaried employees, 4.3 percent were employers, and 3.3 percent had small businesses with no one working for them. According to Shteiwi, professionals, which constituted 15.3 percent of Amman's entire labor force, were expanding the most. In fact, the number of professionals in Amman tripled between 1960 and 1990.[40] This is the population that is voting for the IAF and supporting the activities of the Brotherhood's charity, the ICCS.

THE NGO SECTOR IN JORDAN

The victory of the Muslim Brothers in the 1989 elections was largely attributed to the ICCS—the activities, institutions, and networks it had built up over the years. While the ICCS has held a relatively privileged position among nongovernmental organizations, it has never been the country's sole NGO. In fact, there are so many NGOs in Jordan that the state has seen fit to closely monitor them and to create an umbrella organization, the General Union of Voluntary Societies (GUVS), to which they all must belong.

Despite the fact that the ICCS is a member of GUVS and that one of the roles of GUVS is to provide financial assistance to NGOs, the ICCS's operating budget is larger than that of GUVS. The ICCS is the largest and the most financially solvent of all NGOs in Jordan, with the exception of those NGOs established and patronized by members of the royal family. In addition, the ICCS is by far the largest ISI in the country.

The evolution of NGOs in Jordan—their development and increase—is largely a reflection of the major events—many of which occurred beyond Jordan's borders—that have shaped the country's history: the creation of the state of Israel in 1948 and Jordan's absorption of the area's refugees, the 1967 War and the second massive influx of Palestinian refugees into the country, Jordan's disengagement from the West Bank in 1988, the reintroduction of elections in 1989, the adoption of the IMF's economic Structural Adjustment Programs (SAPs) in 1989, the 1991–1992 Gulf War and the consequent arrival of many returnees to Jordan, and the initiation of the peace process with Israel in 1994.[41] NGOs have established and redefined their agendas in order to respond to each event and its resultant impact on the country's population.[42]

Voluntary work in Jordan began in the early 1930s, and in response to this, the state created its first law legalizing voluntary associations in 1936. By 1958, reflecting the influx of Palestinians refugees in 1948, there were ninety NGOs (including those in the West Bank).[43] This number climbed to over 300 in the early 1970s in response to the impact of the 1967 War.[44] The greatest increase in the number of associations, however, occurred with the lifting of martial law and the introduction of democracy in 1989. From 1989 to 1994, the number of indigenous NGOs increased by 67 percent (compared to a growth rate of only 24 percent between 1985 and 1989). Charitable NGOs grew by 47 percent from 1989 to 1994; from 1989 to 1990 alone they increased by 10.9 percent.[45] In 1997, there were 695 charitable NGOs reaching 475,005 beneficiaries.[46]

NGOs in Jordan are classified into two broad categories: charitable and cultural. The ICCS is a charitable NGO. All charitable NGOs must register with the Ministry of Social Development and follow its regulations, specifically Law 33 of 1966 which establishes the procedures for, regulations of, restrictions on, and enforcements of NGOs.[47] This includes the restriction that all NGOs must limit themselves strictly to the activities for which they were registered and approved and the prohibition of engaging in any political or opposition activities.[48] It also forbids financial and personal gains. To form an organization, charitable NGOs must apply to and receive permission from the Minister of Social Development with input from the governor of the district in which the NGO would be located and from GUVS.[49] In addition, while not explicitly stated in Law 33, all volunteers and administrative board members of a prospective NGO must be approved by security, and by the Ministry of the Interior. The Ministry of Social Development has full discretion to either accept or reject an application. NGOs must restrict themselves to the activities under the purview of the ministry. All NGOs must receive separate permission for each activity, whether it be opening a center for the disabled or establishing an orphanage or a day care center. It is possible that an NGO will not receive permission to conduct all of its activities. NGOs must maintain detailed records of their activities and finances, and they must submit these records on an annual basis. NGOs may also be subject to regular inspections. Ministry officials may also attend any elections to the administrative boards of NGOs and may dissolve an administrative board and appoint a temporary board until new elections are held. Finally, the ministry may dissolve any charitable NGO. Most associations that have been dissolved failed to provide relevant financial records, to hold regular meetings, or to fulfill their stated goals. Others engaged in activities outside their purview. Quintan Wiktorowicz notes that between 1995 and 1996, twenty-nine charitable NGOs were dissolved.[50]

Despite the highly regulated system (unlike Egypt and Yemen, Jordan does not suffer from a serious problem of illegal or unregistered NGOs), the ICCS, while under close surveillance, has benefited from the state turning a blind eye to some of its activities. Its large number of facilities and activities can to a great degree be attributed to the fact that ICCS has not been required to follow all regulations regarding the registration of activities. This gives it a significant advantage over other NGOs, including other ISIs.

ISLAMIC CENTER CHARITY SOCIETY

In terms of its data collection, GUVS does not have a specific category for ISIs. Accurate data on the definition of ISIs—how many there are, and what their activities are—is difficult to ascertain. However, based on the name of the NGO, its specified goals, and, most important, the known affiliations of the director, it can be stated that in 1995 there were forty-nine Islamic NGOs.[51] Of these, thirty-eight were Islamic charitable NGOs (as opposed to cultural NGOs). As is true of other NGOs, ISIs have experienced their greatest growth since 1989. While the increase in the number of ISIs was only 3.3 percent between 1985 and 1989, between 1989 and 1994 the number of ISIs increased by 60 percent. In terms of Islamic charitable NGOs specifically, there was a 50 percent increase from 1989 to 1994 (from twenty-six in 1989 to thirty-eight in 1994), as opposed to a mere 4 percent increase between 1985 and 1989.[52]

As stated above, the Muslim Brotherhood established the ICCS in 1963. Boosted by the influx of oil revenues in the form of remittances and customs and transportation taxes after 1973, the charity activities of the ICCS rapidly expanded during the 1970s. By the early 1990s, the revenues and expenditures of the ICCS far exceeded those of any other Islamic charity in the country. For example, the revenues and expenditures of the ICCS in Amman in 1995–1996 were 2,719,047 JD and 1,148,573 JD, respectively; revenues and expenditures were significantly less for both the Green Crescent Society/Amman and the Islamic Organization for Medical Relief/Amman. The former had revenues of 41,787 JD and expenditures of 41,787 JD and the latter had revenues of 18,078 JD and expenditures of 19,126 JD.[53]

The ICCS's headquarters are located in the area of Amman called Abdali, close to the Muslim Brotherhood's headquarters. The ICCS also has four branches located in Zarqa, Mafraq, Irbid, and Ramtha. In addition to providing mosque facilities, the stated aims of the ICCS focus on education, health, income-generating and training projects, financial assistance for needy families, the care of orphans, and assisting the poor who are sick. Its income-generating and training projects largely focus on sewing, flower arranging, and crocheting. However, the ICCS focuses predominantly on charity activities and not on development efforts per se.[54]

The Center is run by a board of directors consisting of nine people and a general assembly of 120 members.[55] The members of the board of the Center as well as the boards of each of the branches are full-time employees. The Center is thus not run on a volunteer basis.

In addition to the four branches, the ICCS also runs thirty-two committees.[56] Technically, all NGOs must receive licensing before they may establish a new branch. In order to sidestep the licensing process the ICCS has opened "committees" with the tacit approval of the state.[57] This has enabled the Society to significantly expand its operations. These committees operate as any other ICCS facility or center. However, a branch may seek and collect donations independently of Abdali, whereas a committee may solicit donations—but these donations must be sent to the headquarters in Abdali, which in effect filters the money back to the committee. As Laurie Brand states, given the close relations between the regime and the Brotherhood, this preferential treatment of the ICCS is not surprising.[58]

In general, the various branches and committees of the ICCS are expected to be self-sufficient. The Zarqa branch runs its projects independently of Amman and is expected to be financially solvent. While committee projects may initially receive some assistance from Amman, the ICCS does not subsidize projects. ICCS centers and committees, furthermore, do not coordinate efforts with other non-ICCS ISIs. If such coordination of efforts occasionally occurs, it is due to the personal friendships of the respective directors and not as part of a larger strategy.[59] In this sense (as in the case of Egypt), Jordanian Islamists are competing against each other for funds.[60]

The number of people receiving services from the Center is impressive. In 1997/1998, the ICCS ran a total of forty-one education facilities (twenty-two elementary and secondary schools and eighteen kindergartens) and one college.[61] The first school, an elementary school, was established in Irbid in 1959 and the most recent was established in Jebel al-Hussein, Amman, in 1996.[62] Today, the ICCS schools, such as Dar al-Aqsa and Dar al-Arqam, are household names representing the Muslim Brotherhood; they are well-known symbols of the Brotherhood's activities. Since their inception, these schools have been private and relatively expensive. While the ICCS schools must follow the basic curriculum of the Ministry of Education, they appeal to parents who would like a higher-caliber school than the public system offers but do not necessarily have the economic funds to send their children to the private schools of the elite. They desire the additional emphasis on Islamic practice and values in the ICCS schools. The Dar al-Arqam school was opened in 1987 in a high-income area in western Amman. The school is segregated—including separate play yards—and girls are encouraged from a young age (prior to puberty) to wear the *hijab*. All female staff are required to wear *hijab* and modest dress in order to set an example for the students. Teachers and students must perform noontime prayers. During Ramadan, even the youngest children are encouraged to fast, and teachers arrange fast-breaking meals that they take with the students. The schools offer more religious classes than the secular schools run by the Ministry of Education.[63] In addition, teachers integrate Islamic teachings into all subjects. In biology, for example, a teacher would also teach the relevant Qur'anic *hadith*. Outside the classroom, the students have lectures in the mosque on topics of social relevance. Anne Roald found in her in-depth interviews in ICCS schools that the most important goal of the schools is to train the pupils to conduct themselves according to Islamic rules in all spheres of life.[64] The lifestyles of the teachers are therefore a crucial aspect of the education of the pupils. Students are taught a lifestyle rather than an Islamic education in the narrow sense of the term.

The ICCS also has two hospitals and fifteen medical centers housing thirty-two medical clinics and eleven laboratories. In 1997, 283,268 people were treated and 38,018 patients were admitted to the ICCS's facilities. In the clinics alone, 140,343 cases were treated.[65] The Islamic Hospital in Amman is probably the best known of the ICCS's projects. It is a private nonprofit hospital located near the ICCS's central headquarters in Abdali, Amman. The hospital was established in 1982 with seventy beds and thirty employees. Between 1982 and 1997, admissions rose from 2,028 to 33,547.[66] Today, the hospital has over 300 beds, approximately 12,000 employees (including 98 consultants and specialists), 77 resident doctors, 21 interns, and 445 nurses.[67] In addition, the hospital is supported by approximately 300 part-time or referring specialists. It is the largest hospital in Jordan's private-hospital sector (which has fifty hospitals in total) and as such it constitutes one-fifth of the total bed capacity of the country's private-hospital beds.[68] It is Jordan's only private teaching hospital.

The hospital offers some of the most sophisticated medical procedures in the country.[69] Doctors in the Islamic Hospital specialize in one of the following seven areas: internal medicine, general surgery, pediatrics, obstetrics and gynecology, radiology, anesthesia, and endocrinology. The hospital is presently qualified to train doctors in cardiology and gastroenterology. The hospital offers a full range of services: internal medicine (including neurology, hematology, and infectious diseases); surgery (including cardiac, thoracic, and vascular surgeries; plastic surgery; and neurosurgery); obstetrics (including in-vitro fertilization); pediatrics; radiology (the department of radiology houses MRIs, spiral CT scanning, ultrasound, and angiography); anesthesia; emergency medicine; laboratories; nursing; dentistry (including orthodontics); and a pharmacy. Within the seven theaters for surgery, approximately 9,000 surgical operations are performed each year. The hospital also runs a Fund for the Sick and Poor to ease the costs of treatment. The Fund subsidizes approximately 20 percent of medical costs for needy families who qualify.

The hospital has strict criteria for the hiring of its employees. All nurses must be practicing Muslims, have high morals and good conduct, and wear proper Islamic dress. All female employees must wear the *hijab* and long, modest clothing. All employees are required to pray regularly, although this is not enforced or practiced.[70] The hospital attempts to implement gender segregation in which female nurses and doctors treat female patients. While gender segregation is successful at the level of nursing, it has not been fully implemented at the level of doctors for the simple fact that there are not enough female doctors. Patients, it should be noted, may choose whichever doctor they wish, male or female. The hospital also offers optional Islamic educational activities, such as lectures, for employees. The staff is encouraged to discuss Islam with patients, religious literature is available for patients, and Islamic videos and programming are shown on TV.[71]

In addition to its educational and medical facilities, the ICCS has six centers for income generation and training—these six centers house a total of twenty-five projects throughout the country.[72] Three-hundred and seventy-four people received some form of training in 1997.[73] Finally, the

Center also has thirty-three centers servicing the needs of orphans and poor families. The first of these centers was founded in Zarqa in 1970 and the most recent was founded in Marak (Amman) in 1995.[74] In 1997 alone, the ICCS provided financial and material aid to 4,104 poor families and 5,233 orphans.[75]

The ICCS facilities and services servicing this large number of recipients and clients vary greatly in terms of both type and size. Dar al-Arqam and the Islamic Hospital are both examples of its largest projects, as is the Islamic Community College in Zarqa, an all-female college (although previously it had males and females) that was established in 1979 by the ICCS in Amman.[76] The college has approximately fifty to seventy full- and part-time instructors and approximately 900 to 1,000 students and is housed in a large, albeit plain, building attached to a mosque on a dusty road on the outskirts of the city of Zarqa, north of Amman.[77] It offers two-year diploma programs in pharmacy assistance, computer programming, clothing design, accounting, laboratory, child care, *shari'a,* English, and Arabic.[78] Faculty and students are required to dress in Islamic attire, such as wearing a *hijab;* as in the ICCS schools, employees of the college are expected to respect Islam and to set an example for the girls. In addition, all students must take a course in *shari'a.* There are also extracurricular lectures on Islam and activities. Islamic values are integrated into the programs as much as possible. There are, however, male instructors, and the president of the college is male.

In stark contrast to the facilities in Zarqa is the Merkaz Mahqat Sweilah, an example of one of the smallest ICCS charity centers. While the Zarqa branch has, in addition to the college, four schools, two kindergartens, a women's center, and two medical clinics and assists 448 orphans and 245 poor families, the Sweilah center is substantially smaller.[79] It is a very basic center (in need of painting and cleaning) on the second floor of a building in Sweilah, Amman, a working-class area of the city dotted with small-repair and handyman shops. Established in 1991, the center has one full-time director and one part-time administrator.[80] The main room of the center houses a Ping-Pong table and a large box of used clothing to be distributed to orphans. In addition, there are two to three even smaller rooms for classes and the director's office. The center deals almost strictly with orphans; since its establishment, it has expanded the number of orphans it supports from thirty to eighty-nine orphans.[81] It also supports eleven poor families; however, as a nearby mosque distributes *zakat* to needy families, the center has focused it attentions on orphans, who receive approximately 20 JD per month (the customary amount in most centers). The center also has two part-time teachers to provide segregated religious classes for orphans—twice a week for boys and once a week for girls.

FUND-RAISING AND
THE IMPORTANCE OF MIDDLE-CLASS NETWORKS

While the ICCS centers located throughout the country differ quite dramatically in size and services, they all share the fact that they rely on a dedicated staff (particularly their respective directors) and a large number of donors and volunteers for the successful running of their programs. In most cases, when they were asked for the reasons for the success of their branch or committee, respondents immediately stated the name of their director. In fact, as in Egypt, the success of a center (or its lack thereof) is largely, but not solely, due to the connections of a director and his willingness and/or ability to pursue these connections for donations. For example, at the ICCS center in the Baqaʿa Palestinian refugee camp, a very poor and densely populated camp just outside Amman, all employees were unanimous in praising their director for relentlessly raising donations and stating that it was primarily he who was responsible for the fact that the center assists the largest number of orphans in any ICCS location. In 1997, the center assisted 800 orphans in 200 families and 93 needy families.[82] In addition to various classes for orphans and women, the center also runs a medical clinic for the poor.[83] Active directors, such as the director at Baqaʿa, regularly contact their friends and acquaintances, as well as well-known merchants, with phone calls and personal letters. Several centers send out brochures and leaflets—which are printed for free, as a form of donation, by a local merchant—advertising their services and soliciting money. Many donors donate 10 JD to 20 JD on a monthly basis; others contribute on an irregular basis. In some of the branches, the center forms a fund-raising committee designed specifically to research donors and obtain funds. While some centers receive limited funds from GUVS, all of the centers receive the bulk of their donations from merchants and companies.

Donors may give cash, provide a free service, or provide items in kind. For example, at the time of his interview with me, the director at the Baqaʿa center proudly showed me large bags of brand-new school bags for children, coats for the poor, and tins of food all donated by his friends and by merchants and factory owners. In many cases, a center is able to buy clothing at cost from merchants and then donate them to the poor. Women in the women's center in Zarqa go door to door seeking donations and used clothing. The center, Merkaz Nusayba, is the only center in the ICCS run entirely by women and strictly for women and children. In addition to the various courses and lectures they offer, the women also contribute by cooking food and baking goods on various holidays and taking them to the homes of the poor.[84] They enlist various women volunteers to distribute clothing and food to the poor. While women often have far fewer connections to merchants and thus are less able to approach them for substantial donations, they are able to contribute to the center through more local and grassroots methods.

In most cases, the centers are most successful at raising donations when they target friends or merchants by directly approaching and/or writing them and when they specify the actual type of donation. For example, most centers will request financial assistance for a specific orphan. Alternatively, potential donors might be sent a list of orphans, usually ten, with pictures and a letter and be asked to choose which orphan they would like to support.

Even in the most proactive centers, however, donations can fluctuate dramatically from month to month. The highest month for donations is Ramadan, when a center may receive as much as 10,000 JD.[85] In almost all cases, the majority of donors are located in Amman, although donations are received from all over Jordan. In a very limited number of cases, such as at Irbid and Baqa'a, donations are also received from NGOs or individual Muslims who live abroad in Kuwait, Saudi Arabia, Qatar, Britain, Sweden, Holland, Belgium, France, and Germany.

The ICCS demonstrates how important personal connections are in soliciting donations. It demonstrates the ongoing need to create new networks as sources of donations become overused and as new needs arise. One merchant may provide free brochures or may suggest another generous merchant who may be willing to provide school bags. This second merchant may pass on the name of another who may be willing to sell tins of food at cost, and so on. Similarly, the ICCS centers use personal networks to ascertain who needs assistance. The Zarqa Branch, for example, has a team of six social workers who visit homes to assess whether families qualify for assistance. Much of this is also done by word of mouth. If a needy family does not directly approach the ICCS for assistance, a neighbor may tell the ICCS about the family. When visiting one family, the Center may be told about another.

These networks are not disconnected from the activities of the Islamist movement elsewhere; for example, at the universities. A brief (and incomplete) sampling of my own experiences is quite revealing. One Islamist woman I met, for example, had graduated from Dar al-Arqam and was now a teacher there. At Dar al-Arqam she had become good friends with an Islamist woman on the Student Council at the University of Jordan as part of the Islamic List party. This same Student Council member volunteered at an ISI. The mother of the teacher was also active in a weekly Qur'anic lesson, *dars al-din,* and introduced me to the women in another Qur'anic study group located in a nearby mosque. The woman on the Student Council introduced me to her father, an Islamist active in the doctors' syndicate. Through him, I also met other Islamist doctors. The Student Council member also suggested I meet former members of the Student Council, and through her I met an active Islamist at a private Islamic college (not affiliated with the ICCS) outside Zarqa. She suggested that in addition to meeting other Islamist women at this college, I meet the head of the ICCS College in Zarqa. She furthermore recommended that I see her aunt, the head of an ISI! Finally, these networks are linked, at least in the case of men, to the mosques, which act as meeting places and centers for charity and education.

HOW THE MIDDLE CLASS BENEFITS

The networks in which the activities and centers of the ICCS are embedded include not just charity activities but also private schools, kindergartens, and hospitals. These are nonprofit commercial enterprises that cater specifically to the paying middle class, not to the poor. Upon closer examination, we see that ICCS centers are primarily located in urban middle-class areas and provide services to and jobs for the middle class. This means that ICCS centers are located where those with the means to donate and work in its centers are located. Most important, however, ICCS centers are located in these areas where they can best serve and potentially recruit the middle class.

ICCS projects and centers are established one of two ways. The center for orphans in Jebel Hussein, the ICCS center in the Wihdat Palestinian refugee camp, and the small ICCS center in Qwaysama (all located in Amman) were all established by members of the local community who approached the ICCS about establishing a center in their neighborhood. These are smaller centers that focus largely, but not exclusively, on services for the poor. Alternatively, the larger projects such as the Islamic Hospital, which are well-known symbols of the Islamist movement throughout the country, are initiated by the ICCS executive. Either way, ICCS centers are commonly in middle-class areas.

If we begin with an examination of where ICCS facilities are located, we see that in contrast to the charitable NGO community in general, which is evenly distributed between rural and urban communities, the Islamic NGO community tends to be located in urban centers. An overwhelming number are located in the governorate of Amman: thirty-four out of forty-nine, or 69.4 percent.[86] The ICCS adheres to this pattern. The governorate of Amman has the largest number of centers, with a total of seventeen centers and services (approximately 40 percent). The next largest are Zarqa, with seven, and Irbid, with five. Only thirteen services/facilities are located in the remainder of the country.[87] In fact, in the southern cities of Tafila and Ma'an, I was unable to locate anyone who knew where the centers were, and no one ever answered the repeated telephones calls I made to the two centers.

According to the *World Bank Poverty Assessment*, the greatest incidence of poverty and the deepest poverty gaps are in the rural areas of Jordan with the highest concentration of residents in the low-income groups: Mafraq, Balqa, and Kerek. Almost one-third (31.1 percent) of the population in Mafraq is in the poorest decile of the population—almost six times more than in Amman. In other words, you are six times as likely to be poor in Mafraq as you are in Amman. However, while rural areas suffer from the highest concentrations of poverty, urban areas are not immune to poverty. Of the Jordanians in the poorest decile, 67.3 percent live in urban areas. Twenty-one percent of Jordanians in the poorest decile and 24.6 percent in the poorest quintile live in Amman. In other words, while only 5.5 percent of Amman's residents are in the poorest decile, 21 percent of all Jordanians in the poorest decile live in Amman. Amman therefore has the lowest incidence but the second-highest distribution nationwide of people living in the poorest decile.[88]

This means that ISIs, including the ICCS, are concentrated in the areas with the highest distributions of poverty and as such they are able to affect many poor people. Urban areas, however, are also where rapidly growing numbers of the middle class are located—the class that can donate to and support ISIs. In urban areas, particularly Amman, there are more people with the means to donate time and money to ISI activities. As Quintan Wiktorowicz notes, while some Islamic NGOs are located in lower-class areas, most Islamic NGOs are located in middle-class areas.[89]

For example, if we break down the ICCS services according to type, we see that 37.5 percent of the ICCS's health services are offered in the governorate of Amman and 43.75 percent in the governorate of Zarqa. Only two other governorates have health services: Aqaba (6.25 percent) and Balqa (6.25 percent). Amman also houses the lion's share of ICCS educational facilities and centers catering to orphans and poor families: 37.5 percent and 33.3 percent, respectively.[90]

ICCS centers are not just located where the middle-class donors are located, they are situated where the middle class can use them and work in them. In 1997, for example, the Islamic Hospital in Amman provided 9,061 surgical operations, services to 7,386 obstetric patients and 2,568 physiotherapy patients, 50,067 X-rays, and 187,323 laboratory examinations and accommodated 33,547 inpatients and 130,157 outpatients.[91] If we look at the cumulative figures from the time the hospital opened in 1982 to 1997, the figures are impressive: 424,109 admissions, 105,012 surgical operations, 105,739 obstetric patients, 480,989 X-rays, 1,846,785 lab exams, and 1,207,472 outpatients. In the Aqaba Hospital in 1997, 4,471 inpatients and 12,768 outpatients were treated.[92] Between the two hospitals, this comes to a total of 38,018 inpatients and 142,925 outpatients in 1997, all of whom were paying customers.

If we examine the cost of a delivery, for example, the Islamic Hospital appears at first glance to be extremely inexpensive. According to a 1998 price list, the cost of a natural delivery is merely 15 JD. However, the hospital posts its prices by isolating each service. For example: a difficult delivery with incision costs 17 JD; a difficult delivery with incision and twins costs 20 JD; an overnight stay in a third-class room is 8.40 JD; an overnight stay for the newborn baby costs 5 JD; the cost for using the facilities, including meals, is 50 percent of the total cost of the stay; and the cost for each newborn baby who uses the facilities is 30 percent of the total costs. The result is that the fees for a normal delivery of one child with no complications and one overnight stay in a third-class room in the Islamic Hospital is 190 JD. This fee, the equivalent of $267 US in 2001, is clearly not a charity fee. Rather, it is comparable to some of the most expensive private hospitals in the country—although some of the other private hospitals are far more luxurious.[93] Table 3.1 gives a comparison of similar services in a variety of "five star" hospitals.

In comparison, at al-Bashir Hospital, a public hospital located in poorer East Amman that caters to lower-income patients, the cost of a delivery and overnight stay is only 18 JD; 172 JD less than the Islamic Center Charity Society's prices.[94] Moreover, the Islamic Hospital requires all patients to have medical insurance.[95] According to an accountant at the hospital, if a patient is not covered by insurance or if the insurance is not guaranteed, the hospital demands full payment of the fees prior to the procedure. Alternatively, the patient's family is asked to sign a blank check so that the hospital is assured of full payment.[96] In addition, 20 percent is added to the costs if the patient does not have insurance. Yet, Jocelyn DeJong's study of three low-income areas in Amman found that while 70 percent of the population is covered by government, army, or private insurance, only 32 percent of households in the poorer areas of Amman have any form of insurance and, of that group, only 60 percent has insurance that covers the entire household.[97] More alarming, a World Bank study, citing the Jordanian Ministry of Health, states that possibly 70 percent of poor household heads in Jordan are not insured by government or private health care plans.[98]

The ICCS's fees are clearly not prices that Jordan's poor can afford. The World Bank estimates that Jordanian households in the lowest decile have per-capita expenditures of under 223 JD per year and those in the lowest quintile have per-capita expenditures under 294 JD. The World Bank fur-

Table 3.1. Comparison of Hospital Fees for Childbirth in Amman in 2001 (in Jordanian Dinar)

Name of Hospital	Normal Delivery and Overnight Stay
Islamic Hospital	190
Al-Hamaydeh Hospital	160
Qasr Ishbib Hospital	150
Al-Istiqlal Hospital	170
Arab Heart Hospital	180
Al-Takhasoussi Hospital	170

Source: Author's research.

ther estimates that poor households in Jordan (poor households in this case denotes those in the lowest 19.8 percent of the population according to expenditures) spend only 5.4 percent of their total expenditures are on health. In terms of actual expenditure, this means that poor families spend a mere 15.88 JD or less per capita per year on medical expenses.[99] According to the UNDP's *Human Development Report 2000,* 10 percent of Jordanians did not have access to health services during the period 1981–1993.[100]

The Islamic Hospital is thus far beyond the financial means of Jordan's poor. The hospital does try to help poor patients; the Fund for the Sick and Poor assisted 3,160 poor people in 2000.[101] Cumulatively, between 1982 and 1997, the Fund helped a total of 35,580 cases and spent an impressive 3,271,000 JD.[102] But the 20 percent of costs the Fund provides still does not bring the costs into an affordable range for Jordan's poor.[103] In the case of a delivery, this only brings the costs down to 152 JD. Jordan's poor are financially better off going elsewhere for their medical needs. By spreading its assistance out to a greater number of people by only offering a 20 percent reduction to each, the Fund may help an impressive number of people, but it helps each person far less effectively.

Furthermore, the criteria for candidacy for the Fund for the Sick and Poor are vague. One qualifies for candidacy only if the family has an approximate monthly income of 20 JD per person per month or less. Beyond this, candidates are selected by the Fund based on data provided by a team of social workers who conduct inquiries into the family's financial situation. The case studies are based on home visits and interviews with neighbors and friends. A council from the Fund then reviews all the cases. Each of the seven members of the council states the amount of subsidy the patient should receive and a final amount is decided.[104] However, the entire process seems quite arbitrary. Whenever I raised the subject of the Islamic Hospital during my interviews and even among my university friends and their families—almost all of whom were of the educated middle class—I repeatedly heard rumors that the social workers at the hospital use criteria other than economic need. While suspicions that only Islamists (or those who have Islamist sympathies) qualify for the Fund are unsubstantiated, the fact that these rumors exist and are believed is important in and of itself.

The decision to make the Islamic Hospital a commercial one was quite controversial and created debate with the ICCS and even within broader Brotherhood circles.[105] At stake were several issues, the most important of which was the fact that the operating costs of the hospital were much higher than originally anticipated when the idea of the hospital was first conceived in the late 1960s.[106] Also at issue was the desire to create jobs for disgruntled Islamists. As one Islamist told me, the hospital was created in part to create jobs for Islamist doctors who perceived they were being discriminated against in government-run hospitals. Also at stake was a desire by some Islamists to create a powerful symbol of the potency of the Islamist movement. The founders felt that it was necessary that the hospital be of the highest caliber. Because the hospital was established prior to the reintroduction of elections and the ability to create an Islamist political party, this consideration weighed heavily in the minds of many Islamists. Commercialization of the hospital was controversial. Many prominent Islamists felt that operation of the hospital should be in keeping with the mandate of the ICCS, the historical emphasis on social justice in the Muslim Brotherhood, and the Islamic emphasis on service to the poor. In the end, the decision was made to commercialize the hospital, leading one Islamist to state to me that the Muslim Brotherhood had abandoned the poor.

The middle-class bias of the ICCS extends beyond the Islamic Hospital. In addition to its two hospitals, the ICCS also runs fifteen medical centers housing thirty-two medical clinics and eleven laboratories. These charity clinics charge little or nothing. In fact, in 1997, the various clinics offered twelve days of free medical service and saw approximately 10,000 patients during that period alone. Each year these clinics treat approximately 140,000 people.[107] The medical clinic in the Baqaʿa Palestinian refugee camp provides an excellent example of a very successful ICCS charity clinic. The four-room medical clinic is located down the street from the center's main building and is small but quite impressive. The clinic averages 200 patients per month, although numbers can reach as much as 500. It offers the services of a general practitioner, a dentist, and a laboratory. The dentist's office is fully equipped with up-to-date drills and X-ray machines, and the lab has all the basic services and equipment (and is in the process of expanding). Any complicated laboratory tests are sent to Amman. The clinic is run on a strictly charity basis and while it is not free, the fees are kept down to less than 1 JD sometimes. Depending on the procedure, the dentist must also charge the cost of his materials; these he also tries to keep as close to cost as possible. In fact, he gave me one example where he compared the prices he charges to those his fiancée (also a dentist who graduated from the same university, the University of Jordan) charges in the clinic in which she works located in a wealthy area of Amman. While they buy the same materials from the same source, he charges 30 JD for a porcelain tooth while she charges 100 JD. This difference in pricing is not atypical of the ICCS's numerous clinics.

However, not all of these medical facilities cater to the poor. In fact, three of the clinics are located in the ICCS private schools: one in the Farouk school in Zarqa and two in the al-Arqam school system. In 1997, 9,257 of the people treated in ICCS clinics were actually students and staff of the ICCS private school system. Furthermore, while the total number of doctors in the two Islamic Hospitals is approximately 200 (including residents and interns but not including part-time doctors), the number of doctors treating poor patients in the medical clinics throughout the entire country is only thirty-two![108] This figure includes the doctors in the clinics located in private schools. The ICCS has clearly invested the bulk of its educated resources into services for the middle class, not services for the poor.

In the ICCS schools, we see the same picture—a bias toward the middle class in the services ICCS provides. The ICCS has twenty-two elementary and secondary/high schools and eighteen kindergartens with a total of 11,345 students. In addition, it has the Islamic Community College, which serves 641 students.[109] According to the ICCS executive report for 1998, out of the 11,345 precollegiate students, only ninety-three were on scholarships designated for the poor and orphans.[110] In other words, 11,252 students were paying full tuition—ranging anywhere from approximately 120 JD per year (kindergarten) to 545 JD per year (grade ten). Yet according to the World Bank, Jordan's poor households spend only 19.99 JD per capita per year on education.[111] Clearly, these households are not among the ICCS's paying constituency.

In her study of education in Jordan, Anne Roald notes that the ICCS sets its standards according to the area in which it is located. Dar al-Arqam, located in a wealthy district of Amman, has high standards with relatively high fees, while other schools in less economically privileged areas have lower standards with lower fees.[112] (For example, my research indicates that tuition fees are lower in Mafraq than in Amman. However, the majority of Dar al-Arqam schools are located in relatively wealthy Western Amman.) The director of the Dar al-Arqam school in Amman claims that in the mid-1990s the school did a study comparing itself to nine other private schools of comparable standards and found that of the ten schools, Dar-al-Arqam (whose fees average just below 500 JD per year) was the second lowest in

Table 3.2. Comparison of Annual Private School Tuition Fees in Amman
in 2001 (in Jordanian Dinar)

Name of School	4th Grade	6th and 7th Grades	10th Grade
Dar al-Arqam	420	500	545
Dar al-Aqsa	375	430	525
Al-Ramleh	250	350	NA
Al-Resalah	350	400	NA
Al-Yasmeen	250	300	NA
Al-Marwa	200	200	NA
Rahbat al-Wardeyyeh	600	NA	820
Dar al-Ulum al-Islamiyyah	200	200	NA
Ma'muneyyeh	350	NA	500

Source: Author's research.

terms of fees; the highest charged as much as 4,000 JD per year.[113] However, my 2001 study of private schools in Amman (see Table 3.2) found the ICCS schools to be among the most expensive (albeit not the most expensive).

The two ICCS schools are not intended for the poor, but they are not the cheapest private schools in the city. Other than a very limited number of poor children on scholarships, the students are not from poor families. As one teacher at the school stated, most of the children come from well-educated families. Similarly, the controller for private schools for the government-run Private Schools Governing Board noted that the two ICCS schools are in the middle spectrum of the private schools and that they target middle-class students, not those from the lower class.[114]

Similarly, in the Islamic College in Zarqa, tuition fees are substantially higher than other comparable colleges and beyond the reach of the poor. Depending on their field of study, the nearly 1,000 students at the college pay between 900 JD and 1,000 JD in tuition fees per year. In comparison to two other community colleges in Zarqa (one private, one public), the tuition fees of ICCS College are consistently more expensive across the board (see Table 3.3). On the whole, the ICCS is not investing in the educational needs or development of Jordan's poor. Rather, as with the case of its medical facilities, it is catering to the frustrations of Jordan's middle class—the class that makes up the Brotherhood and the IAF.

Through its provision of "charity," the ICCS not only provides services to the paying middle class—schools for their children and medical facilities—it also offers jobs to the members of that class and, in many cases,

**Table 3.3. Comparison of Annual College Fees in Zarqa in 2001
(in Jordanian Dinar)**

Field of Study	Islamic College (ICCS)	Qurtuba College (Private)	Zarqa Islamic College (Public)
Medical Laboratory Technology	988	800	760
Management & Information Systems	1080	900	850
Accounting	910	700	500

Source: Author's research

those members who are sympathetic to the Islamist movement. The Islamic Hospital in Amman employs 1,173 people, and the Islamic Hospital in Aqaba employs 112. In addition to this, there are 81 employees in the medical clinics located throughout the country (32 of whom are doctors). The total number of ICCS employees in the medical facilities (including doctors, nurses, cleaners, and the like) is 1,366. Similarly, the education sector provides numerous jobs, not just in terms of teachers, but also in terms of the large extended support staff and other service providers, such as bus drivers, guards, messengers, cleaners, and maintenance personnel. In the ICCS's kindergarten and elementary and secondary schools, there are 935 employees, and in the college there are 94 employees. In the Dar al-Arqam schools in Amman alone, there are 143 teachers, 45 administrators, 40 messengers, 40 drivers, and 55 other employees.[115] In the Zarqa school system, there are 99 teachers, 14 administrators and 30 additional workers.[116] In total, 2,395 people are hired by the ICCS to work in its private hospitals and schools and its college—most of whom are educated middle-class professionals.

While not all of those who work in the ICCS nonprofit commercial activities are necessarily Islamists (one doctor, in fact, told me quite clearly that he was not), it can be argued that the ICCS commercial centers are clearly established for the benefit of the middle class and that they offer a tremendous source of patronage to those sympathetic to the Islamist movement. In an interview with Quintan Wiktorowicz, for example, the engineer for the construction of the Islamic Hospital in Amman and the former director of the Fund for the Sick and Poor, Ra'if Nijim, estimated that as many as 90 percent of employees at ICCS organizations are members of the Muslim Brotherhood.[117] He argued that as Islamists are repeatedly chosen over qualified candidates, this patronage function brings down the quality of services in Islamic institutions. In addition, I repeatedly heard rumors that the hospital grants all its bids for work to Islamists as well. Similarly, Anne Roald points out in her study of Islamic schools in Jordan that the criteria for the selection of teachers and staff is first and foremost their Islamic commitment, then an Islamic personality, and third, their educational qualifications.[118] My interviews with teachers in the Dar al-Arqam system reveal that not all the teachers have university degrees; many are in fact still university students (first year). They were hired based on their commitment to Islam and the fact that they had been students in the Dar al-Arqam school.

Within the ICCS system, Islamists are paid very well. Roald notes that teachers are paid handsomely in the Dar al-Arqam school system. In my own interviews, doctors repeatedly noted they received better benefits in ICCS clinics than they would elsewhere. The doctors in the Islamic Hospital receive excellent pay and the opportunity to work with some of the finest medical equipment; even doctors in the smallest of clinics received greater incentives to work in them than they did in equivalent clinics elsewhere. The dentist in the clinic in the Baqaʿa refugee camp noted that he had both better pay and better hours there than he had in the private clinics where he had worked previously. He left his previous clinic in Amman because the ICCS clinic offered him good pay, full benefits, three weeks' vacation, and two weeks' sick leave. He also gets Fridays and holidays off and does not work evenings. In his previous clinic, despite catering to a wealthy clientele, he worked seven days per week, including evenings, and did not have vacation pay.

Indirect financial benefits and nonmaterial benefits also accrue to ICCS employees. By being associated with or integrated into the ICCS's social networks, a donor or volunteer may potentially gain access to a new business partner or, based on the friendly connection, receive a discount on some purchase in the future. These trickle-down effects can spread far and wide. Other participants simply benefit from new friendships or new experiences and challenges.

Finally, it cannot be forgotten that the creation of these institutions and working in them reinforces Islamist identity and is an important component in the making of networks of solidarity and trust. This is in and of itself an important source of individual and group satisfaction and tremendous pride. Doctors from the Islamic Hospital to the Baqaʿa refugee camp showed me with pride not just the work they were doing but the high quality of equipment, materials, and medicine they had to work with. Indeed, a strong element of professional pride is integral to the Islamist identity. Participating in ICCS institutions creates a gratifying sense of a mission.

The picture that emerges is one in which the ICCS places its patronage of middle-class Islamists above all other concerns—including, to a large extent, those regarding the poor. The ICCS, particularly its commercial activities but also to a lesser extent its welfare activities, targets Jordan's educated middle class as the membership and voting constituency of the moderate Islamist movement. The ICCS provides the perfect tool for a frustrated middle class armed with the education and skills to provide for its own employment, education, and medical demands and needs. This serves not only to maintain the movement's middle-class membership base but also has the potential to function as a recruitment strategy. Finally, the symbolic importance of top-notch quality medical care is not lost on the ICCS. ICCS initiatives such as the Islamic Hospital create not only a viable but also a highly visible and proud symbol of the Islamist movement and its opposition to the state.

ISLAMIC WELFARE INSTITUTIONS: WHAT THE POOR RECEIVE

To state that ISIs provide numerous benefits to the middle class does not necessarily mean that the poor do not also benefit. ISIs do provide an important service for the poor. No one can deny the help they give. However, upon closer examination, while the numbers are impressive, the services and assistance ISIs offer have far less impact on the lives of the poor than one would assume at first glance. As in Egypt, Jordanian ISIs are not the only source to which the poor turn for help; rather, they are simply one of many services to which the poor must turn. An examination of what the poor receive confirms that it is the middle class and not the poor that is the target of the ICCS.

The dedication of many men and women who address the needs of the poor as well as the necessary and important role the ICCS plays in the lives of the poor cannot be overlooked. The ICCS center outside the city of Kerek is one of only two nongovernmental organizations in the entire Kerek region, despite the fact that Kerek has one of the highest concentrations of people living in the lowest income categories. The one other NGO located in the city of Kerek (where poverty rates are not quite as low as they are in the region of Kerek) deals only with orphans, not with needy families. The ICCS center is very small, but it distributes aid to over 800 needy families; as the only NGO doing so, its role in the community is essential. Similarly, 90 percent of the residents of the Baqaʿa refugee camp live below the poverty line. Reflecting this, the ICCS clinic in the camp deals predominantly with anemia and malnutrition. While there are other medical options in the camp, the clinic's medical services are necessary, as is the education it offers. The dentist and the doctor at the clinic regularly encounter cases of 7-year-olds (and even 2-year-olds) with mouths full of rotting teeth; they both feel that educating the camp's population about hygiene and good health is an important part of their job.[119] In the Wihdat refugee camp, there are no foreign NGOs and no other NGOs serving specifically orphans. The ICCS is the only NGO serving orphaned families, who are often living twelve people to a room. In one case, I witnessed a widow living with all her children in one room with a dirt floor and essentially no furniture. The center is able to give only as little as 30 JD per month to some families, but this family received approximately 50 JD per month, and there was no mistaking the mother's appreciation. These are all important examples of the service the ICCS performs. However a closer examination reveals a second picture as well.

One of the most extensive charity services the ICCS offers is financial (and to a limited degree, material) assistance to orphans and poor families. Essentially, the ICCS centers give orphans 20 JD every month and poor families between 20 and 50 JD per month. Five JD are held back for administrative costs (and what the ICCS refers to as "counseling fees," as they also provide some counseling to orphans), so in actuality orphans receive 15 JD per month and poor families receive between 15 JD to 45 JD per month. In addition, a maximum of three orphans per family may receive financial assistance. An orphaned family (because fathers are the major, if not the only, breadwinner, in a family, an orphan is designated by the ICCS a child under the age of 16 who is without a father) may receive a maximum of 45 JD per month. The criterion for whether one, two, or three orphans in a family receives aid is simply whether or not a donor selects the child. Donors choose orphans based upon a photo and description; lucky families have three children selected (usually by three different donors). Most families do not receive support for three orphans. Therefore, if only one orphan is sponsored, a family receives a total of 180 JD per year. Similarly, poor families may only receive as little as 15 JD per month for the entire family as well as some meat and/or clothing twice a year on religious holidays. (In an effort to reach as many people as possible, those families designated as poor are not those also designated as those with orphans—families usually receive one type of fund or the other.) Yet there may easily be as many as ten to thirteen persons in the family. In fact, while the average family size in Jordan is six persons, among the poor the average family size is nine individuals.[120]

The World Bank records that poor households in Jordan (the bottom 19.8 percent of the population according to expenditures) spend 172.28 JD or less per capita per year on food alone, which translates into 58.6 percent of per-capita expenditures.[121] This amount obviously does not include other necessary household expenditures such as education, medical care, clothing, or housing.[122] While 180 JD per year from the ICCS makes an important difference to one family member, it provides little or nothing for the rest. Indeed, an aid worker for a different organization stated to me that while orphans are "lucky" and relatively well provided for, many poor families cannot fulfill the conditions established by the ICCS in order to qualify for aid, and when they do the assistance they receive is too little. Many poor families fall between the cracks.

Each ICCS center establishes an amount per capita per month that determines which families receive financial assistance. This amount ranges from 15 to 25 JD per capita per month. In other words, if the monthly per-capita income of a family is at or below 15 JD in the case of Zarqa or 19 JD in the case of Jebel al-Hussein, Amman, or 25 JD in Baqaʻa, the family qualifies for financial assistance.[123] This is the amount each center feels is necessary to live. However, this income level is not the only criterion; other factors, such as the number of sons who are of working age, the number of elderly or sick family members, or whether or not there are disabled children, are also taken into consideration. A family with two working members would most likely be excluded, even if the amount the two individuals collectively earn translates to less than 15 JD per family member per month and even if they do not earn enough to support the family adequately. The assessments of social workers play an important role in determining which families at or below the cutoff mark receive monetary assistance. In interviews, ICCS directors made it clear that the views of the social workers are far more important than any set of criteria. The cutoff point may fluctuate so that certain families who have an income higher than the official cutoff mark receive financial aid. This means that many deserving families are not served. This vague set of criteria contributes to the (unverified) suspicions that only those sympathetic to the Islamist movement truly qualify for assistance.

The level of assistance the ICCS offers the poor compares unfavorably to the assistance available from other sources, most notably the state. Poor families receive less from the ICCS than they do from the state-run charity. The state runs its own Islamic institutions, one of the most important of which is the Sunduq al-Zakat in the Ministry of Awqaf. The Sunduq runs approximately 158 *zakat* (alms) committees throughout the country. These are community-based committees that collect *zakat* donations and distribute them and run various services, such as medical clinics, university scholarships, and occupational training for women. They are very similar to the services of the ICCS. In 1995 alone, the number of families that received recurring *zakat* financial support totaled 13,170. In the Wihdat refugee camp, for example, the *zakat* committee provides monthly financial assistance of approximately 50 JD ($72 US at that time) to approximately 600 families.[124] While the refugee camp is also based on charity donations, the level of support it provides averages anywhere from 1.1 to 3.3 times the amount the ICCS provides poor families.

The poor, therefore, have a variety of options from which they may receive financial and other forms of assistance. If they want their needs to be adequately covered, they need to prevail upon the assistance of more than one NGO. Interestingly, the ICCS is aware of this fact and is concerned about double-dipping (as is the state). The ICCS branch in Zarqa has a department of social research that employs three male and three female social workers to research the eligibility of applicants and whether or not they are in fact also receiving assistance from elsewhere, thus having a combined income that makes them ineligible for ICCS funds. The Zarqa branch cooperates with the Ministry of Awqaf in order to see if the applicant is receiving other funds from the government and vice versa. In one case, one family has a combined income of 700 JD per month from various aid agencies and the government! The Zarqa branch is now in the process of setting up a computerized database to coordinate the efforts of various associations and document to whom they are giving assistance. This double dipping challenges the assumption that the poor attribute some form of ideological affiliation or loyalty to the ICCS aid they receive, although interviews must be conducted with the poor to confirm this statement. It would appear that while the poor attribute political loyalty to the ICCS because of the aid they receive, they also attribute some degree of loyalty to the sources of aid they receive elsewhere. Alternatively, they may attribute no loyalty at all.

ISLAMIC COMMERCIAL INSTITUTIONS AND ISLAMIC WELFARE INSTITUTIONS EXISTING SIDE BY SIDE

While the ICCS's commercial institutions have been extremely successful in providing for the needs of the middle class, success has not come without a price. The decision to establish a commercial hospital provoked intense debate within the ICCS and Brotherhood circles. More important is the public's reaction over time—including the reaction of the middle class, the very class that the Brotherhood hopes to recruit—to the ICCS's decision to make the Islamic Hospital and other institutions commercial ones. The two most common colloquial names for the Islamic Hospital (*mustashfa islamiyya*) are the Commercial Hospital (*mustashfa tujariyya*) and the Criminal Hospital (*mustashfa ijramiyya*). I heard these labels in every conversation I had with professionals and university students (professionals in the making), particularly in Amman. Islamists were concerned about it; non-Islamists were angry and pointed to what they felt was a degree of hypocrisy because the ICCS professes concern for the economically vulnerable yet charges high rates. Numerous Islamists admitted to me that they are well aware of these derogatory labels and rumors. One concerned Islamist even stated to me that now that the Islamist movement had "proven" that it could offer these services as an alternative to the state, she preferred that the word "Islamic" no longer be in the title of the hospital because the hospital's high prices provoked a negative reaction; the symbol was starting to become tarnished. With these derogatory terms come numerous rumors concerning exorbitant fees, the ruthless manner in which the hospital supposedly pursues its payments, the withholding of the deceased body from the family for as long as three days if the family has not paid in full, and asking the patients to confirm that they have insurance when they are already in the operating room. One family told me they had been rejected by the Fund for the Sick and Poor and were convinced that it was because of the fact that they did not have strong Islamist sympathies; in their opinion those they saw who were successful applicants were clearly Islamists in dress and manner. Another woman claimed that the operation of a relative had been delayed, even as the surgeon was fully scrubbed and the patient was in the operating room, until it was verified that the patient had health insurance that covered the costs of the operation. In an example that I was able to verify, I spoke to the family of one former patient, who had had his operation in July 1989, that is still angry over the hospital costs more than ten years later. The patient was in and out of the Islamic Hospital for approximately one month, during which time he had a variety of tests and two kidney operations. Much to the family's shock, even after receiving a reduction in price through the Fund, the price was approximately 2,200 JD! It was such a high price for the time period that the family had not even imagined that it could be so exorbitant. Even according to the 1998 price list (ten years later), this operation and hospital stay technically should be less (complicated surgeries over three hours cost 50 JD, intensive care costs 38 JD per night, one night in a third-class room is 8.40 JD, plus the cost of food and usage of the facilities). It is no wonder this family continues to refer to the hospital as the Criminal Hospital!

I repeatedly heard these derogatory names and rumors among the professional middle class. At the heart of the anger is a sense of hypocrisy due to the perception that the Islamic Hospital (and potentially by extension the ICCS and the Brotherhood as a whole) is betraying its values. Because the hospital is part of the ICCS and because of the hospital's own advertising, patients assume the hospital is a charity hospital. The hospital's primary brochure for advertising its facilities is called: "The Islamic Hospital: A Philanthropic Model of Health Promotion in Jordan." Patients expect an Islamic hospital to be inexpensive; Islamism is equated with charity. Indeed,

Islamists expressed their frustration to me that patients arrive at the hospital expecting it to be affordable and, in many cases, even free precisely because it is an Islamic hospital. However, prospective patients arrive at the hospital only to find high prices. They are angry when they find they do not qualify for the Fund or that the amount they qualify for is too little to make much of a difference. I repeatedly encountered the sentiment that the Islamic Hospital was not just charging exorbitant rates but that these high rates were "un-Islamic" and made the hospital just like all the others.[125] The Islamic alternative is not really an alternative. At the heart of labels and rumors lies a growing perception, even among the middle class, of a tension or disjuncture between what Islam and the Islamist movement is believed to stand for—an alternative society based on social justice—and the reality of expensive private commercial (albeit nonprofit) services. Whether these rumors are true or not is irrelevant to a large extent; the rumors themselves create a perceived reality that is negative toward the Islamists even among the very class Islamists are targeting.

CONCLUSIONS

As in the case of Egypt, the social networks that are established in the creation, maintenance, and expansion of the ICCS provide the fabric of which the entire charity is made. It is due to these extensive social networks that a small center with only three employees, such as the Merkaz al-Qasr in the governorate of Kerek, can raise adequate funds to assist 858 poor families, approximately 250 to 350 of which are maintained in a regular monthly basis.[126] The middle-class social networks that make this assistance possible also have a tremendous impact upon the middle class itself—the ongoing process of donating and raising funds ultimately creates a tight net of solidarity. The ICCS networks are further reinforced by the benefits the middle class receives, such as jobs, in the ICCS's charity activities (its Islamic welfare institutions) and, most important, in its Islamic commercial institutions, such as the Islamic Hospital and the Dar al-Arqam private schools, where its members receive services specifically targeted toward them. These services exclude the poor; the poor have little chance of affording them even with various subsidies offered. All profits accrued by commercial activities are invested directly back into the respective commercial activities, not toward the social welfare activities designed for the poor. The examination of the resources that are invested into these Islamic commercial institutions—financially, materially, and in terms of educated labor—strongly indicates that the ICCS (and, by extension, the Brotherhood) strategically prioritizes the middle class over the poor.

This unspoken prioritization has not gone unnoticed and is reflected in the cynical labels employed by ordinary Jordanians, including middle-class Jordanians, for the Islamic Hospital. People immediately understand that one is speaking of the Islamic Hospital when one uses the terms Commercial Hospital or Criminal Hospital. These labels reveal the tension or disjuncture or even hypocrisy perceived by many Jordanians between the ICCS's rhetoric of social justice and its practice of private enterprise for the middle class.

The ICCS's decision to target the middle class is not merely due to the operational needs of its facilities, as in the case of many of Cairo's clinics; it also reflects the demands of its middle-class membership and a strategy to attract additional members. Certainly for those who work in Islamic commercial institutions, it appears to have been successful in terms of long-term commitment and, far more important, the reinforcing of Islamist identity and networks of solidarity. These commercial institutions are built in a spirit of solidarity and pride that both reinforces Islamist identity and is a result of it. It is worth investigating whether this strategy is successful outside of these networks in terms of recruiting new members. The tarnishing of the Islamic Hospital as a symbol of the Islamist movement would seem to potentially support social movement theory: participation in a movement occurs due to face-to-face interaction within social networks, not as a result of impersonal pamphlets or symbols. More important, the case of the ICCS also indicates that, in contrast to social movement theory, membership benefits or selective incentives do not necessarily have a positive impact. The negative labels and rumors associated with the Islamic Hospital indicate that the strategy of targeting or benefiting the middle class is coming into conflict with ICCS's goals of providing charity and the Brotherhood's proclaimed focus on social justice. They result as expectations of what an Islamic Hospital should provide clash with the reality. The very success of an organization at providing benefits can potentially undermine a movement when the instrumental needs of the organization and/or movement override the goals of the social movement organization or when the benefits become the goals in of themselves. In the case of the ICCS, I argue that the widespread recognition and use of the terms Criminal Hospital and Commercial Hospital indicate that the strategy of targeting the middle-class membership is undermining the Islamist movement in Jordan in the long run.

Finally, the success of the ICCS's activities, including those that are specifically aimed at the middle class, is not due just to its middle-class networks and its strategy to provide benefits to the middle class, but also to the state and to historical preferential treatment of the ICCS. The charity is highly dependent upon the state because many of its centers are in fact, technically illegal, and exist only at the whim of the state.

The chapters on Egypt and Jordan have examined the development and importance of middle-class networks to ISIs. They have focused less, however, the dynamics of these social networks—on the impact the provision of social welfare services is having on social networks. In the case study of Yemen, we will examine how the activities of the ISIs bring together, solidify, and create new social networks.

FOUR

The Islah Charitable Society in Yemen: Women's Social Networks, Charity, and Da'wa

---

Each week in Sanaʿa, a fairly unnoticeable yet impressive event takes place. Pouring into the basement of the mosque attached to the Islah Charitable Society's main headquarters, more than 200 women of all ages gather for a lecture by a prominent *shaykh* on the Qurʾan or lessons integral to Islam. I attended this event for the first time after having been in Yemen for a little more than a month. When I first entered the building, I was struck by the huge number of shoes everywhere; women took off their shoes before they entered the huge hall. A few steps farther, upon entering the room, I was again momentarily overwhelmed by what appeared to be a sea of black—women in their black cloaks (*baltohat*) and head-coverings that drape a woman in black leaving only her eyes exposed (*lithma* or *niqab*). At first glance it seemed impossible to tell the women apart, yet children running about the room were easily able to find their mothers sitting in rows on the floor when the time came to settle down and listen to the lecture. I too slowly became able to recognize the shape and movement of the women who had invited me to the lecture. As the basement filled up, women spilled into an upstairs room where they watched the lecture beneath them on a television screen. As there were no men present, this upstairs room also offered them the opportunity to remove their head-coverings and veils.[1] I sat downstairs, with the women who had invited me, against a wall where luckily enough I was easily able to observe the audience. Many women had come early to socialize with one another. In fact, some chitchatted throughout the lecture. Other women made their way through the room seeking donations for the Islah Charitable Society. They were selling coupons for varying sizes of donations; even the smallest amounts were encouraged. When the lecture began, it was familiar in terms of format and was quite interactive. It was at the end of the lecture, during the concluding prayers, that I was most awestruck. One at a time, women began covering their eyes with their hands or veils, rocking back and forth, and crying. The outpouring of emotion by women moved by the beauty of the message was an incredible, and highly personal, sight I had never witnessed before. Yet, as I was to learn, this type of event (both in terms of the lecture and the emotional outpouring) occurs on a much smaller scale in women's homes throughout the city on a weekly or biweekly basis in the form of *nadawat*, or Qur'anic study or discussion groups.

Because I was busy taking in all the new sights and sounds, much of the significance of the evening at that first mosque lecture was lost on me. Only later, as I began attending various *nadawat* in the homes of friends and acquaintances did some generalizable observations begin to emerge. They are usually conducted in the afternoon, and sometimes as many as forty women may arrive for a *nadwa* at the home of a friend or a friend of a friend. Women, sometimes with children in tow, crowd into the hostess's *mafraj*, or "living room," sitting on the floor in a circle around the room. The hostess may conduct the lecture or discussion herself each week or she may invite a different guest speaker, always female, to give a lecture. Afterward, women stay and socialize, talking among themselves before they go home. Here, too, I saw a woman present a story of another woman and her family in particular distress and ask that people donate whatever they could for the family. In response, women collected whatever loose change or money they had in their pockets, wrapped it in a tissue, and passed it forward to the woman collecting donations. While the Islah Charitable Society's weekly lectures are relatively formal events advertised by the Society, private *nadawat* are informal and promoted strictly by word of mouth. As with any gathering in a person's house, some form of invitation, regardless of how informal or secondhand, is needed. It became clear to me that while the women in attendance differed in some aspects—some were members of the Islah Charitable Society, some were members of the Islah Party, and many differed in their outward observance of Islam—many were of the educated middle class. In its essence, I realized, a *nadwa* is social gathering linking various similar social networks together. It is one node in a large web of middle-class social networks. As such, it provides women of the Islah Charitable Society with an excellent opportunity to access those women (and their extended networks) who have the time, skills, and money to work on behalf of the Society.

The Islah Charitable Society, or the Charitable Society for Social Reform, is Yemen's largest NGO. Within it, the Women's Committee is one of six committees that make up the Society. Together with the central (male) headquarters, the Women's Committee provides numerous services for women and children, and, with a substantially more limited budget, it also conducts its own independent initiatives and charity efforts. As I saw in the *nadwa,* in the course of raising and distributing charity, the Women's Committee engages a wide array of women—members and nonmembers, Islamists and non-Islamists—who have material resources and/or facilities, but mostly skills, they can donate to the cause. Through the Committee's work, different social circles are brought together and overlap in various social and charity-directed functions. The Committee reaches women on a regular or irregular basis who would not normally be politically active and through these overlapping social networks brings non-Islamist and Islamist women together. Non-Islamists, Hizb al-Islah (Reform Party) members and Islah Charitable Society members are brought together in ever-tightening social circles and solidarity. These newly established bonds are solidified by the various personal benefits middle-class women receive through participating in Society activities. Society activities give women an important, gratifying, and often rare role outside the home. In doing so, the Committee not only raises charity, it indirectly contributes toward the creation of solidarity and trust among the women. Furthermore, by bringing different social networks together, the activities of the Society can expose women to new worldviews that, for some, may mean the gradual transformation, conscious or unconscious, of an act that is perceived as religious—the act of giving charity—to an act of Islamic activism—an attempt to apply Islam to all spheres of life. The potential for widespread social change lies precisely in this potential transformation of perception or worldview.

ASSOCIATIONAL LIFE IN THE TWO YEMENS

The Republic of Yemen came into being in 1990 as a result of the merger of the former Yemen Arab Republic and the former People's Democratic Republic of Yemen, or North and South Yemen, respectively. The Yemen Arab Republic (YAR) was born out of a revolution to overthrow the previous religious imamic ruler; it existed from 1962 to 1990. The People's Democratic Republic of Yemen (1970–1990) was formed after nationalist forces drove the British colonial powers out of Aden. While the two subsequent political systems were substantially different from one another, the two new states each regarded associational life with suspicion and attempted to tightly control all forms of private nongovernmental associations through prohibition and cooptation. Therefore, despite a relatively long history of associational activity in both countries, associational life did not begin to flourish until the introduction of political liberalization and democratization that came with the unification of the two Yemens.

The former People's Democratic Republic of Yemen was located at the southwesternmost tip of the Arabian peninsula. Aden, its capital, historically commanded a strategic position as a refueling and resupplying base for ships traveling along trade routes from Europe through the Middle East to India. Because of Aden's vital location for trade routes, the British invaded the city in 1839 and made it into a crown colony under direct British colonial rule in 1937.[2] Associational life began with the creation of trade unions in the 1950s and ultimately resulted in the formation of cultural clubs, independent presses, labor and political parties, rural movements, and local self-help groups.[3] Out of these efforts, independence groups and movements arose in the struggle to rid the South of the British. As the British prepared to depart, a brief but bloody civil war ensued between rival groups that dominated the anticolonial struggle and vied for leadership of the new independent country. The result was the final transfer of power to the National Liberation Front (NLF) in 1968 and the eventual birth of the People's Democratic Republic of Yemen (PDRY) in 1970.

Despite the role civil associations played in the success of the South's revolution, NGOs were regarded as suspect by the new socialist regime. It saw independent local initiatives as a threat to the development of a new national socialist consciousness, and it channeled all volunteer and organizational efforts into party-affiliated mass organizations and work cooperatives. As a result, civil society was largely suppressed until the dissolution of the PDRY in 1990.

In northern Yemen, civil society played an important role in the removal of the former imam and the installation of the republican presidential leader in 1962. North Yemen became an independent state after World War I and the consequent collapse of the Ottoman Empire.[4] Imam Yahya, the leader who had united the northern tribes in an independence movement against the Ottoman occupiers, became the autocratic leader of the independent Kingdom of Yemen. From that time until the Revolution of 1962, the Kingdom was ruled by imams, the religiopolitical leaders of the majority Zaydi community of northern Yemen.[5]

Associational life in the North began with political movements that demanded the removal of the ruling religious imam. After the revolution in 1962 and the establishment of the secular one-party presidential republic of the YAR, local associations dealing with social welfare concerns increasingly formed as the country focused on socioeconomic development.[6] Self-help groups providing roads, schools, and water flourished. The most dominant of these were the Local Development Associations. As in the South, however, the new republican regime viewed these local endeavors as security concerns, and most initiatives were brought under increasing government control. In 1985, the Local Development Associations were transformed into local government councils, called Local Councils for Cooperative Development, responsible to the Ministry of the General People's Congress, the president's party.

On the eve of unification, therefore, civil associations were weak, state-directed, and limited in number. Despite prior periods of robustness, associational life played little to no role in the creation of the new united state and the consequent introduction of political liberalization and democratization, including the country's first elections. Women's contributions to associational life prior to unification were also highly circumscribed; however, as with Yemeni men, both Islamist and non-Islamist women activists also have been playing a prominent role in country's burgeoning civil society since 1990.

ASSOCIATIONAL LIFE AND WOMEN

The unification of the former North and South Yemen officially occurred on May 22, 1990. It came about as the result of the agreement reached by the President Ali Abdallah Salih of the YAR and President Ali Salim al-Bayd of the PDRY in November 1989. The decision was wholly inspired and orchestrated by the highest levels of government; in fact, the announcement took most Yemenis and diplomats by surprise. The decision was based on a combination of internal and external factors, including the pressing economic needs of the South due to the loss of Soviet aid after the collapse of the USSR and the discovery of oil in disputed border regions. Although on-again, off-again talks between the two Yemens had been occurring for almost two decades, economic and ideological bankruptcy, popular patriotic sentiments that historically yearned for a united Yemen, and the self-interest of the two leaders finally pushed the two sides toward cooperation and unification.[7] A pluralist democratic constitution offered the new state, which was bereft of both widespread popular support and legitimacy, a legitimizing ideology. Such a constitution had an additional appeal that each side "fancied itself capable of out-maneuvering the other"[8] and thus each was amenable to the transformation of its respective political system and the new distribution of power. The final agreement named Ali Abdallah Salih as president and Ali Salim al-Bayd as vice president. Sana'a, the former capitol of North Yemen, became the capital of the new united Yemen.

The new coalition government embarked on the road of political liberalization and democratization. Within the first year of unification, 150 publications of all hues, hundreds of civil associations, and not less than 38 political parties had formed.[9] For the first time, numerous smaller parties, including the newly formed Hizb al-Islah (the Party of Islah), joined the

General People's Congress (GPC, the party of the North) and the Yemeni Socialist Party (YSP, the party of the South) on the political map.

Hizb al-Islah (the Islah Party), which is also called Al-Tajammuʿ al-Yemeni lil-Islah (the Yemeni Congregation for Reform), was established in January 1991 and is best understood as a coalition of northern-based conservatives who share a common pro–Salih regime stance, an antisocialist stance, and conservative social objectives.[10] Headed by the leader of most powerful tribal confederation of the North, Abdullah al-Ahmar, Hizb al-Islah is a marriage of prominent tribal leaders, businessmen, and several different religious groups. Three major streams can be said to constitute the Islah Party.[11] The first is the tribal stream, represented by the *shaykh* of the Hashid tribes, Shaykh Abdullah Bin Hassan al-Ahmar—who is also secretary-general of the Party. The second is the Muslim Brotherhood, one of the oldest Islamist movements in Yemen, which was introduced by Yemeni students who studied with Hassan al-Banna in Cairo in 1939–1940.[12] The third stream consists of various Yemeni merchants.[13]

In Yemen's first democratic elections in 1993, the Islah Party's program was encapsulated in the slogan "situations have to be reformed, Shariʿa has to rule, and Liberalism has to be rejected."[14] While the implementation of Islamic law took precedence, the Party program also focused on

> the principle of freedom as an Islamic principle, and the principle of power sharing. It also stood by the principles of getting maximum benefit from its resources, adopting economic policies by depending on the local resources, encouraging foreign investment and the national capital, replacing all banking procedures with Islamic ones, re-evaluating the taxation system, adopting freedom in trade and fighting monopolies, developing educational policies in accordance with Islam, and lastly, it regarded the Palestinian issue as the issue of all Arabs and Muslims.[15]

The Islah Party won 62 of 301 parliamentary seats, making it the third and junior partner in a governing coalition with the GPC and the YSP.[16]

The coalition was not to last long. Four years after unification and one year after the elections that brought the coalition to power, a war between the armies of the former North and South broke out.[17] The upshot of the war was the destruction of the YSP and the consequent rise of Hizb al-Islah in the power vacuum that ensued. A new cabinet was formed and Hizb al-Islah was given a number of ministries.[18] In the 1997 elections, however, Islah saw its share of seats decrease to forty-seven.[19]

In both the 1993 and 1997 elections, Yemen's growing civil associations played important roles; for example, in monitoring electoral procedures, training observers, educating voters, encouraging and supporting female candidates, filing candidates, registering voters, and counting votes. Over

2,000 NGOs are registered with the Ministry of Social Security and Social Affairs in Yemen today, and hundreds more are registered with the Ministry of Tourism and Culture. There are potentially 1,000 or more unregistered NGOs. Women are most highly represented in the NGOs specializing in issues related to women, children, and public health. Of the fourteen specialized NGOs dealing with women, children, and family health in a 1996 directory compiled of Yemeni NGOs and quasi-NGOs, six have women as presidents and eleven have women on the board of directors as well as female members.[20]

The task before these women is a daunting one. According to the UN Human Poverty Index, 49.4 percent of Yemen's population (16.9 million) are living in poverty. Yemen's annual growth rate is 3.9 percent (one of the highest in the world) and it is expected to decrease only minimally in the near future. The infant mortality rate is 87 per 1,000 live births, while life expectancy at birth is only 58.5 years. As much as 21.2 percent of the population is not expected to survive to age 40. Only 39 percent of the population has access to safe water, 84 percent of the population has access to health care, and 34 percent of the population has access to sanitation. Literacy among women remains low at 22.7 percent, and only 27 percent of females are enrolled in primary, secondary, or tertiary schools. Although the enrollment statistics for males are higher than for females, they, too, remain low at 70 percent.[21] Only approximately 15 percent of the eligible female population registered to vote in the 1993 parliamentary elections; this number rose to 28 percent in the 1997 elections.[22] Many women do not know that Members of Parliament are elected. The result is that Yemeni women are more likely to be illiterate, they are more likely to suffer from malnutrition or sickness, they are more likely to be untrained or unemployed, and they are more likely to be poorer than are men.

At the time of unification and the introduction of elections in Yemen, the concept of women in public life was relatively alien in the predominantly tribal North, although the sight of women active in public life was more common in the South. Prior to 1990, the majority of women's lives in both Yemens were (and, to an only slightly lesser extent, continue to be) dictated by tribal custom that granted them few of the rights accorded to them under Islam, such as inheritance, and made them subject to the authority of their fathers, brothers, husbands, and sons, who had the right to make decisions concerning their lives. While women's experiences certainly differed according to their ascribed social status, whether they lived in an urban or rural area, and their wealth and legal status (which differed in the former North and South),[23] women's activities were largely restricted to the household and, if they lived in a rural area, the agricultural fields. Traditional attitudes regarding women's "nature" and the symbolic role women played as the "repositories of family honor" meant that women's opportunities in public life were highly restricted.[24] Seclusion of girls and women was a symbol of male respectability; after the onset of puberty, female interaction was strictly limited to contact with other females and close male relatives. Early marriage—often as early as age 13—was encouraged, which meant that the average woman had five or six children before she turned 30 (although this has risen, due partially to better health care, to as many as eight or nine in the 1990s). Regardless of their legal rights, women were largely excluded from the public world and all major political, economic, social, and religious decision-making.

In North Yemen, women were granted the right to vote and to participate in the ruling Party, the General People's Congress, and nominate themselves as candidates for the GPC's Permanent Committee, its highest organizational authority, in 1982.[25] From 1982 to 1986, one woman (out of 338 members) sat on the GPC Permanent Committee; from 1986 until unification, this number was two.[26] Outside of the GPC, there were a small number of women's nongovernmental organizations as well as women engaged in individual efforts to raise standards of living. Their numbers, however, were too limited or their activities too controlled to have a significant socioeconomic or political impact. The most well-known example is that of the Northern Women's Union, which consists of six women's societies concerned with charity and social work that were brought under government control and forged into one national organization.[27]

However, despite these political rights (which are the envy of many sisters in other Gulf countries) and relatively liberal social legislation (allowing women the right to drive and travel, for example), the strong cultural customs and traditions which generally required women to approach members and institutions of authority through male intermediaries, such as their brothers, fathers, or husbands, meant that women who did forge their ways into the public realm did so at a high personal price, suffering conflicts within their families and often painful slander in the workplace and society. While the 1970s and 1980s were decades of tremendous socioeconomic development in the former North (and while they certainly had an impact on Yemeni women), the vast majority of women remained in "traditional" roles as wives, mothers, and rural laborers on the eve of unification.[28] Urban women in the North "covered their faces, left school early, and avoided public places."[29]

On the surface, women in South Yemen played a far more progressive role in public life than the women in the former North. Southern women were allowed both to vote and run as candidates for the country's Supreme People's Council (SPC).[30] All women's grassroots activities were conducted under the auspices of the General Union of Yemeni Women (GUYW) under the direction of the Socialist Party's Secretary of Mass Organiza-tions.[31] The Union therefore became the primary institution responsible for the education and training of women. Entirely run by women, the GUYW established various training centers and literacy campaigns as well as radio and television programs and a magazine dealing with women. In addition to being the vehicle of revolutionary socialization, the Union also assisted in the formulation of state policies, provided informational and decision-making information to state officials, and served as an important avenue of Socialist Party recruitment. The Union was integrated into both state and party structures at all levels. Women representatives from the GUYW sat on the Party central committees at district, directorate, governorate, and national levels. In addition, the GUYW was represented in the state struc-tures—the Union elected a proportion of the members to both the local people's councils and the Supreme People's Council.[32]

Hence, by the time of unification, women in the PDRY not only par-ticipated in all forms of political life but had also entered the workforce and professions in increasing numbers.[33] However, women's public and profes-sional presence was not equally embraced throughout the country. Beyond the city of Aden, women's participation in public life remained exceeding-ly low. In the rural areas of the South, societal norms, like those in the North, discouraged and even condemned women's political participation. Traditional and family authority remained so strong that even progressive cadres and Socialist Party members were known to object to daughters ap-pearing in public or studying outside the village, fearing "public opinion."[34]

Within this political and social context, only a small number of wom-en's nongovernmental organizations, and even fewer Islamist women's NGOs, existed prior to 1990. While Islamist activities were prohibited in the socialist South, a limited number of Islamist women pioneers were ac-tive in the North. In the 1980s, for example, the secular feminists who founded the Northern Women's Union were outvoted in the Sana'a head-quarters by veiled Islamists who argued "that Islam grants women the right to remain at home, rely on male relatives for financial support and legal rep-resentation, study in sex-segregated schools, and refrain from public life apart from charitable activities."[35] Since that time, the Women's Union in Sana'a has continued to be a largely Islamist organization. It was not until the creation of the Islah Charitable Society that Islamist women began to enter public life in large numbers.

THE ISLAH CHARITABLE SOCIETY

Although the word Islah is in its name, the Islah Charitable Society is tech-nically independent from the Islamic party, Al-Tagammu al-Yemeni lil-

Islah. The Society was established in March 1990, prior to the Party, and has its own independent administrative body.[36] It is the most successful humanitarian nongovernmental organization helping the poor in Yemen. The Society is based in Sana'a but it operates branches throughout the country; its most extensive services are located in Sana'a, Aden, Ibb, Dhamar, Hodeidah, Hajja, Taiz, Mukalla, and Say'oon. It is one of the few NGOs that operates in every governorate of Yemen, urban and rural.[37]

The Islah Charitable Society is registered with the Ministry of Social Security and Social Affairs (MSA). Technically, all NGOs must register with the Ministry and abide by Law 11 of 1963.[38] Law 11 provides the legal framework for the establishment, organization, and registration of NGOs and defines their relationship to the state.[39] To register, societies or organizations must have twenty-one people, a board of directors, a general assembly, and election procedures. The meetings of the general assembly must be monitored by an official from the MSA. The MSA has the right to supervise elections and to audit, license, and abolish NGOs. Although NGOs do not need the approval of Political Security to receive a license, persons who have been convicted for violations of moral standards cannot found or participate in activities of societies or any other types of NGO. Associations which violate the law, disturb public order, frustrate moral and Islamic standards, or endanger the political system are prohibited. In its spirit, Law 11 is modeled upon the Egyptian Law 32.

In practice, the application of Law 11 is arbitrary. The MSA seems to have neither the information nor the will to efficiently oversee registration or monitor NGO activities. While many NGOs operate freely without a license, other NGOs accuse the MSA of intervention in their affairs. Whether Law 11 works in an NGO's favor or not depends to a large extent on the relationship between members of the NGO—particularly the founders or heads—and individuals within the MSA. For example, the MSA provides activity licenses for a specific period of time, ranging from six months to three years. The "criteria" that determines whether a NGO receives a license for a shorter or a longer period of time appears to be the degree of influence the NGO's founder has and his/her personal relationship with the authorities. The Yemeni state is committed to subsidizing all NGOs registered with the MSA. Once again, however, the awarding of a subsidy depends on the influence of an NGO's president or founders and on the NGO's relationship with the state. The result is that personal networks, whether for licensing, building, or fund-raising, are pivotal to any charity society—and in particular those of the president or founder of a NGO.

The Islah Charitable Society receives donations from a large variety of sources—one of which is the Islah Party. Most of the Society's financial sources—although not all—are Islamic institutions or persons sympathetic to Islamic causes. A percentage also comes from membership dues. However, a significant degree of the Society's success in raising funds can be directly attributed to the president of the Society, Tariq Abu Lahoom, and his personal contacts among merchants, businesspersons, and government officials. Many of these connections, including Tariq Abu Lahoom himself, are members of the GPC.[40]

The Society raises its funds both within Yemen and abroad. Generally, the local branches of the Society raise all their donations within the country, but the central headquarters has a video and informational package it sends to prospective donors abroad; it also has a newsletter for regular distribution. Donations from Yemeni expatriates and businessmen are central to the Society's ability to raise adequate funds. In addition to targeting personal contacts, the Society also regularly puts up posters advertising events (particularly at the universities), and it occasionally broadcasts on television.

The headquarters of the Society in Sanaʿa employs approximately forty people.[41] Throughout the city there are twenty-one affiliated centers through which aid is distributed to the poor. These centers do not house activities per se but rather are used for the distribution of charity. Volunteers gather at the centers for meetings and visit homes throughout their immediate neighborhoods in order to determine who is in need of aid or other services.

The Society is essentially a charitable society and does not engage in development efforts per se. It primarily organizes volunteers to aid the poor.[42] Its stated goals are to provide social services in the form of financial, educational, health, and counseling assistance to six identified groups: the economically deprived and needy; the orphaned; the handicapped; the mentally and psychologically disturbed; women, children, and the elderly; and victims of economic or natural disasters. By the end of 1995, for example, the Society had sponsored 4,200 orphans throughout the country. It also had 1,500 poor families on its list of permanent regular beneficiaries and as many as 25,000 families on a more ad hoc basis. During Ramadan 1995, as many as 10,000 volunteers (male and female) distributed clothing and other forms of assistance to 397,969 people.[43] Long meal tables were set up by the Society outside various mosques every evening. During the Greater Bairam holiday, 37,340 poor families were given sacrificial meat. Over 1,000 brides and grooms participated in cost-saving mass marriages performed by the Society. From 1992 to 1995, the Society provided 75,500 pupils with school supplies and necessities. During this same period, 32,000 benefited from the Society's ten or more health care centers. In 1994 alone, the Society treated and vaccinated 16,400 individuals in Abyan, Lahaj, Hadramut, Aden, and Shabwah. During the 1992 earthquake, it distributed 1,100 tents and aid to 7,800 families. It also aided 15,000 families in Aden, Lahaj, Abyan, Shabwah, Hadramut, and Sana'a who were victims of the 1994 war in Yemen.[44] The Society's list of its activities and achievements also includes the supplying of clean drinking water to the poor, health lectures, and university scholarships for the needy.

Despite its emphasis on the distribution of aid, the Society has also established various service-oriented facilities when it has perceived a necessity for a particular service, such as a hospital in Sana'a for mentally ill women. The Society is very proud of the hospital, as it should be. It is the only one of its kind in the country and addresses a critical need. The hospital's inpatient facilities have the capacity for sixty beds (at the time of my visit, thirty-one were in use). The women in the hospital are usually brought to the institution by the police, who find the women walking the streets and disoriented. In other instances they are brought by their families. Still other women are transferred from prison, where they were unjustly held due to a lack of facilities for the insane. In fact, the inspiration for the hospital arose after a visit to the central prison in 1991, when members of the Society witnessed firsthand the appalling situation of the women. The first group of patients, approximately twenty-four, were those original prisoners. Most of the women are ill due to a combination of hereditary diseases, life conditions, and accidents or infectious diseases. The one-story hospital is very basic, plain, and clean; it has an activity room, a dining room, a mosque, an instruction room, a kitchen, and four to five bedrooms. All of the rooms are situated around a courtyard with a garden. Approximately seven women sleep in each bedroom, with the exception of one bedroom, designated for relatively affluent families, which has only four beds. While the women are not living in luxury, they are clearly happy and greeted me (indeed, surrounded me!) with tremendous warmth and enthusiasm. There are also outpatient facilities with a small examination room, a bed, and a laboratory. In total, ten female nurses and one social worker and three male doctors work in the hospital. At the time of my visit, the Society was in the process of building a similar hospital for men next door.

Another project that has received acclaim is the Rabassa Literacy Center for Girls and Women in Hodeidah. It is financed by the Hodeidah branch of the Society and run by the Hodeidah Women's Committee.[45] Rabassa is one of approximately six shantytowns in Hodeidah that sprang up after the 1990 Gulf War. It is populated almost entirely by Yemeni returnees from the oil-rich countries of the Gulf, predominantly from Saudi Arabia. As is to be expected, it is an extremely poor district; the inhabitants live in corrugated-metal huts or Tihama-style straw homes. The vast majority of homes have no electricity or indoor running water. Many small children have no shoes or clothes. The poverty of Rabassa is striking when compared to the affluent villas adjacent to it. The literacy center is a relatively small building with a simple sign posted in front stating that it is a literacy school for women. Inside there are four classes, with the girls and women sitting on the floor or sand. Two of the classes are held in two relatively dark rooms with no windows and only an opening for a door. The other two classes are conducted in the open courtyard.[46] Most of the students are under the age of 20. The teachers have small blackboards with which to work; they have no books. The center has no electricity. Like the students, the teachers are generally also from the area (although there are exceptions) and are found through word of mouth. They are technically volunteers; however, they do receive some irregular pay. During my visit, the classes in the Center were crowded with girls. They are forced by poverty to work during the day, and for many this is their only access to education.

The Society also engages in joint projects with the government. In 1995, for example, in cooperation with the government, it distributed thirty ambulances to hospitals and private health centers in the southern and eastern governorates.[47] It has also embarked with the government on income-generating projects such as the building of a private hospital for mothers in Sana'a.[48] By working with government, the Society is able to reach more people and to benefit from the legitimizing effect of power sharing.

Finally, the Society has also invested in other profit-making projects independently of the government. It has established numerous education institutions, the most important of which is the privately run University of Science and Technology (which includes the only dental school in Yemen). In addition to this, the Society has private primary and secondary schools, many of which are quite large. In Hodeidah, for example, the Islah Society school has 1,900 (paying) students. These schools are thus another source of income for the Society.

Society members state that organization and teamwork (the lack of friction and competition) is the key to their success.[49] As the head of the Women's Committee in Hodeidah stated to me, the goals of the Society are the as same those of any of the other NGOs, but the *uslub,* the manner or method, is what makes the difference.[50] As in Egypt and Jordan, it is the attitude and the experiences of the charity providers, and not necessarily those of the recipients, that makes the Islah Charitable Society Islamic.

THE WOMEN'S COMMITTEES
IN SANAʿA AND HODEIDAH

In order to address the needs of its targeted groups, the Society is organizationally divided into six committees: the Neighborhood Activities Committee; the Special Projects Committee; the Orphanage Care and Sponsorship Committee; the Basic Health Services Committee; the Emergency Relief Committee; and the Women's Committee.[51] The Women's Committee is relatively autonomous and conducts its own independent activities on behalf of women and children. The headquarters of the Committee is located in a three-storied building near the old campus of Sanaʿa University.[52] In addition, there are two other, albeit significantly smaller, branches (which are essentially distribution centers) in Sanaʿa. While most of the Women's Committees of the regional branches are extremely small, in Hodeidah, there is a new and quite spacious center recently built by the Hodeidah branch of the Society in a socioeconomically mixed area, close to what is referred to as the commercial area of Hodeidah (and one dominated by villas).[53] Like the men, the women are engaged in two general types of activities. The first is strictly charity, primarily fund-raising and the distribution of clothing or food. The second concerns "profit-making ventures"—offering sewing or English classes for a fee and investing the money back into the Society. This latter type of activity is not geared toward the poor.

Similar to the work of the men, the majority of the women's work is devoted to specific charity events such as providing Ramadan meals, gifts, or clothes for the poor outside of mosques. Independently of the men, the Women's Committee in Sanaʿa supports approximately sixty orphans.[54] The women also conduct hospital and prison visits and provide some training sessions in women's prisons. In order to conduct these activities, they are engaged in a variety of fund-raising events. During Ramadan 1996, for example, the women hosted a fund-raising event for Sanaʿa's elite and the women of the ambassadorial community.[55] The women also independently organize fund-raising events at Sanaʿa University, where they sell donated books and handicrafts made by the poor to students. For other events, they may simply post notices throughout the university campus announcing events and asking for volunteers and donations for orphans. At events such as the weekly Qurʾanic lectures, women collect donations through the selling of coupons representing sums of money. Women may purchase coupons for any amount, no matter how small. In addition to these activities, they also run certain events jointly with the men, such as the weekly lecture for women on the Qurʾan. The women also help organize the mass marriages.

Within the centers, lessons and various services are offered—handicraft workshops, a hairdressing salon, sewing classes, adult literacy classes, Qur'anic study lessons, and day care centers.[56] In Hodeidah, for example, the women's centers offer sewing, knitting, crocheting, English, and typing classes and Braille lessons and hairstyling lessons (although not necessarily on a consistent basis). While they may have the facilities to conduct all these lessons, sewing, hairdressing, and Qur'anic classes are typically taught the most regularly.[57] The new center has numerous professional (industrial) sewing machines in addition to sewing machines designed for home usage.[58] When students become proficient at sewing, they advance to the professional machines and make clothing for retail. Low-income women who become proficient at sewing (some take lessons at the Society, others at the Yemeni Women's Union or elsewhere) are then hired by the Society to sew uniforms at the request of schools and other organizations. The women are paid per piece (as opposed to a salary), and the profits on the sale of the uniforms go back to the Women's Committee toward other projects, such as the support of orphans.[59] In April 2002, there were fifteen low-income women engaged in sewing uniforms. Students pay a fee of approximately 300 YR (Yemeni riyal) for any of the courses offered at the center, and the instructors are generally found by advertising in local schools and elsewhere—usually through word of mouth or through the principal of a school.

The activities in the two centers can be divided into two distinct types —those that are for better-off women (including sometimes middle-class women) and those that are for the poor. An example of services for the former group is the morning kindergarten the Committee runs for approximately twenty children aged 4 to 6. The cost of the kindergarten is 17,000 YR per year. The Committee also runs a two-month summer school during the summer holidays for children that costs approximately 3,000 YR. In a country where the salary of a civil servant is only approximately 8,000 YR, these are relatively large (if not exorbitant) fees.[60] Most of the women who drop off their children are relatively affluent. Even the courses offered by the Women's Committee can be prohibitively expensive for the poor. In a study conducted in 1995, Marina de Regt noted that women who wanted to attend the typing, sewing, or Qur'an classes had to be literate (for the typing classes they have to have finished secondary school), they had to be older than 15 years of age, and they had to pay a monthly fee of 100 to 200 YR. In my 1996 field work, I found that these fees had risen to 300 YR per month. For some poorer women this would be a manageable amount after much saving. However, as de Regt states: "As the activities of the centre are quite expensive, mainly women from better-off families take part in them."[61] These profit-making ventures are not designed for the poor.

THE WOMEN THEMSELVES

Just as the men of the Islah Charitable Society do, the women who volunteer and work for the Society to a large extent represent Yemen's new and slowly growing middle class. Yemen's class and status structure has been rapidly changing over the last thirty years. Social and ethnic background, descent, and status have historically played an important role in Yemeni society, particularly in the northern highlands, and have traditionally been broken down into six basic status groups: the *sa'ada* or *sayyid* families, who claim descent from the Prophet Mohammed; the *quda* families of judges; the *qaba'il*, or tribal families; the *muzayyieen*, who perform service activities; the *akhdam*, who are said to descend from African slaves; and the *muwallideen*, who are of mixed and unknown descent.[62] The strength and importance of these status groups has begun to slowly break down with the expansion of the state, urbanization, industrialization, and increased education. In particular, the 1980s witnessed the slow development of a new middle class as individuals moved to major cities for higher education and jobs. This new middle class has begun seeking careers, largely in urban areas, based on education instead of continuing age-old traditions of their rural forefathers and foremothers. By the 1980s, therefore, we see a new middle class that is primarily composed of high-ranking civil servants, public-sector and private-sector managers, professionals, technocrats, and educated businessmen.

Women are not immune to these changes. Despite continuing high rates of illiteracy in general, many women are going to university and getting higher educations. The first women were graduating from the University of Aden as early as the mid-1960s, and by the 1980s, the number of female university graduates equaled the number of male graduates for all intents and purposes. In 1983, for example, the graduating class of the University of Aden included 398 women and 405 men.[63] In the North, when the University of Sana'a opened in 1973/1974, 8 percent of the total student population was women just four years later. By 1985/1986, this percentage had risen to thirteen, and in the Faculty of Medicine women actually outnumbered men.[64] Today, approximately 105 per 100,000 women in Yemen are enrolled in some form of tertiary education; for every 100 males in tertiary education, there are fourteen females.[65]

It is largely these educated middle-class women who volunteer and work for the Charitable Society for Social Welfare. The Women's Committees of the Islah Charitable Society in Sana'a, Hodeidah, and the branches elsewhere are generally regarded as charity groups for rich women. This, however, is largely not true. While some of the women holding positions of authority in the Committee are from well-known families and/or are related to prominent tribal men in both Yemen and in the Islamist political party, Hizb al-Islah, the majority of women active in the Islah Charitable Society are neither wealthy nor well-known. They are, however, predominantly (albeit not solely) of the educated middle class. The majority of women are either in university, have a university degree, or are in secondary school with the intention of going to university. Either because of the extended family with whom they live (who can look after their children when they are out) and/or the relatively good salaries their husbands make, these are the women with the luxury of time (and with the educational skills) to engage in charity work.

This profile is most accurate in Sana'a. There are, of course, some regional variations. In Hodeidah, for example, we find that many of the young women who join the Islah Charitable Society, as literacy teachers in particular, are returnees from Saudi Arabia—those Yemenis who lived, worked, and were often born in Saudi Arabia and were forced to return to Yemen because of the 1991 Gulf War. These women do not as a whole have a university education. They do, however, perceive themselves as having had a better education in Saudi Arabia than that available in Yemen and see themselves as educated. These women often strive for opportunities they view as commensurate with their education. The families of these women, whose members are relatively well-educated, were of the middle class in Saudi Arabia, and have the ambitions of the educated middle class, are now often reduced to living in poorer areas, having had to flee Saudi Arabia without much of their wealth or belongings. The women of these families have their education to offer the Society.

SOCIAL NETWORKS AND
THE ISLAH CHARITABLE SOCIETY:
THEIR ROLES AND RELATIONSHIPS

Although the Islah Charitable Society supports various services for women, such as sewing lessons or literacy classes, the majority of the work of the volunteers is devoted to raising donations and distributing charity, such as Ramadan meals or clothes for the poor.[66] It is largely through informal social networks that they are able to do both of these. Most commonly, Committee members enlist women through informal face-to-face contact. The number of women who work full-time for the Society is relatively small; however, through their efforts, many women assist the Committee on an irregular basis. They may be students at an Islamic university and may know someone in the Society—a friend or teacher—and decide to help with an event. For example, during Ramadan, one woman on the

Committee, in the spirit of giving, may negotiate with a retailer she knows on behalf of the Committee to buy material at the wholesale price. Another woman on the Committee may then find a seamstress who agrees to sew clothes for orphans for free as a Ramadan gift. Through similar methods, Committee women approach individuals and businesspersons for new and used books in order to hold book sales at the university to raise funds. Through word of mouth, the friend of a Committee member may know of a high school student or teacher who is willing to conduct literacy or sewing classes in the late afternoon. In this informal way, the Committee raises money or goods and reaches networks of women of many ages with differing levels of skills, resources, education, and commitment to providing for Yemen's poor.

Women in the Hodeidah Committee, for example, readily acknowledge that the personal nature of the fund-raising is an important element in its success. This, they note, is reflected in at least two ways. First, as stated above, the women find volunteers through very personal methods—largely though informal social networks. Second, the women try to make the fund-raising as personalized as possible. For example, donors are told exactly where the money is being directed, and, if possible, even which specific child (in the case of orphans) they are supporting. Fund-raising is therefore highly personalized and targeted.

NADAWAT

An in-depth examination of Qur'anic study groups, *nadawat,* provides insight into how Society women use social networks to accomplish the goals of the Society. *Nadawat* are essentially social gatherings, and as such, they are the most formal aspect of a social network and provide a focal point for analysis. *Nadawat* are particularly revealing windows through which to view the activities of the Society and how these activities play an important role in the creation of networks of trust and solidarity and, potentially, an Islamist worldview, because they are held on a regular, often weekly, basis and many of them bring together a greater number of different social networks than would otherwise be the case in a typical social gathering of one circle of friends. While many *nadawat* are closed and are attended only by a small group of friends, others connect relatively large numbers of women from different circles on a regular or irregular basis, many of whom may be meeting each other for the first time. They are thus a meeting ground for old and new friends and a link between different social networks. Certainly a woman who is wholly secular in her views would not typically attend a *nadwa,* and in this sense the selection of *nadawat* as a unit of analysis is biased. However, *nadawat* do attract women with varying degrees of religious conviction and link together social networks that include many secular women within them. *Nadawat* may also be considered somewhat atypical social gatherings, in that both the Islah Charitable Society and the Islah Party independently host *nadawat* themselves and consider them to be an important aspect of their outreach programs. Although many women in the Society and in the Party do not attend *nadawat,* they are an important example of how women in the Society use social networks as the primary means of finding human and material resources. They are also an example of the type of informal links that connect the institutions of the Islah Charitable Society and the Islah Party together through the people who attend them and, potentially, transfer ideas.

Nadawat generally focus on how to apply Islam in one's daily life; how to be a better Muslim. Subjects may include a discussion of the meaning of Ramadan or the evils of jealousy.[67] A *nadwa* can be as small as four women or as large as forty women, and females of all ages attend.[68] Many women have a regular *nadwa* they attend; however, they may drop in on a *nadwa* on a more casual basis. Some *nadawat* are clearly closed, while others are much more open to whomever wishes to attend. In general, while a certain core group of women may be regulars, the women at a *nadwa* may not all know each other. Women who meet at university or at charity events may learn of *nadawat* or a regular may bring a new friend with her.

In the larger sense, therefore, *nadawat* are informal social gatherings that bring friends together or link several social networks together on a regular basis. There is no formal membership, no regular attendance policies, and no set expectations—women attend these gatherings as often or as little as they wish. Women of different degrees of religious conviction attend. While many of the women are deeply pious, the social nature of the gatherings draws together women with differing attitudes toward Islam (or different degrees of identification with Islam).

Nadawat form an important part of women's informal networks. They provide religious solace and guidance, an education in reading and in Islam, an emotional outlet, a social life outside of the home, and a support group. They also provide an arena where a woman can go for advice or find out where (or to whom) she can go to solve a problem. *Nadawat* furthermore form an important link in the transmission of knowledge and education from female religious scholars to the next generation. Young girls generally learn about Islam at home, but those who desire to learn more generally seek out a *nadwa* in someone's home.

Although *nadawat* are open to all women, their social nature generally dictates that women of similar situations in terms of education and socioeconomic class gather together. In general, they are found in social circles of educated middle-class women, not among the uneducated poor. I have found no evidence of any among the poor. This social categorization rein-forces itself as new members join a *nadwa*.[69] In bringing various networks of women together in a fairly large group, *nadawat* create a tight commu-nity of overlapping social circles where women can socialize, establish friendships, and learn about Islam. They thus link middle-class women—non-Islamists, members of the Society, and those active in the Hizb al-Islah—together.

HIZB AL-ISLAH AND *NADAWAT*

Women in Hizb al-Islah are represented by the Women's Sector of the Party. Theoretically speaking, the Women's Sector in Hizb al-Islah operates as a parallel organization to the main party (the male part).[70] Since 1998, seven women have been on the Party's highest executive council, the Majlis al-Shura.[71] However, women continue to be most active in the Women's Sec-tor, where their predominant goal is to recruit women to the Party.

To a large extent, the Women's Sector focuses its efforts in two related areas. The first area seeks to expand the female membership of the Party. The women are involved in hosting informational events, in education, in recruiting, and in canvassing, for example. They produce newsletters, dis-tribute literature, and raise funds. In addition, at election time, they instruct women in their electoral rights and assist in the registration and voting process.[72] The second area is the education women receive about their rights and duties according to Islam and its laws—*da'wa*. This may include lec-tures on health education or women's right to work according to Islam. The Women's Sector is thus engaged in trying to create a new picture of society, to change traditions—to enact social change.

Within the Party, *da'wa* is primarily conducted through *nadawat*. The Women's Sector uses *nadawat* in two ways. It may send a speaker to a *nadwa* or *qat*-chewing session[73] in someone's home or it may host a *nadwa*, usually at the university or at the Sector's headquarters.[74] While the hosting of *nadawat* within the Women's Sector headquarters is an explicit Party strategy, it cannot always be said that women who lead *nadawat* at the uni-versity or act as guest speakers at *nadawat* within homes are acting on be-half of the Party as part of a larger strategy to usurp *nadawat* for Party purposes. The very nature of *da'wa* creates an almost indistinguishable line between those activities undertaken on behalf of the Party and those that form part of an individual's personal fulfillment of *da'wa*. The promotion of Islam, which lays the foundations for the Islamist message, is an impor-tant part of these women's lives regardless of whether or not they are formal members of the Party or under the directives of Islah.[75]

The type of women who joins the Islah Party is generally younger than the women in other political parties, is middle class, has university ambitions or a university degree, and is deeply religious. She may have a husband or relative within the Islah Party, but this often not the case. She is usually not from an influential family, or *bayt,* although there are exceptions to this generalization. This description must be qualified by stating that there are regional differences—the level of education and political awareness among Islahi women in Sana'a, Taiz, and Aden differs, for example.[76]

On average, women in Hizb al-Islah are in their late teens or early twenties. The leaders, however, tend to be older—in their thirties. The women in Islah generally do not have children yet or have small children. In a country such as Yemen where extended families are very strong, middle-class women have an extensive network of female relations to take care of the children while they are out at school or volunteering for the Party for part of the day.[77]

An understanding of the type of woman who joins Hizb al-Islah would be incomplete and inaccurate if it did not include the simple fact that these women are also deeply religious. Working for the Party is seen as a religious duty. It is, if you will, an act of faith. It is for this reason that the women are so successful in their various activities. That the women are, on the whole, more pious than the men is often acknowledged by male members of the Party.

But women join the Party for the same reasons many people engage in politics throughout the world: to participate in the democratic process and to improve and develop their societies. The Islah Party and the women in it feel that they can improve their country by educating the population about Islamic rights and duties and facilitating the eventual application of Islamic law. Because women are deemed to be responsible for the family and the family is the building block of society, Islahi women argue that it is natural that women participate in society and be involved in politics.

Thus, women in the Party and the Society can be considered to be of similar socioeconomic backgrounds. As are women in the Society, women in the Party tend to be young. In general, most of the Party women are educated—they have university ambitions or a university degree—and are of the middle class. Although they generally have not attended Westernized private schools, they have attended state schools or private Islamic schools. These are the women who have the greatest exposure to the ideas and intellectual debates of Islamist movements throughout the Middle East.[78] These women form relatively homogeneous middle-class social networks from which the Society gets its work done and indirectly participates in the creation and spread of new worldviews based on an activist understanding of Islam. It is through social events, such as *nadawat,* that this process occurs.

NADAWAT AND
THE ISLAH CHARITABLE SOCIETY

The Islah Party is not the only organization to recognize the important potential role of *nadawat*. *Nadawat* also play a pivotal role in the raising and distributing of charity. Technically, it cannot be said that the Islah Charitable Society has an explicit or even implicit strategy of using *nadawat*, or any other social events, for its purposes. The process is far more informal and natural. For example, Society members are able to reach women at *nadawat* to ask for their support of a Society cause, such as Ramadan clothing for orphans, through several means. At the end of the *nadwa* a Society member may ask for donations for a family in need. Members of the Society may discuss their efforts on behalf of the Society while socializing with other women. Or it may be at a *nadwa* that Society members ask about and learn of a retailer or seamstress who would be amenable to donating efforts and goods. *Nadawat* present an impromptu meeting place for Society members to finalize plans and distribute materials among themselves. These processes happen at any social gathering.

In this manner, *nadawat* offer Islamic Charitable Society members direct and indirect means for enlisting people and gaining participants. Society activities do not demand a serious commitment from women. Women may participate at their own time and pace. Networks of women who have different degrees of commitment to the Society and to Islamist ideology are linked together to provide charity and services for the poor. Society members do not have to, nor do they, explicitly or directly "use" *nadawat* by openly encouraging women to join the Society or by making announcements on its behalf. There is no form of pressure. The process is far more natural and subtle—through regular socializing among like-minded women and through emulation of women doing good work in the name of Islam, Society members are able to achieve their goals.

This ease with which women are able to participate in Society activities, as opposed to political events sponsored by the Islamists, is furthered by the fact that Society activities, as religious activities, are firmly rooted in the social fabric of Yemeni society. The degree to which they are political depends on the political significance each woman attributes to her actions. While the acts of one woman who donates money to the Society once a year and the acts of another who raises money for the Society by helping to host a fund-raising event are relatively similar acts, the meaning the two women may attribute to these acts could be significantly different. It may be a simple act of charity, a concerted effort to "live" Islam in all aspects of one's life, or a political act to help demonstrate the viability and superiority of the Islamist alternative. Society activities do not force a woman to state her position publicly or to overtly challenge social norms.

Giving charity is a regular occurrence for most Yemeni women. It is not uncommon for a woman to visit a friend in her home to collect money for another friend or neighbor who is having financial difficulties. (It is also common for women to try to employ poorer neighbors on an irregular basis in order to provide her with some form of income. While the "employer" may not have much money herself, she may hire a poorer friend to apply henna to her hands or feet in preparation for a celebration, for example.) These acts of charity are done on an informal basis, largely through social networks, as part of everyday life. For most women these are simple acts of charity that do not require much thought and that a good Muslim performs. Many women in the Society regard their activities in the same light. Yet some women view these same acts in a different light. There is a difference between those who perceive activities in the Society as religious acts and those who perceive these activities as a part of a larger worldview in which a good Muslim is an activist, one who attempts to apply Islam to all spheres of life. The latter view has both social and political implications. Within the Society, women who hold both views regularly come into contact with each other.

Chart 4.1 traces the interactions or ties of fifteen women in Sana'a who are active in the Islah Charitable Society, a *nadwa* (in the home), and/or the Hizb al-Islah. I met each of the women in one or more of these three institutions. The chart traces the primary institutional ties these women have—where they work or study, volunteer, and socialize. I make a distinction between interactions or ties that are regular and consistent (for example, the woman is a full-time employee or member or volunteer) and those that are irregular or occasional (for example, a woman attends a *nadwa* on an irregular basis). The former are represented by a solid line and the latter by a broken line. In Chart 4.2, I grouped these same ties of interaction according to social networks.

I focused on two *nadawat* to make the charts more reflective of the different *nadawat* in the city and the social circles and networks they attract. To be included, a woman needed to go to one of these three institutions just once. While I chose these women randomly, I selected them in part because they belonged to social networks that I was able to learn about in intimate detail. In this sense, the charts cannot be considered fully representative.

Having said that, the ties that bind these fifteen women, not all of whom know each other, reveal clearly the multiple and diverse social networks that are connected to the Islamic Charitable Society in a regular or occasional manner and, indirectly, to each other. In Chart 4.2, we see that just from this small sample, the Society has accessed five different social net-

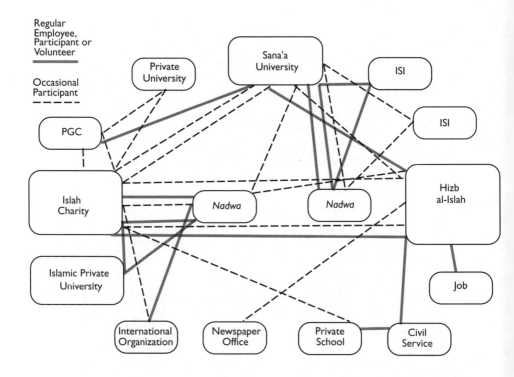

Regular
Employee,
Participant or
Volunteer

Occasional
Participant

Private
University

Sana'a
University

ISI

PGC

ISI

Islah
Charity

Nadwa

Nadwa

Hizb
al-Islah

Islamic Private
University

Job

International
Organization

Newspaper
Office

Private
School

Civil
Service

Chart 4.1. Institutional Ties of Fifteen Women in Sana'a

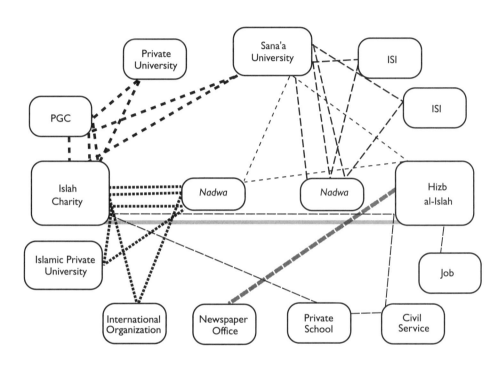

Chart 4.2. Institutional Ties of Fifteen Women in Sanaʿa Grouped According to Social Networks

works to raise resources and volunteers; two of the networks are quite large and quite distinct. As Chart 4.1 demonstrates, some of these women attend a Society event or donate to the Society once per year at most. Others are full-time volunteers. Some are active members in the president's party, the GPC, and others are active in Hizb al-Islah. In these five social networks we find women who hold diverse understandings of the meaning of their activities in or for the Society. While *nadawat* are not the only social events through which the Society reaches women (in fact, some of the women do not attend *nadawat* at all), the charts demonstrate the close ties between *nadawat* and Islamic social institutions. In both *nadawat*, there are strong ties to religious charitable institutions and vice versa.

Furthermore, while the charts confirm that there are direct links between the Society and Hizb al-Islah, the majority of these ties are indirect through a *nadwa*, Sana'a University, or a combination of both. The predominance of the university is no surprise given that both the Society and Hizb al-Islah have their respective headquarters close to the university's two campuses and are very active on campus. Indeed, students are mobilized on behalf of the Society at social gatherings or events at the university. The interlocking nature of these social networks, even highly diverse ones, provides a conduit for the Society to reach large numbers of women and for ideas to travel from one social network to another. It also provides the opportunity for new social networks to develop.

Depending on a women's degree of involvement, new bonds of friendship develop between women as they work together to achieve a goal, be it sewing clothing or donating books. New circles of women who are developing a common activist understanding of *da'wa* and engaging in *da'wa* may be created. While women generally do not mix party politics into their *nadwa* discussions, during the social segment of the *nadwa*, an Islahi woman may quietly approach another and suggest that she join her at another *nadwa* or social event on a different day.[79] At this second *nadwa*, she may be introduced to a social group which is more openly supportive of Islah or Islamist goals. This may happen at any social gathering. Women who become engaged in Society or Party activities develop new and strong friendships with one another. They may even find a husband who supports and encourages their activities through Party or Society networks.

Girls and women thus may slowly enter new Islamist networks that encompass many aspects of life—networks that eventually lead them to withdraw from their previous childhood friends. It may also alienate them from their families. In one case I encountered, a young woman rejected her parents' advice and married the man of her choice, an Islamist. In another case, a father spoke to me about his concern that his daughter had developed new friends and, as a result, had become increasingly critical of her family's secular ways. He was considering moving her to a different school where she would meet new people and engage in new social circles and events. As they become more involved in *da'wa* activities, women may spend increasing amounts of time with new friends with whom they are jointly engaged in these activities. And most important, they become immersed in a new worldview, an Islamist worldview. This reconfiguration of social circles thus both breaks down and builds upon existing social networks to create new subgroups bound by an activist understanding of Islam and a commitment to *da'wa* activities. In the terminology of social movement theory, these women slowly become engaged in a process of negotiating and renegotiating a collective identity—an Islamist collective identity based on an activist understanding of *da'wa*. Within these new social groups and networks, the Islamist ideology is reinforced through both word and deed. Whether these women become formal members of Islah is relatively irrelevant—their active support for Islamist ideology has a far bigger impact than simply garnering votes for Islah. As social networks based on an activist understanding of Islam develop and expand, the women in the networks are engaged in a grassroots process of social change.

These newly established bonds are solidified not only by the satisfaction of jointly working for Islam but by the various personal benefits—largely nonmaterial—middle-class women receive. Society activities, as well as those of the Party, can involve a variety of activities including lecturing, organizing events, learning about one's social and political rights, helping others, and fund-raising. They thus give women a strong sense of worth and self-satisfaction—something women do not generally receive elsewhere, especially at a young age. Quite simply, these activities involve a great deal of personal growth and ultimately offer women an important and gratifying role outside the home. Fulfilling *da'wa* through the Society provides meaning and direction for young women, particularly educated young women. It gives a sense of self-worth to its members as they become active and take on challenging projects, and it creates a tremendous feeling of solidarity as friends jointly engage in creating a new society.

Furthermore, participation in Society activities may be a means to improve one's class status. Women returnees in Hodeidah are often recruited as literacy teachers, an occupation that enables them to improve their class status by taking up professional employment—employment they feel is commensurate with their education. For educated women who are living in slum areas, struggling to adapt to new economic realities in Yemen, the Society can sometimes offer the best opportunity for improvement—economic and otherwise.

At the same time, members and participants remain within the dominant cultural norms as they increasingly conduct activities outside the home. They avoid the pressure and criticism from which more liberal female activists suffer. Working for a charitable society is a legitimate reason to go outside alone and freely conduct work.[80] The importance of charity work for the Islamist movement lies precisely in the fact that it does not challenge prevailing cultural norms. Furthermore, Society work is not political work per se. In a conservative and largely tribal society such as the one we find in Yemen, families regard politics and public roles for women as inappropriate and many women shy away from overt political participation. In this sense, Society activities provide an important stepping-stone toward greater acceptance of women's participation in public life and potentially even in political activities. Entering public life through the safety of the Society may be a woman's main aim in some cases; religious aims may be secondary.

Even if a woman attending a *nadwa* chooses not to participate in the activities of the Society, at the *nadwa* she witnesses regular examples of activist *da'wa* around her—the Society activities conducted through *nadawat* or the *nadwa* itself. Through *nadawat*, Islamist women (although they are not necessarily "Party women") are able to provide an example and an environment in which *da'wa* is actively practiced through word and, most important, deed. *Nadawat* are forums that focus on the Qur'an and Islam and do not on the whole discuss politics.[81] However, the act of *da'wa* itself is ideologically and politically significant even if undertaken in isolation from the larger (verbal) political message. The act speaks as loudly as the words. *Da'wa* does not need to be explained in terms of its relevance to the Islamist ideology or agenda—the very act is a concrete example of a different understanding of what it means to be a good Muslim: an activist Muslim is a good Muslim. In this way, women slowly adopt an Islamist worldview.

The creation of new social groups supportive of the Islamist worldview and directly or indirectly supportive of the Islah Party is due to the personal fulfillment of *da'wa* and the sense of joint purpose and solidarity it creates among women through participation in Society activities. The Society indirectly provides the forum for women to meet and the activities which provide a sense of fulfillment and belonging. In doing so, the Society contributes to a process of breaking down and rebuilding Yemen's social fabric in accordance with the Islamist vision.

CONCLUSIONS

Throughout Yemen's cities we find overlapping networks of middle-class women's circles. Women educators and students and their social, religious, political, and family circles overlap at school, on university campuses, at lectures in mosques, at Qur'anic study groups, on social occasions, at the Islah Charitable Society, at Party meetings and activities, and at work. Members of the Islah Charitable Society find volunteers (and/or donations) from among the women present at the *nadawat* they attend. A teacher at an Islamic university may ask one of her students to lead a *nadwa*. A friend active in giving *nadawat* in the dorms on behalf of Hizb al-Islah may be invited to host one in the home. A woman attending one *nadwa* may be invited to visit another. Women at the lectures at the Society's headquarters may learn of a *nadwa* or meet someone from the Party. These uncoordinated networks create overlapping activities, memberships, and friendships.

The Islah Charitable Society is thus embedded in precisely the type of homogenous social networks found in social movements around the globe. It is through these networks that women in the Society find both volunteers (participants) and donors. In one case, for example, a woman introduced her new daughter-in-law to the Society and brought her to the women's headquarters in Hodeidah for a tour. Admittedly, the class base of all the women in these extensive networks is not fully consistent. We see lower degrees of education in many of the women in Hodeidah and in the south, for example. The women in these networks differ in a number of ways. Some women are far more affluent than the majority; some women with highly influential tribal roots have lower levels of education; some women have busy careers and others have none. Yet beyond these exceptions, we find a common thread—these women are largely of the new educated middle class and have university degrees or university ambitions. It is no coincidence that in Sana'a the women's headquarters is located very close to Sana'a University.

The fact that these networks are dominated by the educated middle class does not mean that all the donors are also of the middle class, and presumably most donors contribute on a relatively small scale. As Putnam states, all networks have both horizontal and vertical ties.[82] The central headquarters of the Society (the men's part of the organization) has been particularly successful at eliciting large donations from extremely wealthy benefactors both in Yemen and abroad.[83] As also is the case in Jordan, women work at a more grassroots level than men in the Society; however, the women have also benefited from some very generous philanthropists. Some of the women's fund-raisers explicitly target elite women. And in Hodeidah, the new women's center was bought (including the land) and built by one of the city's most successful merchants and a Member of Parliament for the GPC. But the day-to-day work and raising of money, materials, and skills is done through middle-class networks with the relatively small contributions of many women. As in Egypt and Jordan, the networks are the bread and butter of the Society.

Most important, these very same networks are essential to the building of social capital—trust and solidarity—and, as social movement theory predicts, a vital component in the negotiation and renegotiation of an Islamist identity. Through their activities, women engage large and different social networks of women in the process of *da'wa*—accessing sources of charity and distributing charity. In reaching large numbers of women, the Society indirectly brings women with various degrees of commitment to the Society in contact with Islamist women. As women become more involved in Society activities, a sense of teamwork, solidarity and mission develops. For some women, this means gradually breaking away from their previous social circles and creating new social circles based on Islamist worldviews—ones rooted in an activist concept of *da'wa*.

Whether participation in the Society leads to membership in the Party (and thereby acts as a stepping-stone) is extremely difficult to determine—and in many ways is irrelevant. Membership between the two organizations overlaps substantially (or at least those in attendance at their respective meetings overlap). At the same time, we find numerous women who support the Islah Party and may in fact participate in many of its events, we find women who are not card-carrying members of the Party, and we find many women who have nothing to do with the Party. The fact that women may participate in Party activities and yet not join it is due to a variety of reasons—one is the simple fact that they do not see it as necessary. Because they view their activities as largely an extension of their religious practice, many women do not deem formal membership to be important. In one case I know of, the (male) Party leadership directly contacted a particularly active woman in the Society and asked her to consider joining the Party. This, however, is highly unusual. Participation in Society can quite naturally lead, and for many does lead, to contact with Islamists and potentially to the gradual spread of an Islamist worldview—one shared by many in the Party.

The networks of solidarity that work together to raise funds and establish services for the poor are further reinforced with the rewarding activities the Society has to offer women. Without challenging dominant social norms, middle-class women find within the Society opportunities to enter public life, fulfill their perceived religious duty, and even potentially raise their social status. While the women in the Society do provide a much-needed service for the poor, they too benefit enormously from their activities. These are largely nonmaterial benefits such as friendships and self-confidence, and they are certainly important in luring, securing, and retaining active women, the vast majority of whom are volunteers, in the Society. However, the Islah Charitable Society also offers numerous (relatively expensive) private schools and day care centers that are not intended for the poor. It is no surprise that the head of the Women's Sector in Hodeidah sends her children to a school established by the Society. These commercial institutions offer additional benefits to the middle class and help to extend the networks.

Although in Egypt and in Jordan these private charity activities have raised critical eyebrows (even among those who are intended to benefit from them), they have not done so as of yet in Yemen. Their success is of important symbolic value to the movement. However, these commercial initiatives are relatively new and take place on a small scale in Yemen; their long-term impact on the movement remains to be seen.

FIVE

The Significance of Being Middle Class

The three case studies in this book strongly challenge the concept of Middle East exceptionalism that prevails in political, social, and economic analyses of the region. In all three cases we find ample evidence that social movements in the Middle East, and specifically Islamist movements, behave as social movements do elsewhere. ISIs are embedded in a complex web of social networks through which they find participants—volunteers, donors, and employees—and secure important contacts and donations. As social movements do elsewhere, these networks are dominated by one social category that reproduces itself over and over again within the social movement. Most social movements are composed of strong horizontal but weak vertical ties. In the case of ISIs, I argue that this social category is the middle classes, predominantly members of the professional or new middle class. Middle-class ties are forged and strengthened because of the operational needs of the ISIs and the instrumental needs of the Islamist movement. By providing "five star" services, such as schools, summer camps, and hospitals and employment for professionals, ISIs benefit the middle classes—the backbone of the Islamist movement. While ISIs are "charities," they cater to the middle class. It is within these horizontal networks of clients, doctors, teachers, and directors that ties of solidarity, trust, teamwork and a sense of mission are developed. And it is within these middle-class ties that the potential lies for the introduction and the expansion of Islamist networks. However, an examination of ISIs and their associated networks indicates that they lie at the heart of a social movement that seeks less to radically reorganize dominant institutions and social arrangements than to coexist and compete with them. Most important, the strategy of catering to middle-class needs undermines the movement in the long term.

As with social movement organizations elsewhere, social networks are pivotal in the day-to-day functioning of ISIs, which rely on social networks for donations, for volunteers, and for employees. Through word of mouth, Islamist women in Yemen locate and rely on volunteer seamstresses to sew Ramadan clothing for the poor. Directors of Islamic Center Charity Societies in Jordan visit, phone, and write their friends at home and abroad for monetary and material donations, such as school bags and uniforms and canned food. And in Egypt, Islamic clinics generally do not advertise for doctors and nurses but rely on social networks—the friend of a friend of a friend—to staff their clinics. The very fabric of ISIs is made up of the ongoing development and maintenance of social networks—interpersonal ties that are constantly being created and/or solidified in order to prevent their discontinuation or, to use Diane Singerman's term, overuse.[1]

Central to this process are the directors of ISIs and their contacts. Without connections to donors or even government officials, ISIs struggle to establish and maintain themselves. They rely on the social ties of their directors and boards of directors to help hasten the registration process, obtain building permits, procure donations, find doctors and other employees, and locate willing volunteers. The ISIs who offer the largest facilities and services are those whose directors have contacts with large donors such as a major bank or a benefactor living in the Gulf, with civil servants who can ensure (or even overlook) the registration process, or with merchants who are willing to donate food or clothing. As one doctor said to me of his director: "He is the head and the shoulders of the Association." Without the leadership, drive, and connections of his director, the ISI would struggle or cease to exist. It is no coincidence that the most impressive Islamic medical clinics in Cairo are located in those areas where those with the means to donate reside.

As the literature on social movements demonstrates, people generally associate with those similar to themselves. This means that social networks are generally homogeneous. This homogeneity is recreated within social movement organizations. The day-to-day needs of ISIs dictate that they are composed of people with the time, skills, and/or means to devote—whether on a regular or ad hoc basis—to ISI activities. Their operational demands thus require a predominance of networks best able and willing to fulfill these needs. In the case of ISIs, this social category is the middle classes, primarily the new middle class—doctors, teachers, and other professionals whose needs are not being met (or are being poorly met) elsewhere.[2] ISIs therefore must be understood within a larger context of overlapping, growing, contracting, and evolving middle-class social networks that link middle-class volunteers and employees and their respective social networks with each other and with other institutions. Indeed, the political significance of ISIs can only be fully understood in light of the middle-class networks in which they are embedded.

ISIs are able to attract middle-class employees, volunteers, and donors not just because they appeal to altruistic values. As Doug McAdam and Ronnelle Paulsen state, interpersonal ties not only encourage the extension of an invitation to participate, they also ease the uncertainty of participation.[3] Social bonds raise the costs of not joining and at the same time provide incentives or rewards for participation. Women in Yemen find that as their friends become increasingly involved in charity activities (and the nature of their social networks begins to change), they feel excluded if they choose not to participate. The feeling of exclusion (or the potential negative reactions of one's friends if one does not join) raises the costs of nonparticipation. At the same time, ongoing participation in a social group provides what McAdam refers to as solidarity incentives.[4] Quite simply, when people participate in social networks, they have incentives to maintain the gratifying social relations they experience there.[5]

One gains other nonmaterial rewards when one joins a social movement organization such as an ISI, even if the apparent goal of the ISI is to volunteer and help others. For example, through their activities on behalf of the Islah Charitable Society, Yemeni women benefit from a socially acceptable justification for getting out of the house, organizing various charity drives, and attending meetings—opportunities they might not otherwise have. Similarly, in her work on female dervishes in Turkey, Catharina Raudvere notes that women's associations offer more than spiritual benefits. She finds that they provide networks of economic contacts as well as a basis for other important relations.[6]

Much like the Moonies, the Hare Krishnas, the Mormons, and Nichiren Shoshu, ISIs also offer material rewards. Working as a doctor in an Egyptian medical clinic means a second income. Working as a teacher in an Islamic private school in Jordan means better pay. ISIs often strategically lure and secure employees and volunteers by offering material incentives.[7] In Jordan, medical clinics associated with the ICCS regularly adopt a strategy of purchasing limited pieces of top-of-the-line equipment rather than numerous pieces of cheaper and perhaps lower-quality equipment. Because of better hours and better pay, doctors are willing to travel to work in a refugee camp. In Cairo, a large portion of the doctors who work in the city's mosque-based clinics are simply there for the money. As Asef Bayat states with regard to the Islamic associations that run the clinics: "For many involved in them, these associations simply provided a job or, for some, even a business."[8] This is further confirmed by Carrie Rosefsky Wickham's research on Islamist recruitment among university-educated youth in Egypt. She argues that most graduates initially join Islamist networks because of various social, psychological, and emotional benefits conferred by participation.[9]

The result is an extensive and growing network of social ties and connections with both Islamists and non-Islamists.[10] A woman who is a volunteer in an ISI may approach a woman at her Qur'anic study group about sewing clothing for Ramadan. Through their children, a teacher in an Islamic school may have increased contact with a doctor in an Islamic hospital. As a consequence, the doctor develops ties with the teacher's friends from university. This in turn may lead to contact with Islamist students running for student council. Or it may lead to contact with college professors at an Islamic university. To ensure the survival of their clinics, clinic directors and boards of directors may create networks within the government bureaucracies in order to circumvent arbitrary bureaucrats and government regulations and to obtain all necessary licenses.[11]

Ultimately we find the strengthening of previous social bonds and the development of new social bonds, and this in turn leads to new benefits. In Yemen, the Islah Charitable Society organizes mass marriages and helps defray the costs of marriage. In Jordan, the Afaf Marriage Society (which was established by a Muslim Brother/IAF member but is not part of the ICCS) offers the same services.[12] Participants may find their future partners through ISI-related social networks. A merchant who sends his/her children to an Islamic school may come into contact with a supplier who may give him/her preferential treatment or prices.

The forging of these new networks may cause strains in family relations. As a woman enters new Islamist circles and increasingly develops a new worldview, relations with her non-Islamist family may become strained. She may question her family's religious practices at home or marry an Islamist she meets through someone in her new social networks as opposed to someone her parents choose for her. To a certain extent, it can be said that she leaves one family in order to join another.

ISIs also include a significant number of Islamic commercial institutions that cater to the relatively wealthy middle class. In Jordan, the majority of Amman's uninsured poor go to the Al-Bashir Hospital, where it costs 18 JD for childbirth (without complications) and one overnight stay; the middle class goes to the Islamic Hospital, which charges 190 JD for a delivery (no complications and a one-night stay in one of the hospital's third-class rooms).[13] In addition, patients at the Islamic Hospital must have insurance. The Islamic Hospital is one of the most expensive in Jordan, and it is clearly inaccessible for the poor. It has plans to expand its services and increase its personnel, and the costs of medical treatment will most certainly rise to (or exceed) those of other private hospitals.[14] Dar al-Arqam and Dar al-Aqsa are similarly exclusive, albeit not the priciest, schools in Amman. The same can be said of the private Islamic university, the University of Science and Technology, in Yemen. These schools address a perceived need for a superior education (and one with a more extensive religious curriculum) than that of the state schools and fees that are more accessible than those private schools of the "velvet circles."

In this regard, these middle-class networks are not only driven by the day-to-day demands of ISIs but also by the instrumental needs of the Islamist movement. The ICCS in Jordan made a decision to create a hospital with some of the best facilities and the highest prices in the country. The motives behind this decision were dictated by the needs of and pressures from within the Islamist movement, not the goals of the ICCS. The hospital was created as a symbol of the Islamist challenge and in order to provide jobs for unemployed and underemployed Islamists, most of whom are professionals. In Jordan, these middle-class professionals are often Palestinians as opposed to East Bank Jordanians—those who are most systematically excluded from positions within the government and state-run institutions. ISIs are thus often a tool by which the moderate Islamist movement can respond to the needs of its constituency, the middle class.

The purpose of this book is not to argue that the poor do not benefit in ISIs—they do—but to argue that the long-term political significance of ISIs lies in the horizontal, and not the vertical, ties that are forged in ISIs and through their activities. Vertical ties to the poor do exist in ISIs; however, they are weak. It is the middle class, not the poor, that benefits from charity activities and nonprofit "five star" services, receives employment, and develops friendships. And horizontal ties are often nurtured at the expense of vertical ties.[15]

The catering by the Islamist movement to the middle class is not new. Vickie Langohr's study of the Muslim Brotherhood in rural Egypt between 1930 and 1952 produced similar findings to my own. She argues that the success of the Brotherhood during this time period, given the context of the existence of other groups competing for the same potential members and the difficulties all groups had in obtaining resources, was due to its strategy of targeting and recruiting members who possessed the necessary resources to expand the movement. Thus, while peasants (who constituted the bulk of the rural population) were largely absent from Brotherhood membership lists, teachers who could provide meeting places, chairs, and possible recruits (students); traders who could provide financial resources; and judges who could defend Brothers brought before the court dominated the list.[16] She goes on to observe that an examination of Brothers' letters reveals that the Brothers regarded the full incorporation of the underprivileged into their ranks as threatening because they feared it would drive away potential members who had rich resources to offer. Langohr states that while more research needs to be done, it appears that the peasantry was not welcomed by the leadership of the branches.[17]

Amani Kandil and Sarah Ben Nefissa concur. In a more contemporary example, they note that a key reason for the financial success of *jam'iyat is-lamiyya,* Islamic associations, in Egypt today is that they position themselves in areas where large parts of the population have money that can be redistributed. When they do help the poor, it is the poor people located in middle-income or affluent areas. Researchers agree that Islamist charity efforts are not designed for the poor. As Asef Bayat states: "Although the episodes of Cairo earthquakes in 1991 and flooding in upper Egypt in 1994 pointed to the Islamists' attempt to build a social basis among the poor, these were largely occasional activities."[18]

Bayat provides further evidence from outside the three case studies discussed in this book. In his study of the Iranian revolution, he notes that a review of eighty-eight sermons, messages, and letters by the Ayatollah Khomeini reveals that in the fifteen years prior to the revolution, he made only eight passing references to lower-class people, compared to fifty references to educated youths, students, and universities.[19] Bayat argues that while the new Islamist leaders portrayed the revolution as the revolution of the downtrodden, the urban poor and the disenfranchised remained on the margins of the revolutionary campaign almost until the end. A review of the statistics of those killed in the street events during the revolution attests to the fact that the urban poor joined late and participated in limited numbers: out of a sample of 646 people killed in Tehran in the street events from August 23, 1977, to February 19, 1978, only nine (just over 1 percent) were from the shantytowns. Islamist agitators, Bayat states, largely ignored the underclass, concentrating instead on the political and intellectual training of educated groups of young people, chiefly students.[20]

Within ISIs and their associated networks, the middle class has access to friendships and a feeling of family-like relations, of teamwork. It is this growing sense of teamwork, trust, solidarity and a sense of mission that marks ISIs as different from other NGOs. The significance of ISIs lies not in the actual services they provide—many NGOs do the same—or in some form of Islamic "framework" within which they provide the services, for by and large there is none. Rather it lies in the intangible accumulation of social capital—trust, solidarity—that develops among the providers of charity.

In fact, there is nothing particularly unique about an ISI when you first walk into one. In terms of their function, the services they provide, and the way in which they are organized, they are very similar both to past charitable efforts and other contemporary philanthropic efforts in the region, including those of the state. For example, when I asked Egyptian directors about the philosophical or inspirational roots of their endeavors, their answers were quite revealing. While they spoke of the grassroots welfare activities of the early Muslim Brotherhood, directors of Cairo's Islamic clinics also mentioned other sources of inspiration, such as the first private voluntary medical care organization established in 1909 by Princess 'Ayn al-Hayat Ahmad. Based upon the generous donations of the women of the royal family from their private incomes, the Mubarra Muhammed 'Ali (the Muhammed 'Ali Benevolent Society) founded a network of hospitals and outpatient clinics for the poor.[21] As the director of one clinic's association said to me:

> Our centers are derived from the old system. For example, long ago there was something called the *mubarra*; those *mubarrayat* were really ideal examples for offering services to the really poor people. . . . So these clinics like ours have been established to revive the *mubarrayat's* services.[22]

Even from the perspective of the directors, today's Islamic clinics are a continuation of earlier philanthropic efforts and not something new or different. While the organizers may be of different classes, the end result is the same.

In all three case studies, there is also little or no evidence that ISIs are different from secular associations. There is little that makes them Islamic. For example, we find no conscious attempt within the Islamic clinics in Egypt to create an alternative decision-making or organizational structure. There is no conscious attempt to create the foundations for an Islamic vision of society. The majority of clinics have few or no Islamic guidelines or regulations, and they do not require Islamic duties or modes of conduct from their staff. The clinic directors seek the best possible doctors they can hire, regardless of politics.[23] The decision-making and organizational structures within the clinics are ones which are suited to efficiency and quality of health care; they are not designed to plant the seeds of a new understanding of state and society.[24]

Medical anthropologist Soheir Morsy agrees. She examines the nature and type of medicine being practiced in Islamic medical clinics and argues that we find the reproduction of Western biomedicine—a very similar form of medicine to the form being practiced in other clinics and hospitals in the Middle East and the West—not an attempt to implement an Islamic approach. In one of a very few studies specifically on Islamic clinics, she argues: "One does not detect even a partial commitment to a renaissance of Islamic medicine." Rather, she states, when stripped of their cultural façade, Islamic clinics and health care are firmly supported by the well-entrenched pillars of high-tech, curative, individually centered Western biomedicine.[25] And while the doctors' syndicate in Egypt has taken part in several conferences throughout the Arab world concerning the topic of Islamic medicine, this has been more an attempt to take part in actual international debate in medicine than an attempt to invent a specifically Islamic medicine.[26]

The case of the ICCS in Jordan indicates that there is little to distinguish the activities of ISIs from the of the state's *zakat* committees. *Zakat,* one of the five pillars of Islam, requires that all Muslims with the financial means to do so donate approximately 2.5 percent of his/her annual income for charity. While most states in the Middle East no longer collect a mandatory *zakat* tax, they have established *zakat* committees to which citizens may voluntarily give. These committees collect and then redistribute *zakat* to the poor. In Jordan, *zakat* committees are essentially voluntary organizations that are established, run, and staffed by private citizens and are registered under the Sunduq al-Zakat in the Ministry of the Awqaf.[27] They are tightly controlled by the Sunduq al-Zakat and, as Quintan Wiktorowicz states, are essentially pseudo-governmental institutions. For all intents and purposes, however, *zakat* committees are indistinguishable in their activities and procedures from ISIs. Just as the ICCS centers do, *zakat* committees employ teams of social workers familiar with the local community that assess which individuals and families are eligible for aid. This is conducted largely by going from door to door and by keeping in touch with the events of the neighborhood. A form very similar to the one used by the ICCS centers is filled out for each applicant. Much like the ICCS, the *zakat* committee considers income, family size, and age of the children in order to determine who qualifies. Although the bulk of the *zakat* committees' funds are directed toward financial aid, much like the ICCS, they also provide social services. Wiktorowicz describes a medical center operating at reduced prices that was established by the local *zakat* committee in the Wihdat refugee camp that is very similar to the ICCS clinic down the road.[28] In fact, on my way to visit the ICCS clinic in the Wihdat camp, I accidentally went to this clinic run by the local *zakat* committee. It took me several moments and questions before I realized that I was in the wrong spot, so similar were their activities and appearances.

Wiktorowicz arrives at the same conclusion as I do in his study of ISIs in Jordan. What differentiates Islamic NGOs from their secular counterparts, Wiktorowicz argues, is not the particular Islamic nature of their activities, but the belief of volunteers that they are promoting Islam through their work. It is therefore an insiders' belief in the mission, more than the activities themselves, that distinguishes them.[29] The priority is the services themselves, not a specific Islamic message or a political agenda.[30]

What marks ISIs as different from other social welfare NGOs is a feeling of solidarity, of a mission, of teamwork among the care providers, particularly the directors. Networks of shared meaning are created through the provision of charity—raising donations, locating seamstresses, contacting merchants, distributing aid, or providing medical care. Communities of participants accept, internalize, and promote a particular set of values in these networks.[31] The act of participating in charity activities, even on an ad hoc basis, brings different middle-class networks together. In this manner, ISIs indirectly facilitate the potential expansion of Islamist worldviews and networks. ISIs do more than foster a participant's self-identity with the ISI and its mission; it can also play a role in a participant's identification with the Islamist vision.

In Jordan's Islamic Hospital, for example, the pride of the directors as they provide top-quality health care in the name of Islam confirms research elsewhere that actors are simultaneously the subjects of structures and acting subjects. While actors operate within the constraints of opportunities provided by social movement organizations and network structures, they are also involved in the creation of identities. Paraphrasing Alberto Melucci, Susan Phillips states that "a social movement is the *process* of the social construction of reality because, in the course of the repeated activation of relationships that link SMOs, a collective identity is formed and reinforced."[32] She goes on to elaborate that while the construction of a collective identity may, in part, be a result of the intentional and instrumental attempts by social movement organizations to mobilize consensus, it is also the product of "emotional recognition that occurs in unplanned ways through friendship bonds and direct participation in collective action."[33] It is the slow dissemination of that vision and its values that lies at the base of the Islamist social movement and of potential gradual social change within the Middle East.

While the poor benefit as recipients of services of Islamic welfare institutions, they are excluded from the social networks which lie at the heart of the Islamist movement. They are simply not participants in middle-class networks. In Yemen, we see the homogeneity of *nadawat. Nadawat,* themselves rooted in social networks, attract middle-class women; I know of no evidence to indicate that *nadawat* occur among the uneducated poor in Yemen. In Islamic medical clinics in Egypt, the poor have access to the clinic directors and indeed may regularly visit directors in their offices and express their views; however, on the whole, the poor are not in the general assemblies or on boards of directors. They are not privy to the social networks, those networks of solidarity, and a sense of mission that would encourage their participation.

The poor choose to use numerous facilities and services, public or private, Islamist or secular, and often simultaneously, regardless of ideological persuasion. In Jordan, ICCS centers have social workers who (often in conjunction with the government) research potential recipients of charity in order to ensure that they are not receiving charity from more than one source. In some of these cases, the "poor" were found to have a combined income from several charity sources that reached several hundred Jordanian dinars—enough for a very comfortable middle-class lifestyle, at least in economic terms. In Egypt, poor patients living in *sha'abi* areas may go to several clinics—government, Islamic, and/or private—as well as a traditional *shaykha*. In addition to government clinics that are free and/or cheap (albeit crowded), Egypt's poor can also take advantage of the grassroots services offered by Al-Azhar, the center of Islamic scholarship in Egypt.[34] These services are similar to those offered in Islamic welfare institutions. In the 1990s, a growing number of private charities or soup kitchens were established by Egypt's benevolent affluent.[35] The poor are not only not integrated into ISI networks, they must also actively seek the aid of numerous NGOs and other sources in order to have their financial, material, medical, and educational needs met.

This book thus challenges a dominant view, held particularly by observers of Egypt, that sees the strategy of moderate Islamism, particularly the Muslim Brotherhood, as two-pronged. This view sees its activities in the political parties and its activities in the professional syndicates, where it dominates most of the governing councils, as part of a strategy to target the educated middle class and its efforts in ISIs as part of a strategy to reach out and recruit the poor.[36] This study takes a contrary view—the two prongs, both of which benefit the middle class, are but one.

There is no doubt that middle-class Islamists have mobilized on behalf of the poor in times of crisis and that mass mobilizations by Islamists, such as protests, contain members of the middle classes and the poor. However, this study strongly indicates that the poor are not mobilized on a sustained basis. To ascribe a unified mobilization strategy or a unity to the mobilizations themselves would be false. ISIs cannot be regarded strictly as political tools established for recruitment purposes. They are established for a variety of reasons, and their volunteers, donors, and employees are associated with them for a variety of reasons. In all three case studies, we find projects initiated from both the top down and from the bottom up—from members of the respective executives establishing "trophy clinics" or "five star" hospitals and schools and from local community members establishing services for their local communities. The ICCS in Jordan operates on two levels. One is the ICCS executive committee that initiates projects from the top down. These are the large commercial projects such as the Islamic Hospital that are designed for the middle class. The ICCS's numerous committees, however, are initiated largely from the bottom up. Much as they do at the Islamic clinics in Cairo, community members approach the ICCS about establishing some service in their area. (In some cases, the ICCS identifies a person in a community and encourages him to gather community members and raise money for a center.) At this second level, we also do not see a policy to mobilize the poor. Rather, we see services established to help the poor out of a strong sense of religious obligation. (The ICCS executive also established the Fund for Sick and Poor out of this sense of religious obligation to the poor.) Whether the actions that proceed from this sense of obligation are acts of charity or are part of a larger attempt to Islamize society is irrelevant in the sense that neither perspective views the poor as objects of mobilization. I would argue, therefore, that the day-to-day events of ISIs cannot be conflated with other events, such as protests, involving Islamists and the poor. We must break down these various events and institutions—protests, crises, ISIs, and so forth—and examine their different agendas, locations, and participants.

My research on ISIs in Egypt, Jordan and Yemen further indicates that ISIs do not present an alternative model for reorganizing society, one that stands on contrast to the state and challenges it. To the contrary, I argue that ISIs are highly dependent upon the state and seek to work within the existing institutions and arrangements, not to alter them. Indeed, ISIs have little cause to challenge the state; they receive from the state their permits, financial aid, and, often, preferential treatment above other NGOs. The Egyptian government provides three types of assistance to civil associations: direct payments, technical assistance, and material support.[37] I found that financial assistance received by Islamic clinics from MOSA could range from twenty to several thousand LE. One clinic where I conducted interviews received 1,000 LE ($350 US at the time) from MOSA; its entire operating budget was 106,000 LE. This association was also extremely fortunate in that it also received additional funds for its other (nonmedical) activities, such as its youth club. While statistics show that less than 40 percent of civil associations are aided by the Egyptian government or other institutions (and many of the clinics I visited received nothing),[38] these donations are "quite often the difference between survival and extinction for certain associations."[39]

Furthermore, the Egyptian government can also place civil associations in a privileged category of "general" or "public" interest that protects organizations from confiscation of their funds. Since 1967, an increasing percentage of associations in this category have been Islamic. In 1985, thirteen of the seventeen associations that were designated as public interest were Islamic.[40] In Jordan we also see preferential treatment of ISIs; the state turns a blind eye toward the ICCS's creation of committees which technically bypass the state's law concerning registration. When I asked the director of the Dar al-Arqam school why the ICCS is successful and he replied that it was because of the king, he was not exaggerating.[41]

In all three case studies we see ISIs entering into joint ventures or projects with the government, thus rendering them a pillar in the state system. In Egypt, the government regularly refers patients to the Mustafa Mahmoud hospital complex. The Religious Association of Imam Abu al-Azm in Cairo jointly runs a working mothers program with the government. In Yemen, the Islah Charity has established the Mothers' Hospital with the Yemeni government. And in Jordan, the ICCS coordinates its activities with the government in order to ensure that there is no abuse of its welfare services.

A large percentage of ISI employees and volunteers in all three countries are employed in government or public institutions. In Egypt, the primary income of the majority of doctors working in Islamic clinics comes from the government. Work within the clinics is purely supplementary. Only 25 percent of doctors are in private practice; the majority of the rest are employees of the Ministry of Health.[42] Islamic clinics have not provided doctors with an opportunity to break away from their reliance on the state. In fact, they have to a certain extent deepened this dependence as doctors work during the day in a government health care facility and at night in ISIs that are reliant on the state for licensing and fund-raising.

In fact, in her examination of Islamic clinics in Egypt, Soheir Morsy argues that Islamic clinics and the doctors working in them "do not represent an explicit antagonistic challenge to political authority." Rather, she says, "Within the existing power structures the service orientation of Islamic associations provides opportunities for members to gain legitimacy and consequently to share power." Because Islamic clinics play a role in maintaining an indispensable component of the social welfare package in Egypt, ISIs are not only gaining legitimacy *in,* but also affirming the legitimacy *of,* the social system. Far from representing an alternative health care strategy that challenges state authority, Islamic health care, as Morsy states, is a vehicle for its providers to share power with the state.[43] Quintan Wiktorowicz agrees in his analysis of Jordan's Islamic NGOs. He argues that overall, Islamic NGOs are nonconfrontational in nature and generally supportive of regime policies. They do not "seek a radical transformation of the political system."[44]

A comparison of ISIs indicates that this is precisely what the professional middle class who works in and benefits from ISIs wants—a piece of the state pie. While ISIs represent a challenge to the dominant classes, this threat seeks less to replace them than to share power with them. Women in the Islah Charitable Society in Yemen carry with them a worldview that ultimately envisions dramatic social change—that of a state and society based on Islamic laws and social mores. The opportunities the Society (and the Party) offers women outside the house also carry the potential for an increased and new role for women in society and politics. However, one of the strongest appeals of working in the Society lies in the fact that these activities are socially condoned. The importance of the socially acceptable nature of Islamist activities is confirmed by research on Islamist women elsewhere. In her study of Islamist women in Turkey, for example, Yesim Arat finds that Islamist movements often provide women with a vehicle by which to assert their autonomy and build social networks outside the house. She argues that because of the nonthreatening nature of networks, women with ties to Islamist movements may actually gain influence within the family and within society as their religious credentials force family members, including fathers, brothers, and other men, to give greater weight to their opinions.[45] At least for the time being, therefore, the future Islamic state and society that appears to be emerging through the activities of the women in the Islah Charitable Society is one which involves less change and greater consolidation of moral values. It is the reassertion of a very familiar moral community.

Asef Bayat's discussion of Islamist gatherings in Egypt in the 1980s and 1990s is relevant. As he states:

> Beyond improving material conditions, the Islamist movement in Egypt also offered alienated constituencies an alternative social, cultural, and moral community within which the rival secular and western culture seemed less threatening. . . . These communities provided the traditionalists both with an expression of discontent and a moral safety net. The ritual of weekly gatherings that spread across the small and big cities reflected not only a cultural protest but also materialized a Durkheimian social solidarity, security, and moral integration—the contradictory conditions to which Arlene Macleod referred when she called the new veiling among Cairian women a way of "accommodating protest."[46]

It is for reasons such as these that Bayat refers to the Islamist movement in Egypt, and I would add also in Jordan and Yemen, as a social movement without a revolution. It is a pervasive Islamist social movement that has brought about significant changes within civil society but one that has failed to alter the political structure.[47] Instead of leading to a sudden revolution, movements without revolutions both coexist and compete with the dominant institutions and social arrangements. *Ultimately, movements without revolutions do not or cannot undo political authority.*[48]

In the wake of September 11, 2001, it is difficult to state what the impact of the terrorist attack and the resulting attack on terrorism has been on ISIs. The moderate nature of Islamism may in fact be further asserting itself. While more research needs to be done on the aftereffects, my general impression, based on informal discussions with those working in the charities, at least in the case of the Islah Charitable Society in Yemen, is that ISIs have experienced an upsurge in volunteerism since September 11th. These volunteers are largely seeking to assert an understanding of Islam that stands in contrast to the violence of Islamist extremism. It is an Islam that stands for justice and caring. While much has been said in the media regarding the role of hidden networks in planning of the attacks on the World Trade Center, the impact of those attacks may have been to further strengthen moderate Islam in the region.

At the same time, the impact of September 11th may also further strengthen the role and importance of social networks in ISIs. One year after the attacks, the Islamic Hospital in Amman is still suffering from a decrease in donations. According to the former director of the hospital's Fund for the Sick and Poor, donors are reluctant to contribute money to charities and projects that claim to be Islamic because they are concerned about future accusations of abetting terrorism.[49] While more research needs to be conducted on this issue, this may mean that personal connections may becoming increasingly vital to the solicitation of donations. It also may mean that ISIs will have to rely on the state more for additional funding and other material sources.

The professional middle-class nature of ISIs indicates strong vested interests—professionally, personally, and politically—in the state. I would argue that catering to professional middle-class needs undermines the movement in the long run. The prioritization of middle-class needs above those of the poor is creating a growing sense that Islamic charities are not fulfilling the spirit or values of Islam. This is not to imply that Islam does not approve of commercial ventures or private business. Islam looks favorably on economic and earthly matters, encourages commercial activities, sanctions the right to private property, and emphasizes an individual's right to pursue self-interest in economic activities. But the three case studies indicate that Jordanians, Egyptians, and Yemenis, including those of the middle classes, expect ISIs to reflect Islam's concern for social welfare and social justice, to be economically affordable, and to keep the needs of the poor in mind.

In Jordan, the common references to the Islamic Hospital as the "Criminal Hospital" or the "Commercial Hospital" speak volumes. Rumors abound concerning patients waiting on operating tables until the hospital administration has verified that the patient has private health insurance before surgery begins. More disturbing are the rumors of the hospital refusing to grant bereaved families the bodies of the deceased until all hospital costs have been covered. At the heart of these rumors lies the tension between the public's expectation of an Islamic institution and the realities of a private (albeit nonprofit) commercial business. As one Islamist stated to me, people have an expectation that Islamic services should all be free or extremely cheap because Islam stands for social justice; however, a quality hospital cannot remain in existence without charging the required fees. This same Islamist went on to say that perhaps the hospital would be better off not using the word "Islamic" in its name. This Islamist does not stand alone. The decision to have the Islamic Hospital run on a commercial basis provoked heated debate and protest within Islamist circles.[50] The debate revolved precisely over the issue of the role of the ICCS, which is directly related to the clientele the hospital should be serving. Many Islamists continue to feel that the Brotherhood has abandoned the poor.[51]

In Islamic clinics in Egypt we find a similar tension as revealed by the complaints of former patients. Precisely because Islamic clinics claim to be Islamic, they often appear to be judged more harshly than their non-Islamic counterparts. Despite the relatively inexpensive (albeit rising) examination fees in Cairo's Islamic clinics, a significant minority of former patients complain that the fees are too high and clinics have become too commercial. While they are appreciative of the efforts of Islamic clinics, at the heart of their disgruntlement lies the perceived tension between the expectation of low fees, which they feel is in keeping with Islam, and high (or rapidly rising) fees, which they view as commercial and un-Islamic. In Yemen, we see the recent introduction of relatively expensive summer camps, day care centers, schools, and universities by the Islah Charitable Society that are bound to evoke the same negative sentiments.

While more research needs to be conducted, these negative assessments indicate that catering to middle-class needs may in fact be undermining the Islamist movement in unforeseen ways—at the ballot boxes in associational, syndicate, local, and national elections where Islamist promises may be examined with different, perhaps jaded, eyes. I would argue that at a very minimum, this sense of betrayal or hypocrisy is creating a greater gulf between those inside and those outside of Islamist networks of shared meaning.

The case study of ISIs indicates that in contrast to the dominant literature which regards benefits and selective incentives as necessary and strictly beneficial, benefits may both help and hinder a movement. When the goals of the movement are prioritized above those of the ISI and the constituency of the movement is prioritized over the constituency of the ISI, the benefits or incentives targeted for the movement constituency may in fact hinder a movement in the long run. This occurs in the case of ISIs where the constituency of the social movement (the middle class) is different from the proclaimed constituency of the ISI (the poor). The case of ISIs indicates that only when the fit between the stated goals of the movement and NGO is tighter or more similar can we say that benefits are beneficial.

In the case of ISIs, where the fit is looser, the prioritization of the middle class over the poor has alienated potential members, including those of the middle class, who perceive hypocrisy and a betrayal of ISI goals. The fact that many ISIs are expensive and geared toward the paying middle class is perceived as a betrayal of the goal of ISIs as charities and of the fact that these charities claim to be Islamic.

The study of ISIs is thus central to our understanding of social and political change. By shifting our gaze toward the horizontal ties in which ISIs are embedded—those ties created in the establishment and ongoing functioning of the institutions—we redirect our attention to the importance and significance of the middle class to the ISIs themselves, the Islamist movement in general, and the politics of the three countries under study. ISIs are not hotbeds of cross-class recruitment. Neither, however, can they be regarded as arenas for the recruitment of the middle classes. While ISIs cater to the middle classes, largely the new or professional middle class, there is not necessarily a direct link between middle-class services and recruitment. The significance of ISIs lies in the social networks in which they are embedded—the networks that bind middle-class people together and in which they form a sense of solidarity and mission. This gradual accumulation of social capital, and the concomitant potential changes in social values and identity, cannot be said to be automatic or inclusive of all middle-class ISI participants. However, it is a vital element in the process of social change the Middle East is undergoing.

NOTES

1. ISLAMIC SOCIAL INSTITUTIONS, SOCIAL MOVEMENT THEORY, AND THE MIDDLE CLASSES

1. I chose the term "Islamic social institution" as opposed to "Islamic nongovernmental organization" or "Islamic voluntary association" for several reasons. The most important reason is that both of the latter terms explicitly connote voluntary activity and/or charity for the poor. As the three case studies will demonstrate, many Islamic nongovernmental organizations have in fact established private institutions that may be nonprofit but are not for the poor. Rather, they are private enterprises for the paying middle class. I also did not want to presuppose voluntary activity, as my data reveals that a high percentage of those working in ISIs are in fact paid employees. Finally, the term "nongovernmental" is problematic because it is debatable whether or not Islamic social institutions, indeed any nongovernmental associations, in the Middle East are in fact "nongovernmental." I chose to use the term "Islamic" social institutions as opposed to "Islamist" social institutions in order not to presuppose that those who establish and/or work in Islamic social institutions are all politically motivated Islamic activists. My choice of the term Islamic social institution is also based on the fact that there is no consistent definition for Islamic nongovernmental organizations within the literature. The terms nongovernmental organization (NGO) and private voluntary organization (PVO) are generally used interchangeably within the literature; the exception is the literature on Egypt. Data on Egypt treats PVOs as a subcategory of NGOs, and the term PVO excludes professional syndicates and unions to which membership is mandatory by law in Egypt. Within this book, I do the same. With the exception of the data on Egypt, where I use the two terms as employed by prominent researchers on Egypt, I consider the terms NGO and PVO to be interchangeable. For the sake of clarity, I generally adhere to the term NGO.

2. Sami Zubaida, "Islam, the State and Democracy: Contrasting Conceptions of Society in Egypt," *Middle East Report* 179 (November–December 1992): 9.

3. Ibid., 9–10.

4. Alain Roussillon, "Entre al-Jihad et al-Rayyan," in *Modernisation et nouvelles formes de mobilisation sociale* (Cairo, Egypt: Dossiers du Centre d'Études et de Documentation Économiques, 1991), 45.

5. See also Zubaida, "Islam, the State, and Democracy," 9.

6. Mustapha K. al-Sayyid, "A Civil Society in Egypt?" *Middle East Journal* 47, no. 2 (Spring 1993): 233.

7. Bert Klandermans, "The Social Construction of Protest and Multiorganizational Fields," in *Frontiers in Social Movement Theory,* ed. Aldon D. Morris and Carol McClurg Mueller (New Haven, Conn.: Yale University Press, 1992), 77–103.

8. Doug McAdam, John D. McCarthy, and Mayer N. Zald, "Social Movements," in *Handbook of Sociology,* ed. Neil J. Smelser (Newbury Park, Calif.: Sage Publications, 1988), 695–738.

9. Anthony Oberschall, "Loosely Structured Collective Conflict: A Theory and an Application," *Research in Social Movements, Conflicts and Change* 3 (1980): 45–68.

10. See Quintan Wiktorowicz, ed., *Islamic Activism: A Social Movement Theory Approach* (Bloomington: Indiana University Press, forthcoming); Quintan Wiktorowicz, *The Management of Islamic Activism* (Albany: SUNY Press, 2001); Carrie Rosefsky Wickham, *Mobilizing Islam* (New York: Columbia University Press, forthcoming); Ziad Munson, "Islamic Mobilization: Social Movement Theory and the Egyptian Muslim Brotherhood," *Sociological Quarterly* 42, no. 4 (2001): 487–510; Charles Kurzman, "Structural Opportunity and Perceived Opportunity in Social-Movement Theory: The Iranian Revolution of 1979," *American Sociological Review* 61 (February 1996): 153–170; and Gehad Auda, "The Islamic Movement and Resource Mobilization in Egypt: A Political Culture Perspective," in *Political Culture and Democracy in Developing Countries,* ed. Larry Diamond (Boulder, Colo.: Lynne Rienner, 1993), 379–407.

11. This process took place throughout and beyond the Ottoman Empire, albeit at different times in different regions.

12. Halim Barakat, *The Arab World: Society, Culture, and State* (Berkeley: University of California Press, 1993), 77.

13. Alan Richards and John Waterbury, *A Political Economy of the Middle East* (Boulder, Colo.: Westview Press, 1990), 47.

14. Barakat, *The Arab World,* 81–87.

15. Richards and Waterbury, *A Political Economy,* 43.

16. James A. Bill and Robert Springborg, *Politics in the Middle East,* 5th ed. (New York: Addison, Wesley, Longman, 2000), 87.

17. Sheila Carapico, *Civil Society in Yemen* (Cambridge: Cambridge University Press, 1998), 78–79.

18. Barakat, *The Arab World,* 76.

19. Richards and Waterbury, *A Political Economy,* 47.

20. Ibid.

21. Ibid., 48.

22. Sarah Ben Nefissa-Paris, "L'état égyptien et le monde associatif," *Égypte/Monde Arabe* 8 (4ème trimestre 1991): 108.

23. Historically, there have been three kinds of *awqaf:* religious *waqf* for the mosque maintenance and services; philanthropic *waqf* for public works and buildings such as hospitals; and family *waqf,* where the proceeds of the *waqf* went first to the descendants of the dedicator and the surplus went to the poor. John Esposito, ed., *The Oxford Encyclopaedia of the Modern Islamic World* (New York: Oxford University Press, 1995), 313. For an in-depth discussion of *waqf,* see Hamilton Alexander R. Gibb and Harold Bowen, *Islamic Society and the West,* vol. 1, *Islamic Society in the Eighteenth Century, Part II* (London: Oxford University Press, 1957); and Majid Khadduri and Herbert J. Liebesny, eds., *Law in the Middle East,* vol. 1, *Origin and Development of Islamic Law* (Washington, D.C.: The Middle East Institute, 1955).

24. Amina el Azhary Sonbol, *The Creation of a Medical Profession in Egypt, 1800–1922* (Syracuse: Syracuse University Press, 1991), 4–6; see also Carapico, *Civil Society in Yemen,* 69–73.

25. See Richards and Waterbury, *A Political Economy,* 409–422; and Barakat, *The Arab World,* 87–94.

26. In Yemen, the education changes were largely in response to the exclusionary policies of the old religious kingdom.

27. Richards and Waterbury, *A Political Economy,* 411.

28. Dietrich Rueschemeyer, Evelyn Huber Stephens, and John D. Stephens, *Capitalist Development and Democracy* (Cambridge: Polity Press, 1982), 52.

Notes to pages 10–14 | 165

29. Hanna Batatu, "Class Analysis in Syria," in *Arab Society: Social Science Perspectives,* ed. Nicholas S. Hopkins and Saad Eddin Ibrahim (Cairo, Egypt: The American University in Cairo Press, 1987), 381.

30. Richards and Waterbury, *A Political Economy,* 411–413.

31. Amani Kandil, "The Status of the Third Sector on the Arab Region," in *Citizens: Strengthening Global Civil Society,* ed. Miguel Darcy de Oliveira and Rajesh Tandon (Washington, D.C.: CIVICUS World Alliance of Citizen Participation, 1994), 127. See also Amani Kandil, *Civil Society in the Arab World: Private Voluntary Organizations* (Washington, D.C.: CIVICUS, 1995), 38.

32. Robert Latowsky quoted in Denis J. Sullivan, *Private Voluntary Organizations in Egypt: Islamic Development, Private Initiative, and State Control* (Gainesville: University Press of Florida, 1994), 16.

33. Marina de Regt, "Yemeni NGOs," in *Women and Development in the Middle East: Perspectives of Arab NGOs and Project Participants,* ed. Inge Arends (Amsterdam: Middle East Research Associates, 1995), 111.

34. As stated above, data on Egypt treats PVOs as a subcategory of NGOs; the term PVO excludes professional syndicates and unions which individuals must join by law in Egypt.

35. See Saad Eddin Ibrahim, *An Assessment of Grassroots Participation in the Development of Egypt* (Cairo, Egypt: The American University in Cairo Press, 1997), 4, 28. There is a vast literature dealing with NGOs, voluntary associations, "the third sector," nonprofit organizations, and civil society. Much of this literature draws attention to the middle-class bias within NGOs. In their comparative study of NGOs in the developing world Anheier and Salamon note that the strength of the nonprofit sector in the developing world is dependent upon the strength of the urban middle class—the class most active in establishing and staffing NGOs. Helmut K. Anheier and Lester M. Salamon, "Conclusions: Towards an Understanding of the Nonprofit Sector in the Developing World," in *The Nonprofit Sector in the Developing World: A Comparative Analysis,* ed. Helmut K. Anheier and Lester M. Salamon (Manchester and New York: Manchester University Press, 1998), 358.

36. Ibrahim, *An Assessment of Grassroots Participation,* 52, 66–67.

37. Researchers Kandil and Ben Nefissa furthermore note that Islamic voluntary associations are the most important type of social welfare association in Egypt presently—particularly the charity services for children, mothers, and families. Amani Kandil and Sarah Ben Nefissa, *Civil Associations in Egypt* (Cairo, Egypt: Al-Ahram, 1994), 100, 111.

38. Amat al-Alim as-Suswa, Deputy Minister of Information, interview with the author, Sana'a, Yemen, February 2, 1996.

39. Islamic Center Charity Society, telephone interview with the author, Amman, Jordan, December 6, 1998.

40. This figure does not include the community college in Zarqa. Islamic Center Charity Society, interview with the author, Zarqa, Jordan, December 6, 1998.

41. Dale Eickelman and James Piscatori, *Muslim Politics* (Princeton, N.J.: Princeton University Press, 1996), Chapter 2. Concept taken from Eric Hobsbawm, "Introduction: Invention Traditions," in *The Invention of Tradition,* ed. Eric Hobsbawm and Terence Ranger (Cambridge: Cambridge University Press, 1983), 1–14.

42. Eickelman and Piscatori, *Muslim Politics,* 46.

43. Adapted from Karin Ask and Marit Tjomsland, "Introduction," in *Women and Islamization: Contemporary Dimensions of Discourse on Gender Relations,* ed. Karin Ask and Marit Tjomsland (New York: Berg, 1998), 2.

44. Eickelman and Piscatori, *Muslim Politics,* 35–36.

45. Sana Abed-Kotob, "The Accommodationists Speak: Goals and Strategies of the Muslim Brotherhood of Egypt," *International Journal of Middle East Studies* 27, no. 3 (August 1995): 321–339.

46. The Muslim Brotherhood was formed in 1928 in Ismailiyya, Egypt, by Hasan al-Banna. Al-Banna's thinking largely continues to guide the actions of the Egyptian Brotherhood, its sympathizers, and much of moderate Islamism today. Al-Banna founded the Society of Muslim Brothers (Muslim Brotherhood) as an educational movement to reform the hearts and minds of Egyptians, which had been corrupted and degraded due to "their subordination politically, economically and culturally to the dominant foreigner." Sami Zubaida, "Islamic Fundamentalism in Egypt and Iran" in *Studies in Religious Fundamentalism,* ed. Lionel Caplan (London: Macmillan, 1987), 34. Egyptians therefore had to be guided back to the true religion and away from the corrupt aspirations and conduct of the European powers. According to al-Banna, this decline was perpetrated not only by the regime but also by al-Azhar, Egypt's center of Islamic teaching and scholarship. He felt that while the regime was the puppet of European powers, al-Azhar had failed as an exponent of a living and dynamic Islam and had not been vigorous enough in its resistance to encroachment on Islamic values by foreign ideas. Furthermore, the *ulema,* the body of Islamic scholars, had failed to speak out against social injustices and exploitation. As a result, Egypt had fallen into religious, cultural, political, economic, social, legal, and moral decadence and impotence. Richard P. Mitchell, *The Society of Muslim Brothers,* 2d ed. (New York: Oxford University Press, 1993), 212. With its growing popularity, the Society developed an elaborate hierarchy with branches throughout Egypt and rapidly involved itself in political, economic, and social activities. By 1949, there were 2,000 branches of the Brotherhood throughout Egypt with approximately 500,000 active members and as many as 500,000 sympathizers. Mitchell, *Society of Muslim Brothers,* 328.

47. Gehad Auda, "The Islamic Movement and Resource Mobilization in Egypt: A Political Culture Perspective," in Diamond, ed., *Political Culture,* 386.

48. Mitchell, *Society of Muslim Brothers,* 290. See also Ann M. Lesch, "The Muslim Brotherhood in Egypt: Reform or Revolution?" in *The Religious Challenge to the State,* ed. Mathew C. Moen and Lowell S. Gustafson (Philadelphia: Temple University Press, 1992), 183.

49. Lesch, "The Muslim Brotherhood in Egypt," 183.

50. Abed-Kotob, "Accommodationists Speak," 326–327.

51. Saad Eddin Ibrahim, "The Changing Face of Islamic Activism," *Civil Society* 4, no. 41 (May 1995): 5.

52. There are also ideological differences, such as the radicals' understanding of *jahiliyya* (ignorance, barbarism) and *jihad* (holy struggle). See Gilles Kepel, *Muslim Extremism in Egypt* (Berkeley and Los Angeles: University of California Press, 1984), 43–59; and Sullivan and Abed-Kotob, *Islam in Contemporary Egypt,* 42.

53. John Waterbury, "Egypt: Islam and Social Change," in *Change and the Muslim World,* ed. David Cuthell, Philip Stoddard, and Margaret Sullivan (Syracuse, N.Y.: Syracuse University Press, 1981), 53.

54. Mitchell, *Society of Muslim Brothers,* 329–330.

55. Carrie Rosefsky Wickham, "Islamic Mobilization and Political Change: The Islamist Trend in Egypt's Professional Associations," in *Political Islam: Essays from Middle East Report,* ed. Joel Beinin and Joe Stork (London and New York: I. B. Tauris, 1997), 121–122.

56. Eric Davis, "Ideology, Social Class and Islamic Radicalism in Modern Egypt," in *From Nationalism to Revolutionary Islam,* ed. Said Amir Arjomand (London: Macmillan, 1984), 141. While empirical field studies of the class base of moderate Islamists remain limited in number, Kurzman's unpublished survey of the empirical literature on Islamic activists confirms that there are two social bases for Islamism today. The first consists of students and graduates of secular institutions of higher education, in particular young men from modest backgrounds. The second social basis consists of less-educated rural residents who have had some contact with "modern" institutions, especially oil-based capitalist enterprises. As Kurzman states, these two groups may overlap. Higher education may be one

of the means of modern contact for the sons of rural families. Charles Kurzman, "Who Are the Islamists?" unpublished article, University of North Carolina at Chapel Hill, 1996. In her research on Islamist women in Egypt, Soraya Duval also found that although there were women from all strata of society at the Qur'anic study meetings of the Muslim Sisters, there was also a large middle-class presence among Islamist women. She found that the majority of women were between 20 and 30 years of age. Soraya Duval, "New Veils and New Voices: Islamist Women's Groups in Egypt," in Ask and Tjomsland, eds., *Women and Islamization,* 59.

57. Ahmad Jamil Azm, "The Islamic Action Front Party," in *Islamic Movements in Jordan,* ed. Hani Hourani (Amman, Jordan: Al-Urdun al-Jadid Research Center, 1997), 101–103. For the breakdown according to occupation of the first Shura (Consultative) Council, the 1993 Executive Bureau, the second Shura Council, and the second Executive Bureau of the Islamic Action Front, see appendixes on pages 128–131, 132, 134–137, and 138, respectively. Marion Boulby argues that the rise of the Muslim Brotherhood in Jordan can be directly attributed to the growing numbers of middle-class would-be professionals and civil servants that have emerged from the country's universities with the rapid expansion of Jordan's education system in the past two to three decades. Boulby, *The Muslim Brotherhood and the Kings of Jordan: 1945–1993* (Atlanta, Ga.: Scholars Press, 1999).

58. Bernard Lefresne, "Les islamistes yéménites et les élections," *Maghreb-Machrek* 141 (juillet–août 1993): 30–31.

59. These figures stand in sharp contrast to the national statistics for education. According to United Nations Development Programme (UNDP) statistics for 1999, adult literacy (the percentage of adults over the age of 15 who can read) is only 45.2 percent and the combined primary, secondary, and tertiary gross enrollment ratio is only 51 percent. UNDP, *Human Development Report 2001: Making New Technologies Work for Human Development* (New York: Oxford University Press, 2001), 176, 143.

60. Boulby, *Muslim Brotherhood and the Kings of Jordan,* 74.

61. Bayat and Denis note that Cairo's poor squatter areas, or *ashwaiyyat,* are not exclusively poverty belts but are also where many middle-class urbanites, professionals, and civil servants live. Asef Bayat and Eric Denis, "Who Is Afraid of Ashwaiyyat? Urban Change and Politics in Egypt," *Environment and Urbanization* 12, no. 2 (October 2000): 198.

62. Al-Sayyid, "A Civil Society in Egypt?" 233.

63. Malcolm Kerr, "Egypt," in *Education and Political Development,* ed. James S Coleman (Princeton, N.J.: Princeton University Press, 1965), 187.

64. *Al-Wafd,* April 12, 1987. Roy also confirms this in the case of Islamic NGOs in Palestine and quotes a high-ranking Ministry of Interior official who admitted to her: "We 'look the other way' with many Islamic institutions because they provide excellent services and this helps [the Palestinian National Authority] a great deal." Sara Roy, "The Transformation of Islamic NGOs in Palestine," *Middle East Report* 214 (Spring 2000): 26.

65. See Eickelman and Piscatori, *Muslim Politics.* See also Oliver Roy, *The Failure of Political Islam,* trans. Carol Volk (Cambridge, Mass.: Harvard University Press, 1994), Chapter 6. Today, this questioning of Muslim authority has extended to a questioning of the right of traditional authorities, the *ulema,* to interpret sacred texts for other Muslims and the consequent rise of alternative and competing sources of sacred authority; see Eickelman and Piscatori, *Muslim Politics,* 70.

66. Pamela E. Oliver, "Bringing the Crowd Back In: The Nonorganizational Elements of Social Movements," *Research in Social Movements, Conflicts and Change* 11 (1989): 6; see also Gerald Marwell and Pamela E. Oliver, "Collective Action Theory and Social Movements Research," *Research in Social Movements, Conflicts and Change* 7 (1984): 4–7.

67. Klandermans, "The Social Construction of Protest," 94.

68. Mayer N. Zald and Roberta Ash as quoted by McAdam, McCarthy, and Zald, "Social Movements," 717.

69. Adrian F. Aveni, "Organizational Linkages and Resource Mobilization: The Significance of Linkage Strength and Breadth," *Sociological Quarterly* 19 (Spring 1978): 187.

70. Ibid., 188. For a discussion of strength and breadth, see 189–190.

71. Doug McAdam, "Micromobilization Contexts and Recruitment to Activism," in *International Social Movement Research*, vol. 1, *From Structure to Action: Comparing Movement Participation across Cultures*, ed. Bert Klandermans, Hanspeter Kriesi, and Sydney Tarrow (Greenwich, Conn.: JAI Press, 1988), 136.

72. James A. Kitts, "Not in Our Backyard: Solidarity, Social Networks, and the Ecology of Environmental Mobilization," *Sociological Inquiry* 69, no. 4 (Fall 1999): 554.

73. Myra Max Ferree and Frederick D. Miller, "Mobilization and Meaning," *Sociological Inquiry* 55, no. 1 (Winter 1985): 45; McAdam, "Micromobilization Contexts and Resource Mobilization," 137.

74. Ibid., 145–146, 149–150. McAdam's research deals specifically with high-risk activism, as opposed to less risky, more moderate activism such as Islamic charities.

75. Kitts, "Not in Our Backyard," 569.

76. David A. Snow, Louis A. Zurcher, and Sheldon Ekland-Olson, "Social Networks and Social Movements: A Microstructural Approach to Differential Recruitment," *American Sociological Review* 45 (October 1980): 791, 796.

77. Rodney Stark and William Sims Bainbridge, "Networks of Faith: Interpersonal Bonds and Recruitment to Cults and Sects," *American Journal of Sociology* 85, no. 6 (1980): 1386.

78. Ibid., 1376.

79. Ibid., 1379.

80. Ibid., 1380, 1382, 1389, 1390–1392.

81. Ibid., 1397–1389.

82. Doug McAdam, "Culture and Social Movements," in *New Social Movements: From Ideology to Identity,* ed. Enrique Larana, Hank Johnston, and Joseph R. Gusfield (Philadelphia: Temple University Press, 1994), 36–37.

83. For a brief overview of the literature, see Bert Klandermans and Dirk Oegema, "Potentials, Networks, Motivations, and Barriers: Steps towards Participation in Social Movements," *American Sociological Review* 52 (August 1987): 520.

84. Doug McAdam and Ronnelle Paulsen, "Specifying the Relationship between Social Ties and Activism," *American Journal of Sociology* 99, no. 3 (November 1993): 644.

85. As Klandermans and Oegema state in their study of the 1983 peace demonstrations in The Hague, informal social networks linked to social movements act as guardians of the movement's principles by forcing people to overcome their reservations and act according to their principles. Klandermans and Oegema, "Potentials, Networks, Motivations, and Barriers," 530.

86. Lofland and Stark in Stark and Bainbridge, "Networks of Faith," 1378–1379, 1382. Similarly, McAdam argues that while ideological affinity pushes someone to participate, it is not sufficient. What is also needed is integration into supportive networks. Doug McAdam, "Micromobilization Contexts and Resource Mobilization," 151.

87. McAdam and Paulsen, "Specifying the Relationship," 655.

88. The literature is generally in agreement that people seldom join movements per se; rather, they typically participate in movement activities and gradually become members. Snow, Zurcher, and Ekland-Olson, "Social Networks," 795. However, there is some recent dissent concerning recruitment patterns. Jasper speaks of the "moral shock" that induces members to join a movement. James M. Jasper, *The Art of Moral Protest: Culture, Biography, and Creativity in Social Movements* (Chicago: University of Chicago Press, 1997).

89. McAdam, "Micromobilization," 139. See also McAdam and Paulsen, "Specifying the Relationship," 643; Kitts, "Not in Our Backyard," 552, 567; Snow, Zurcher, and Eckland-Olson, "Social Networks," 798.

90. Stark and Bainbridge, "Networks of Faith," 1387.

91. Klandermans, "The Social Construction of Protest," 88.

92. Klandermans and Oegema, "Potentials, Networks, Motivations, and Barriers," 526.

93. Ibid. See also Charles Tilly, *From Mobilization to Revolution* (Reading, Mass.: Addison-Wesley, 1978), 62–63.

94. Suzanne Staggenborg argues that successful social movements recruit from institutions and organizations where people with common lifestyle preferences interact. Suzanne Staggenborg, "Life-Style Preferences and Social Movement Recruitment: Illustrations from the Abortion Conflict," *Social Science Quarterly* 68, no. 4 (December 1987): 779–797.

95. Mario Diani and Giovanni Lodi, "Three in One: Currents in the Milan Ecology Movement," in *International Social Movement Research,* vol. 1, *From Structure to Action: Comparing Movement Participation across Cultures,* ed. Bert Klandermans, Hanspeter Kriesi, and Sydney Tarrow (Greenwich, Conn.: JAI Press, 1988), 104–107.

96. Ben Schennink, "From Peace Week to Peace Work: Dynamics of the Peace Movement in the Netherlands," in *International Social Movement Research,* vol. 1, *From Structure to Action: Comparing Movement Participation across Cultures,* ed. Bert Klandermans, Hanspeter Kriesi, and Sydney Tarrow (Greenwich, Conn.: JAI Press, 1988), 264–268.

97. Maria Helena Moreira Alves, "Interclass Alliances in the Opposition to the Military in Brazil: Consequences for the Transition Period," in *Power and Popular Protest,* ed. Susan Eckstein (Berkeley and Los Angeles: University of California Press, 1989), 278–298.

98. Dietrich Rueschemeyer, Evelyn Huber Stephens, and John D. Stephens, *Capitalist Development and Democracy* (Cambridge: Polity Press, 1982), 8.

99. Robert D. Putnam, *Making Democracy Work: Civic Traditions in Modern Italy* (Princeton, N.J.: Princeton University Press, 1993).

100. For definitions of social capital, see Putnam, *Making Democracy Work,* 167; and James S. Coleman, *Foundations of Social Theory* (Cambridge, Mass: Harvard University Press, 1990), 300–321.

101. Putnam, *Making Democracy Work,* 174–175.

102. Ibid., 173.

103. Bert Klandermans, "The Formation and Mobilization of Consensus," in Klandermans, Kriesi, and Tarrow, eds., *From Structure to Action,* 175.

104. Alberto Melucci, *Nomads of the Present: Social Movements and Individual Needs in Contemporary Society,* ed. John Keane and Paul Mier (Philadelphia: Temple University Press, 1989).

105. Steven Pfaff, "Collective Identity and Informal Groups in Revolutionary Mobilization: East Germany in 1989," *Social Forces* 75, no. 1 (September 1996): 98–100, quote on page 100.

106. While Melucci's theory sees this process as occurring prior to the emergence of the "visible" social movement or mass mobilization, scholars have noted the ongoing activity and importance of submerged networks in identity creation. Mueller conceptualizes a form of feedback mechanism in which, rather than outgrowing social networks, a social movement will pass through several levels or stages and back again. Carol M. Mueller, "Conflict Networks and the Origins of Women's Liberation," in *Social Movements: Readings on Their Emergence, Mobilization, and Dynamics,* ed. Doug McAdam and David A. Snow (Los Angeles: Roxbury, 1997), 170. Wiktorowicz argues that under certain conditions social movements may never develop formal institutions and may chose to remain at the level of informal networks. Wiktorowicz, *Management of Islamic Activism.*

107. While the issue is not dealt with directly, studies implicitly imply that preexisting ties do not matter once someone has been recruited. As a whole, studies do not deal with preexisting ties after recruitment.

108. Alternatively, those who know numerous other people who are participating in a social movement, such as the peace movement, stand a much higher chance of being asked if they are participating and of getting negative reactions if they are not. The costs of non-participation, which may include losing one's friends, are thus very high. Klandermans and Oegema, "Potentials, Networks, Motivations, and Barriers," 527.

109. Debra Friedman and Doug McAdam, "Collective Identity and Activism: Networks, Choices, and the Life of a Social Movement," in *Frontiers in Social Movement Theory,* ed. Aldon D. Morris and Carol McClurg Mueller (New Haven, Conn.: Yale University Press, 1992), 161.

110. Karl-Dieter Opp and Christiane Gern, "Dissident Groups, Personal Networks, and Spontaneous Cooperation: The East German Revolution of 1989," *American Sociological Review* 58 (October 1993): 661.

111. McAdam, "Micromobilization Contexts and Resource Mobilization,"135.

112. Stark and Bainbridge, "Networks of Faith," 1381, 1384.

113. Ibid., 1393.

114. Ibid., 1393–1394.

115. Snow, Zurcher, and Eckland-Olson, "Social Networks," 795.

116. Mancur Olson, *The Logic of Collective Action* (Cambridge, Mass.: Harvard University Press, 1965), 133; Hanspeter Kriesi, "The Organizational Structure of New Social Movements in a Political Context," in *Comparative Perspectives on Social Movements: Political Opportunities, Mobilizing Structures, and Cultural Framings,* ed. Doug McAdam, John D. McCarthy, and Mayer N. Zald (New York: Cambridge University Press, 1996), 156.

117. The poor do receive some limited financial aid from the hospital.

118. Kriesi, "Organizational Structure," 156.

119. Frances Fox Piven and Richard A. Cloward, *Poor People's Movements* (New York: Vintage Press, 1979), 310.

120. In her examination of Kuwaiti women's organizations, both secular and religious, Haya al-Mughni notes a similar phenomenon. She states that in almost all women's organizations in Kuwait, the *rab'a* (a tight network of friends and kin) is an important source of control and a strategy for perpetuating power. In order to retain their influence and avoid a redistribution of power, the leaders bring their own friends and relatives into the organization. Leadership positions have therefore remained in the hands of a relative few and it is these few who have gained popularity and prestige. Leaders meet with government officials, give interviews to the press, and travel all over the world to attend conferences on women's issues. As al-Mughni states: "Given all these privileges, it is perhaps not surprising that they are so reluctant to give up their positions and return to anonymity." Haya al-Mughni, *Women in Kuwait: The Politics of Gender* (London: Saqi Books, 2001), 119.

121. I use these terms as originally employed by Asef Bayat. See Bayat, "Revolution without Movement, Movement without Revolution: Comparing Islamic Activism in Iran and Egypt," *Society for Comparative Study of Society and History* 40, no. 1 (January 1998): 136–169.

122. Olson defines a selective incentive as a form of benefit that a nonmember cannot obtain. This meaning of the term selective incentives applies to some, but not all, of the benefits that participants in ISIs receive.

123. Maren Lockwood Carden, "The Institutionalization of Social Movements in Voluntary Organizations," in *Research in Social Movements, Conflicts and Change,* 11 (1989): 143–161. In her research on the women's movement in the United States, Carden argues that voluntary organizations may or may not share the same ideology and goals as the social movement to which they ostensibly belong. Carden found that many voluntary groups have very specific or narrow goals, such as helping an identified needy group such as homeless families, but do not always realign their organizational activities in keeping with the larger social movement that is pursuing social problems or the welfare of deprived people in gen-

eral. The goals of the social movement organization and the social movement may not always fit, and tensions may arise between the social movement organization and the social movement. Carden found that members in voluntary organizations join an organization to pursue *its* goals and not the goals of the social movement.

124. Wiktorowicz agrees. See *Management of Islamic Activism,* 85.

125. The case studies of ISIs in Egypt, Jordan, and Yemen appear to confirm a growing body of research that argues that the poor avoid becoming trapped in any system of authority that may limit their options elsewhere. See, for example, Asef Bayat, *Street Politics: Poor People's Movements in Iran* (New York: Columbia University Press, 1997).

126. Poor patients and members of the community will drop by the director's office and discuss concerns. See Janine A. Clark, "Islamic Social Welfare Organizations in Cairo: Islamization from Below?" *Arab Studies Quarterly* 17, no. 4 (Fall 1995): 11–28.

127. Bayat, "Revolution without Movement," 157. See also Bayat, *Street Politics.*

2. ISLAMIC MEDICAL CLINICS IN CAIRO

1. Denis Sullivan and Sana Abed-Kotob, *Islam in Contemporary Egypt: Civil Society vs. the State* (Boulder, Colo.: Lynne Rienner, 1999), 28–29.

2. As "official" proof of the Mustafa Mahmoud Association's high-quality services, the government-run Medical Agency regularly sends patients there for kidney dialysis. Iman Roushdy Hammady, "Religious Medical Clinics in Cairo" (Master's Thesis no. 885, American University in Cairo, 1990), 207.

3. Augustus Richard Norton, "Introduction," in *Civil Society in the Middle East,* ed. Augustus Richard Norton (Leiden: E. J. Brill, 1995), 1: 23.

4. According to Sarah Ben Nefissa-Paris, the first PVOs were established by religious or ethnic communities, but by the beginning of the twentieth century, associations without any particular community affiliation were being created. Sarah Ben Nefissa-Paris, "L'état égyptien et le monde associatif à travers les textes juridiques," *Égypte/Monde Arabe* 8 (4ème trimestre 1991): 109. The first PVO in Egypt was the Greek Benevolent Society of 1821. The first Egyptian PVO was formed in 1868, while the first association with an Islamic reference in its name, the Association of Islamic Benevolence, dates to 1878 (108). See also Saad Eddin Ibrahim et al., eds., *An Assessment of Grassroots Participation in the Development of Egypt* (Cairo, Egypt: The American University in Cairo Press, 1996): 37–38.

5. Mohammed Ali, the great nineteenth-century Egyptian ruler and reformer, recruited French physician Antoine-Barthelmey Clot (Clot Bey) to design his military and civilian public health services and establish the first School of Medicine at Qasr al-Aini in 1837. After Mohammed Ali's death, the government continued to finance health services and medical education. When British colonial rule began in 1882, the new government retained control of the profession. Under the British, however, it suited the needs of the colonizers, not the Egyptians. Amira el-Azhary Sonbol, *The Creation of a Medical Profession in Egypt, 1800–1922* (Syracuse, N.Y.: Syracuse University Press, 1991), 106–132.

6. The Ministry of Health continued to run public hospitals, but the better hospitals were all privately owned. Each of the major European communities—for example, Greek, Jewish, Italian, and Anglo-American—raised funds and built their own hospitals. Nancy Elizabeth Gallagher, *Egypt's Other Wars: Epidemics and the Politics of Public Health* (Syracuse, N.Y.: Syracuse University Press, 1990), 10.

7. Ibid., 3–4.

8. Ibrahim, *An Assessment of Grassroots Participation,* 38.

9. Ibid., 58.

10. Sylvia Chiffoleau, "Le désengagement de l'État et les transformations du système de santé," *Maghreb-Machrek* 127 (janvier–mars 1990): 89. See S. van der Geest for an in-

teresting discussion of the manipulation of health care by states in order to bind groups into the larger political unit, penetrate the local level, and legitimize the state. S. van der Geest, "Health Care as Politics? 'Missed Chances' in Rural Cameroon," in *State and Local Community in Africa,* ed. Wim van Binsbergen, Filip Reyntjens, and Gerti Hesseling (Brussels: Centre d'Etude et de Documentation Africaines/Afrika Studie-en Documentatiecentrum, 1986), 241–260.

11. Chiffoleau, "Le désengagement," 86; Joe Stork, "Political Aspects of Health," *Middle East Report* 161 (November–December 1989): 5.

12. In 1994 there were 2,209 rural basic health units, most of them devoid of materials or personnel. Egyptian Preparatory Committee for the 1995 International Women's Forum, *Report of the Egyptian NGOs for the Forum on Women Beijing 1995: Egyptian Women's Status from Nairobi to Beijing* (Cairo, Egypt: Egyptian Preparatory Committee with the cooperation of UNICEF, USAID, and the Social Fund, 1995), 27.

13. Chiffoleau, "Le désengagement," 89. In the late 1980s, health care costs constituted approximately 2.5 percent of Egypt's budget; the military commanded just under 20 percent. Stork, "Political Aspects of Health," 7. See also Sylvia Chiffoleau, "Islam, Science et Médecine Moderne en Égypte et dans le Monde Arabe," in *Santé, Médecine et Société dans le Monde Arabe,* ed. Elisabeth Longuenesse (Paris: L'Harmattan, 1995), 35. In 1993–1994, Egypt's National Planning Institute reported that the Ministry of Health's budget had dropped to 1.9 percent of the national budget. A. Okasha and T. Okasha, "Mental Health in Cairo (al-Qahira)," *International Journal of Mental Health* 28, no. 4 (Winter 1999–2000): 67. See also Egyptian Preparatory Committee, *Report of the Egyptian NGOs,* 28.

14. Egyptian Preparatory Committee, *Report of the Egyptian NGOs,* 27–28. These are 1994 statistics. The government sector consists of all the departments and agencies of the Ministry of Health and its affiliated departments in governorates and villages, as well as the hospitals and remedial and research institutions affiliated with other ministries, foremost among which are the Ministry of Defense, the Ministry of the Interior, and the Ministry of Education. Ultimately it is the Ministry of Health that is solely responsible for preventative health measures and health orientation in Egypt. This system is presently under review.

15. A. K. Nandakumar, Mukesh Chawla, and Maryam Khan, "Utilization of Outpatient Care in Egypt and Its Implications for the Role of Government in Health Care Provision," *World Development* 28, no. 1 (January 2000): 188. This study states that 99 percent of Egyptians technically have access to a government health facility within 5 km (193, although on page 188 this source cites this statistic as 95 percent rather than 99 percent). A 1996 World Bank study states that 99 percent of the population has access to health care. World Bank, *Social Indicators of Development* (Washington, D.C.: World Bank, and Baltimore: Johns Hopkins University Press, 1996), 102.

16. Chiffoleau, "Le désengagement," 89–90. See also Sylvia Chiffoleau, "Itinéraires médicaux en Égypte," *Revue Tiers Monde* XXXVI, no. 143 (juillet–septembre 1995): 521.

17. Chiffoleau, "Le désengagement," 88.

18. Patients complain that doctors treat them poorly in government hospitals and are often absent or tardy. Patients also complain that doctors tend to concentrate their time on the patients in their private practices rather than on those in the government hospitals. Theresa el-Mehairy, *Medical Doctors: A Study of Role Concept and Job Satisfaction—The Egyptian Case* (Leiden: E. J. Brill, 1984), 31. See also Nandakumar, Chawla, and Khan, "Utilization of Outpatient Care in Egypt," 193–194. Patients commonly complain about the following six issues regarding government hospitals: the behavior of the staff and the treatment of the patients, the absence of doctors on call during working hours (evidence of the carelessness of some doctors), long waits for doctors to arrive, poor meals in hospitals, poor sanitation and other services, expensive visitors' fees, and the preference and extra attention for private patients over patients in public hospitals. El-Mehairy, *Medical Doctors,* 31.

19. This figure does not include mosque and church clinics and pharmacies, which are also technically private although they are not private practices. Nandakumar, Chawla, and Khan, "Utilization of Outpatient Care in Egypt," 190.

20. The aim of the program is to reorient Egypt's state-directed economy toward market forces, the private sector, and external trade. The case for privatization in Egypt rests, as Said el-Naggar states, on two bases: the size of the public sector and its performance. Egypt is presently burdened with a huge public sector which dates back to Nasser's early years of nationalization and import-substitution strategies. By 1984–1985, the public sector employed 1.35 million people—more than 10 percent of the entire workforce and approximately 25 percent of the nonagriculturalist workforce. It also employed 2.8 million civil servants. By the mid-1980s, therefore, about two-thirds of the nonagriculturalist workforce in Egypt was on the state payroll, and these figures do not include the 400,000-member armed forces or the 150,000-strong police force. Compared to other developing countries, Egypt ranks as one of the highest in terms of the relative importance of its public sector in the economy. In 1990, the public sector accounted for 70 percent of total investments, 80 percent of manufactured imports, and 55 percent of GDP. The inefficient performance of this massive public sector is reflected in its statistics. In the mid-1980s, the public sector accounted for 90 percent of Egypt's foreign debt. Of the total public-sector debt, a conservative estimate put the share of public enterprises (excluding financial and defense sectors) at about one-third. From 1973 to 1983–1984, public companies consistently registered deficits ranging from approximately 3 percent to 7 percent. This deficit was and is financed from the national budget and the banking system and by direct borrowing from abroad. When one takes the debt-service payments into account, by 1984–1985, the net annual burden of public enterprises on the balance of payments was more than $4 billion US annually or more than 40 percent of total current foreign-exchange receipts. These figures also do not include the Petroleum and Suez Authorities. The public sector in Egypt has hence been a major contributor to Egypt's slowdown of economic growth, its poor export performance, its heavy external debt, the widening gap between the food it produces and the food it imports each year, and its unhealthy dependence on foreign assistance. El-Naggar notes that other factors have also contributed to the poor performance of the Egyptian economy but that the public sector remains of major importance. Egypt's Economic Reform and Structural Adjustment Programme has therefore focused on cutting back on the public sector and spending with the sale of public enterprises, the reduction of bureaucracies, the removal of subsidies, and cutting budgets, including the health budget. Said el-Naggar, "Prospects and Problems of Privatization," in *The Political Economy of Contemporary Egypt*, ed. Ibrahim M. Oweiss (Washington, D.C.: Center of Contemporary Arab Studies, Georgetown University, 1990), 50, 55–56, 63; John Waterbury, "The Political Context of Public Sector Reform and Privatization in Egypt, India, Mexico, and Turkey," in *The Political Economy of Public Sector Reform and Privatization,* ed. Ezra N. Suleiman and John Waterbury (Boulder, Colo.: Westview Press, 1990), 141, 296.

21. Egypt has achieved positive results in the areas of macroeconomic stabilization, the correction of price distortions, financial liberalization, and the removal of trade barriers. Because of this economic restructuring program and the huge infusion of aid after the 1991 Gulf War, government spending has decreased, its revenue has increased, the budget deficit and external debt have decreased, and inflation rates have lowered. Saad Eddin Ibrahim, "Governance and Structural Adjustment: The Egyptian Case" (unpublished paper, Ibn Khaldoun Center for Development Studies, Cairo, November 1994), 15–17; "The Year in Review," *Civil Society* 7, no. 73 (February 1998): 5–17. See also Karen Pfeiffer, "How Tunisia, Morocco, Jordan and Even Egypt Became IMF 'Success Stories' in the 1990s," *Middle East Report* 210 (Spring 1999): 23–27. Pfeiffer also notes that Egypt has been particularly successful in privatization and in reducing inflation, budget deficit, debt service, and foreign aid.

22. Cassandra, "The Impending Crisis in Egypt," 11–13; Amos Elon, "One Foot on the Moon," *New York Review* (April 6, 1995): 34; Saahir Lone, "Government Cracks Down on Militants," *Civil Society* 4, no. 39 (March 1995): 9; Simon Brindle, "Egypt: A High Rise Economy," *The Middle East* (January 1995): 25–26.

23. UNDP, *United Nations Development Report 2000* (New York: UNDP, 2000), 170. The UNDP rates poverty according to: 1) the probability at birth of not surviving to age 40; 2) the adult illiteracy rate; and 3) the deprivations in economic provisioning measured by the percentage of the people without access to safe water and health services; and 4) the percentage of children under the age of 5 who are underweight (147).

24. "The Year in Review," *Civil Society* 7, no. 73 (Feb 1998): 11. The Egyptian Planning Institute bases its calculations on expenditures per capita needed to meet minimum food requirements. Similarly, an independent study conducted by Patrick Cardiff, which defined the poverty line as the necessary cost to obtain the minimum calories and protein for an average Egyptian household (the ability to purchase a minimally nutritious diet), found that the incidence of poverty was 44.29 percent of the population in 1995–1996. Patrick W. Cardiff, "Poverty and Inequality in Egypt," *Research in Middle East Economics* 2 (1997): 12, 29. See also Pfeiffer, "Success Stories," 26. The definition of poverty and how one measures it is a subject of considerable debate among governments, international agencies, and PVOs. The IMF defines poverty as an income of less than one dollar per person per day (adjusted for local purchasing power). According to this definition, only 7.6 percent of Egypt's population lives in absolute poverty (1995). In another independent study, Richard Adams notes that the depth and severity of poverty have increased in Egypt. Basing his data on a modified UNDP Human Poverty Index, he cites the share of the population living in poverty in urban Egypt as 22.5 percent and in rural Egypt as 23.3 percent in 1995–1996. Richard H. Adams, Jr., "Evaluating The Process of Development on Egypt, 1980–97," *International Journal of Middle East Studies* 32 (2000): 260–263, 272. For a discussion of the difficulties in determining poverty levels, see Cardiff, "Poverty and Inequality in Egypt," 5–6.

25. Egyptian Preparatory Committee, *Report of the Egyptian NGOs,* 28. Budgetary figures can vary dramatically, depending on the source and the method of calculation. For example, one report indicated that in the fiscal year 1995 (the last year for which audited accounts were available as of 1999), Egypt spent 3.7 percent of its gross domestic product on health care. According to this article, overall public spending accounted for only 44 percent of total health financing; the balance came from private sources. Almost 80 percent of public expenditures for health care comes from general tax revenues, 14 percent from social insurance premiums, and the rest from external donor assistance. Nandakumar, Chawla, and Khan, "Utilization of Outpatient Care in Egypt," 188. Egypt's expenditure of 3.7 percent of the GDP on health care is considered a moderate level of spending for the nation's level of income. A. K. Nandakumar, Michael R. Reich, Mukesh Chawla, Peter Berman, and Winnie Yip, "Health Reform for Children: The Egyptian Experience with School Health Insurance," *Health Policy* 50, no. 3 (January 2000): 156.

26. Egyptian Preparatory Committee, *Report of the Egyptian NGOs,* 28. While national and international agencies cite a decrease in the number of beds, the Egyptian government claims there has been a minimal increase in the number of hospital beds. According to the Central Agency for Public Mobilization and Statistics, the number of beds in Ministry of Health hospitals and in other government hospitals increased by 0.8 percent and 0.4 percent, respectively, between 1989 and 1993. Government of Egypt, *Statistical Yearbook Arab Republic of Egypt* (Cairo, Egypt: Central Agency for Public Mobilization and Statistics, June 1994), 146. A Johns Hopkins study published for the World Bank states that between 1980 and 1985 and 1989 and 1994, the population per hospital bed grew from 483 to 517. World Bank, *Social Indicators of Development,* 103.

27. Egyptian Preparatory Committee, *Report of the Egyptian NGOs,* 28. See also World Bank, *Social Indicators of Development,* 103.

28. For details on the extension of Egypt's health insurance to cover all schoolchildren (Law 99 of 1992), see Nansakumar, Reich, Chawla, Berman, and Yip, "Health Reform for Children," 155–170.

29. Chiffoleau, "Le désengagement," 87. See also Egyptian Preparatory Committee, *Report of the Egyptian NGOs,* 28.

30. There are also traditional practitioners such as midwives and barbers, although they are legally banned.

31. Chiffoleau, "Le désengagement," 94–95.

32. Ibrahim, *An Assessment of Grassroots Participation,* 45–46, 64, 66, 113–115. Welfare PVOs constitute 74.5 percent of all Egyptian PVOs. Many CDAs were established by (or taken over by) the government during the Nasser era and were staffed and funded directly by the government with a view, at least from the government's point of view, toward implementing the state's development program.

33. According to Ibrahim, MOSA estimates the number of community-based PVOs in 1990 at 12,832 plus an additional 160 national PVOs with branches in various governorates. Ibrahim, *An Assessment of Grassroots Participation,* 62. Researchers Amani Kandil and Sarah Ben Nefissa put the number of voluntary associations at 11,313. Amani Kandil and Sarah Ben Nefissa, *Civil Associations in Egypt* (Cairo, Egypt: Al-Ahram Center for Political and Strategic Studies, 1994), 91, 111.

34. Ibrahim, *An Assessment of Grassroots Participation,* 64–65. According to Ibrahim, 74.5 percent of all PVOs are welfare organizations and the remaining 25.5 percent are CDAs. According to MOSA, in 1991, 3,453 of Egypt's 12,832 associations (PVOs and CDAs) were located in Cairo (65). The majority are in urban areas, with the largest number in Cairo.

35. Ibrahim, *An Assessment of Grassroots Participation,* 69–70, 113–114. Based on an in-depth study of 40 PVOs as well as interviews with MOSA, Ibrahim's study estimates that the total number of beneficiaries from all PVOs in 1992 was approximately 5.5 million citizens.

36. Statistics on Islamic associations and their clinics must be treated with caution. Sarah Ben Nefissa-Paris notes that there are a variety of sources from which one may obtain statistics on PVOs in Egypt and that each of them varies in the numbers they provide and what criteria and typology the researchers used (and they are often unspecified). In addition, many registered associations are not actually functioning. Ben Nefissa-Paris, "Le mouvement associatif," 23, 34. See also Kandil and Ben Nefissa, *Civil Associations in Egypt,* 87–90.

37. Ibrahim, *An Assessment of Grassroots Participation,* 52, 66–67. The greatest increase in the number of PVOs appears to have occurred in the 1970s and 1980s after Sadat's reintroduction of the multiparty elections and the process of democratization. Moheb Zaki's study of Egyptian civil society notes that the steepest increase took place in the first three years after the political opening created by Sadat's reintroduction of the multiparty system in 1976. Moheb Zaki, *Civil Society and Democratization in Egypt, 1981–1994* (Cairo, Egypt: Konrad-Adenauer Stiftung and the Ibn Khaldoun Center, 1995), 58–60. This is confirmed by Ibrahim's study, which states that the steepest rate of increase occurred in the first three years following the political opening in 1976. Ibrahim, *An Assessment of Grassroots Participation,* 62. According to Sarah Ben Nefissa-Paris, 3,165 associations were created in the 1970s, 31 percent of which were Islamic; in the 1980s, 3,946 associations were established, 34 percent of which were Islamic. Ben Nefissa-Paris, "Le mouvement associatif," 27. Ben Nefissa-Paris defines Islamic associations by name (whether or not the name contained a reference to Islam) and location (whether or not it was beside a mosque). See page 24 for more details. This increase also indicates the significant impact of Egypt's political and eco-

nomic liberalization and of Sadat's and Mubarak's historic compromise (albeit for different reasons) with the country's Islamic activists. In contrast to Nasser before him, Sadat made Islam central to his personal and political image. He encouraged Islamic groups and activities in an effort to counteract the popularity of Nasserite groups. Muslim Brothers were released from jail, Islamic presses flourished, and Islamic student groups soon came to dominate university campuses. According to Carrie Rosefsky Wickham, these processes furthermore coincided with the influx of oil money—money that came into private, not state, hands—which put excess money in the pockets of Egyptians to donate to Islamic institutions. Between 1973 (and the OPEC crisis) and 1985, an estimated 2.7 million Egyptian migrants worked outside the country. Carrie Rosefksy Wickham, "Political Mobilization under Authoritarian Rule: Explaining Islamic Activism in Mubarak's Egypt" (Ph.D. diss., Princeton University, 1996), 440–441. Despite the crackdown after Sadat's assassination, Mubarak continued the policy of liberalization throughout the 1980s as part of his intensified efforts at political liberalization and state disengagement from the economy. The leading political idea throughout the 1980s was that of self-help as Mubarak attempted to alter public opinion and expectations about the role of the state in society and the economy.

38. Kandil also notes that the greatest number of Islamic associations are in Upper Egypt. In Ibrahim, *An Assessment of Grassroots Participation,* 67.

39. Ibid. In their 1994 study, Kandil and Ben Nefissa record the number of Islamic PVOs in Egypt as 2,996. Kandil and Ben Nefissa, *Civil Associations in Egypt,* 111, 117. They state the number Islamic PVOs in Cairo as 476 out of a total of 2,976 Islamic PVOs. On page 115, they list the percentage of Islamic PVOs in Cairo as 21.43 percent.

40. Soheir Morsy, "Islamic Clinics in Egypt: The Cultural Elaboration of Biomedical Hegemony," *Medical Anthropology Quarterly* 2, no. 4 (December 1988): 356. Hammady's unpublished survey, however, found that there were 241 voluntary associations offering medical services in Cairo, 91 of which were Islamic. In Sylvia Chiffoleau, "Les Formes de la Prise en Charge Médicale en Égypte," in *Médecins et Protections Sociale dans le Monde Arabe,* ed. Brigitte Curmi and Sylvia Chiffoleau (Beirut and Jordan: Centre d'Études de Recherches sur le Moyen-Orient Contemporain and the Institut Français de Recherche Scientifique en Cooperation pour le Developpement, 1993), 126.

41. Ibrahim, *An Assessment of Grassroots Participation,* 81. The majority of viable PVOs are active in the field of social welfare. Such PVOs are mainly active in the areas of health care, child care, and family planning (75–76).

42. Al-Jam'iya al-Shar'iya is one of the oldest Islamic associations and is one of the largest, best-organized, and most centralized. It was originally founded in 1912 by Shaykh Khattab al-Sobky (1858–1933). Hammady, "Religious Medical Clinics," 34.

43. Sullivan and Abed-Kotob, *Islam in Contemporary Egypt,* 33–34.

44. Denis Sullivan, "Islam and Development in Egypt," in *Islam, Muslims, and the Modern State,* ed. Hussin Mutalib and Taj ul-Islam Hashmi (New York: St. Martin's Press, 1994), 223.

45. Sarah Ben Nefissa-Paris, "L'état égyptien et le monde associatif," *Egypt/Monde Arabe,* 8 (4ème trimestre, 1991): 111–112.

46. As will be discussed later in this chapter, Law 32 is presently in the process of being eliminated and/or revised.

47. Excerpts from a report published by the Middle East and North Africa Programme of the Lawyers Committee for Human Rights and the Egyptian Organization for Human Rights, December 1991, "Restricting the Human Rights Movement in Egypt: Legal Restrictions on Independent Non-Governmental Organizations," *Civil Society* 5 (May 1992): 6. See also Ben Nefissa-Paris, "L'état égyptien," 118.

48. Middle East and North Africa Programme of the Lawyers Committee for Human Rights and the Egyptian Organization for Human Rights, "Restricting the Human Rights Movement," 6. See also Ben Nefissa-Paris, "L'état égyptien," 118.

49. Ben Nefissa-Paris, "Le mouvement associatif," 21.

50. Saad Eddin Ibrahim, "Egyptian Law 32 of 1964 on Egypt's PVOs and PFs: A Critical Analysis, 1994" (unpublished paper, page 3 of Executive Summary, Ibn Khaldoun Center for Development Studies, Cairo); for more details, see pages 17–19.

51. Ibid., 23–25.

52. Ibid., 24, 48.

53. Ibid., 48–49.

54. Kandil and Ben Nefissa, *Civil Associations in Egypt,* 273; see also Ibrahim, *An Assessment of Grassroots Participation,* 60–61 for a discussion of Islamic public-interest PVOs.

55. Middle East and North Africa Programme of the Lawyers Committee for Human Rights and the Egyptian Organization for Human Rights, "Restricting Human Rights Movement," 7–8.

56. Ibrahim, "Egyptian Law 32 of 1964," 53.

57. Many PVOs, including ISIs, avoid getting certain types of registrations because MOSA's regulations often serve to suffocate PVOs. Many PVOs are also opting for registering as civil or professional companies instead of registering as PVOs and falling under the control of Law 32. As companies, they are liable to taxation on their revenues, but they feel that taxation is preferable to the arbitrariness of Law 32 and MOSA bureaucrats. Human-rights PVOs also often choose to register as legal practices as opposed to registering with MOSA. Many donors are willing to fund civil companies, and OXFAM encourages PVOs of all types to register as companies.

58. Cassandra, "Impending Crisis," 21.

59. In 1984, Islamists won seven out of twenty-five seats in the national doctors' syndicate, and since 1988 Islamists have consistently won the majority of seats. Alain Roussillon, "Entre Al-Jihad et Al-Rayyan: Phénoménologie de l'Islamisme Égyptien," *Modernisation et mobilisation sociale, Égypte-Brésil, Dossier du CEDEJ* (1991): 51.

60. Mustafa K. al-Sayyid, "A Civil Society in Egypt?" in *Civil Society in the Middle East,* ed. Augustus Richard Norton (Leiden: E. J. Brill, 1995), 1: 285–286; see also al-Sayyid, "Egypt: Parliament Pushes Union Law Through," *Civil Society* 15 (March 1993): 3–7.

61. Cassandra, "Impending Crisis," 16. See also Ibrahim, "Electoral Politics in Egypt," 6.

62. Ibrahim, "Electoral Politics in Egypt," 6, 129.

63. Ben Nefissa-Paris, "Le mouvement associatif," 31–32;and "L'état égyptien," 119.

64. Middle East and North Africa Programme of the Lawyers Committee for Human Rights and the Egyptian Organization for Human Rights, "Restricting Human Rights Movement," 7.

65. MOSA argued that deregulating Law 32 or loosening its grip over PVOs would only serve the interests of Islamic extremists, who would then be able to establish PVOs as covers for illegal activities against the government and the state. Ibrahim, "Law 32 of 1964," 57. This fear was well exemplified by MOSA's reaction to the October 12, 1992, earthquake in Cairo and to the success of ISIs at addressing the needs of its victims. When ISIs were on site helping the survivors (the majority of whom were poor) well before MOSA or any other association, MOSA officials issued a ban on all PVOs dispensing aid directly to the earthquake victims. Instead, all aid was to be channelled through MOSA and/or the Egyptian Red Crescent. See also Ibrahim, *Cairo Papers in Social Science,* vol. 19, no. 3, *An Assessment of Grass Roots Participation in the Development of Egypt* (Cairo, Egypt: The American University in Cairo Press, 1997), 53.

66. "The Year in Review: Rigged Elections, Terrorism and Stagnant Peace Process," *Civil Society* 7, no. 73 (January 1998): 11.

67. Andrew Tabler, "Another Year on the Civil Society Treadmill," *Cairo Times,* June 8–14, 2000, 10.

68. In his study of grassroots participation in Egypt, Ibrahim notes that over 50 percent of NGOs and CDAs began as informal initiatives. Ibrahim, *An Assessment of Grassroots Participation,* 27. The typical process of founding and recruiting starts with a small group of citizens from the community. Out of thirty-five PVOs on which data was available, ten (29 percent) started with fewer than ten people, and another seventeen (49 percent) began with fewer than fifty. About 80 percent of the PVOs under investigation were each initiated by fewer than fifty people (104–105).

69. Kandil and Ben Nefissa confirm this observation. In their 1994 study, they state that the key reason for the financial success of certain Al-Jam'iyya al-Islamiya in general is that they position themselves in areas where large portions of the population are holders of higher degrees and in places where there is an excess of money to be redistributed. Kandil and Ben Nefissa, *Civil Associations in Egypt,* 281.

70. As stated above, Islamic clinics are most highly concentrated in neighborhoods with large numbers of Christians and church-based clinics.

71. Ibrahim, *An Assessment of Grassroots Participation,* 75–76, 28.

72. Ibid., 105.

73. Ibid., 87–98, 97, 117. Quote on page 117. In eighteen out of thirty-five (51 percent) of PVOs Ibrahim studied, founders did not exceed twenty-five people. In four cases, the number of founders was over 100.

74. Denis Sullivan, *Private Voluntary Organization in Egypt* (Gainesville: University Press of Florida, 1994), 23.

75. Diane Singerman, *Avenues of Participation: Family, Politics, and Networks in Urban Quarters of Cairo* (Princeton, N.J.: Princeton University Press, 1995), 253–254. A recent study on the Cairo neighborhood of Manshiet Nasser confirms that "there is a polity and a long tradition of communities reaching into and mobilizing one or another government institution of their behalf." Belgin Tekce, Linda Oldham, and Frederic C. Shorter, *A Place to Live: Families and Child Health in a Cairo Neighborhood* (Cairo, Egypt: The American University in Cairo Press, 1994), 34. Even the lower classes have connections and networks, based on family, friends, army service, and mosques, that are located at different levels of the bureaucracy. Community members use these connections to facilitate the provision of services, such as clinics, for their neighborhoods.

76. Robert J. Latowsky, "Financial Profile of Egypt's PVO Sector, June 1994" (unpublished paper 33, The World Bank, Washington, D.C.), 33.

77. See Ibrahim, *An Assessment of Grassroots Participation,* 51–52.

78. Hammady states that religious medical clinics are regularly able to overcome bureaucratic handicaps such as getting various licenses through informal relations such as family members and the support of various state officials. Hammady, "Religious Medical Clinics," 232.

79. Wickham, "Political Mobilization under Authoritarian Rule," 475–476.

80. Zubaida, "Islam, the State and Democracy," 7. Civil servants may also act independently on informal and formal (private) affiliations, such as prior ties of kinship or acquaintance or perhaps mutual economic interest or ideological commitment, and contradict their prescribed roles as public servants. As one Egyptian development worker exclaimed to Sullivan: "It is not the *government* which is controlling society, but *government officials.*" Sullivan, *Private Voluntary Organizations,* 44. Similarly, Wickham argues that as a result of low barriers to entry, minimal socialization, and low pay, state employees are more likely to retain, and potentially act upon, private interests and orientations; at the same time, the weakness of internal monitoring and enforcement mechanisms has limited the regime's ability to identify and sanction such behavior. Wickham, "Political Mobilization under Authoritarian Rule," 475.

81. Singerman, *Avenues of Participation,* 254; Ibrahim, *An Assessment of Grassroots Participation,* 109–110. Ibrahim notes a large discrepancy in amounts of annual revenues

among PVOs. He notes that based on 1991 figures, the annual revenue of PVOs may vary from those that have annual revenue of under 5,000 LE (approximately $1,500 US at the time) to over 1 million LE (approximately $300,00 US).

82. Ibrahim, *An Assessment of Grassroots Participation,* 73, 112, 74–76, 109. Ibrahim also notes that PVOs in Cairo have much larger resources than those elsewhere and that their major source of income is the sale of services. Quoting estimates from the Central Agency for Public Mobilization and Statistics, Ibrahim states that in 1991 (domestic) donations to PVOs were approximately LE 3 million, most of which went to organizations providing charity as opposed to CDAs (76). MOSA confirms that nearly half of Egyptian PVOS receive income solely from dues and donations (74).

83. Ibrahim, *An Assessment of Grassroots Participation,* 110, 74–76. USAID is the largest foreign donor. See also Sullivan, *Private Voluntary Organizations,* 27, 31–32.

84. Latowsky uses a simplified version of MOSA categories. See Latowsky, "Egypt's PVO Sector," 7.

85. Latowsky, "Egypt's PVO Sector," 26.

86. Ibrahim, *An Assessment of Grassroots Participation,* 67. In 1991, Coptic associations constituted approximately 9 percent of all PVOs.

87. Article 17 of the By-Laws (Presidential Decree 932 of 1966) exempts religious PVOs from the need for such permission, "so long as donations are collected within places of worship, in boxes or plates during religious functions, and for the purpose of spending it on its own activities." Thus, religious PVOs can collect funds throughout the year without a permit. For Christian Copts this can be once a week on Sunday, for Muslims it can be five times daily. Ibid., 52–53. Taxation provides another example of state policies at cross-purposes. On the one hand, the state has tried to encourage self-help initiatives by raising the ceiling on tax deductions on donations from 3 to 7 percent in 1980. On the other hand, the state removed previously accorded tax breaks for imported equipment after 1986 and reductions for water and electricity. Ben Nefissa-Paris, "Le mouvement associatif," 22. See also *Al-Wafd,* April 12, 1987.

88. Many reports indicate that Islamic PVOs receive illegal funding from abroad, yet without proof these reports are mere speculation. Zaki, *Civil Society and Democratization in Egypt,* 63.

89. Ibrahim, *An Assessment of Grassroots Participation,* 106–107.

90. Hammady, "Religious Medical Clinics," 96–97. Hammady also notes that most physicians were introduced to the medical centers in question through personal connections—mainly through colleagues or friends.

91. Hammady states that doctors in the Mustafa Mahmoud medical facilities receive 25 percent of the total value of their diagnostic tickets (the tickets each patient must purchase from the administration according to the value of the necessary services) in addition to their salaries. Alternatively, they are allowed to see their own private patients (during specific hours) at the Mahmoud clinic. Ibid., 224.

92. In general, medical students had reservations about the adequacy of their education. Several said that their education was sufficient for general practice, indicating that additional education would be necessary if they wanted to specialize. Many students complained of the lack of practical experience because of insufficient facilities and the large number of students. Some doctors felt that their professors were not the most highly qualified people to teach at the university because it pays poorly and is unable to keep top doctors. The classrooms are also crowded. El-Mehairy, *Medical Doctors,* 67. El-Mehairy notes that 88 percent of her respondents indicated a desire for additional education and/or training. A Ministry of Health survey revealed that doctors were very frustrated with the bureaucracy with which they had to deal. Doctors also cited the fact that they were dissatisfied with their salaries, so much so that they either give up medicine, are regularly absent, or start charging for medicine (68, 88–89).

93. Chiffoleau, "Itinéraires médicaux," 529. In 1995 it cost approximately 10,000 LE to equip a medical practice/private office.

94. An estimated 70 percent of Egyptian doctors are under 35 years of age. Only 25 percent are in private practice while the overwhelming majority of the rest are employees of the Ministry of Health. Sami Zubaida, "Religion, State, and Democracy: Contrasting Conceptions of Society in Egypt," in *Political Islam: Essays from Middle East Report,* ed. Joel Beinin and Joe Stork (New York: I. B. Tauris, 1977), 58. Furthermore, only 8 percent, predominantly university professors and specialists, have lucrative private practices. Alain Roussillon, "Entre Al-Jihad et Al-Rayyan: Phénoménologie de l'Islamisme Égyptien," 51–52. See also *al-Sha'b,* July 29, 1986.

95. Chiffoleau, "Le désengagement," 97.

96. Ibid.

97. Chiffoleau, "Itinéraires médicaux," 522.

98. Chiffoleau, "Le désengagement," 95. Fergani cites the average annual salary for a doctor in 1988 as 2,507 LE and notes that this number conceals the bipolarization of the profession. Nader Fergani, "Médecins et ingenieurs sur le marché du travail en Égypte," *Maghreb-Machrek* 146 (October–December 1994): 45.

99. In December 1988, the Islamist leadership of the Medical Syndicate conducted a survey of nearly 250,000 doctors in twelve governorates and found that nearly two-thirds stated that their salaries were not enough to cover their living costs. Carrie Rosefsky Wickham, "Islamic Mobilization and Political Change: The Islamist Trend in Egypt's Professional Associations," in *Political Islam: Essays from Middle East Report,* ed. Joel Beinin and Joe Stork (New York: I. B. Tauris, 1977), 123.

100. Hammady confirms that religious medical centers offer supplementary employment for the majority of doctors. Most work in a variety of private and public hospitals as well. Hammady, "Religious Medical Clinics," 98.

101. Chiffoleau, "Itinéraires médicaux," 519–521.

102. Ibid., 519, 521. Between 1970 and 1980, approximately 20,000 doctors left to work abroad, predominantly in the Gulf (527).

103. This is indirectly confirmed by Nandakumar, Chawla, and Khan, whose extensive study of outpatient care in Egypt indicates that Egyptians' preference for private practice over public practitioners is exacerbated by the government's policy of allowing the doctors it employs to simultaneously open a private practice. As a consequence, doctors spend less time in their government jobs as their private practice grows. Nandakumar, Chawla, and Khan, "Utilization of Outpatient Care in Egypt," 194. Hammady confirms that doctors prefer religious medical clinics because there is less bureaucracy and because they are able to practice in their areas of specialization. Hammady, "Religious Medical Clinics," 124.

104. Sullivan and Abed-Kotob, *Islam in Contemporary Egypt,* 33. Hammady's study of religious medical clinics in Cairo confirms this lack of religious motivation for working in the clinics. She found that aside from the relatively good secondary income that they receive (most doctors work full-time in a hospital during the day), the majority of interviewees expressed their positive opinion of the different medical centers in question because of the good teamwork and the friendly atmosphere that prevails among all staff members. Others reported that they preferred the clinic because of the convenient schedules and the convenient location of settings. Hammady, "Religious Medical Clinics," 102–103. The majority of nurses, according to Hammady, preferred their center because of its good schedule and because they lived nearby (106, 108). Both Morsy and Wickham note the importance of a second income to doctors/employees who work in Islamic clinics and associations. Morsy, "Islamic Clinics in Egypt," 362; Wickham, "Political Mobilization under Authoritarian Rule," 529.

105. Having stated that the clinics provide an important source of income to doctors, it is important to note that this does not necessarily reflect a strong loyalty to the clinics (how-

ever, the doctors generally show strong loyalty and dedication to the patients in these clinics). There are no contracts regulating the working relationship between the doctors and the associations. This is because the majority of doctors work on a part-time basis in the clinics, and the associations are not obliged by law to formalize the working relationship. Hence doctors do not have the legal right to any promotions regardless of their academic qualifications or seniority. Doctors can also be fired without warning or compensation. Many doctors independently interviewed by Hammady and myself were frustrated by their low wages even as the clinics where they work became increasingly more successful and/or charged more. On the other hand, the lack of a contract allows doctors to leave when they wish. Younger doctors appreciated this when they needed to write their exams. Hammady, "Religious Medical Clinics," 223–224. See also *Al-Wafd,* April 12, 1992.

106. This happens in government hospitals as well as in Islamic clinics. El-Mehairy, *Medical Doctors,* 89.

107. Ibrahim, *An Assessment of Grassroots Participation,* 69.

108. Ibid.

109. Inge Arends, "Egyptian NGOs," in *Women and Development in the Middle East: Perspectives of Arab NGOs and Project Participants,* ed. Inge Arends (Amsterdam: Middle East Research Associates, 1995), 37.

110. Despite this, in a limited number of clinics, the fee is waived for certain members of lower socioeconomic groups so that the association can have broader representation across classes.

111. These estimates of the size or quality of clinics are imprecise and are based largely on impressions; however, it is interesting to note that a World Bank study found that the PVO sector as a whole is dominated by weak low-income PVOs. Only 65 percent of registered PVOs are active and are community oriented, and of these, 25 percent are very weak and, in many cases, active only part-time. Twenty-seven percent have limited success as providers of one to two small but regular services and one to two minor, periodic activities. Latowsky, "Egypt's PVO Sector," 32. At the other end of the scale, 5 percent have one to four major service programs, expansive facilities, and institutionalized relationships to the local community. These are strong and active organizations with full-time programs and administrative support staff (33).

112. This number decreases to approximately 15–20 percent for the medium-sized clinics and decreases to close to 0 percent for the larger wealthier clinics.

113. Louise G. White, "Urban Community Organizations and Local Government: Exploring Relationships and Roles," *Public Administration and Political Development* 6, no. 93 (1986): 243–244.

114. Timothy Mitchell, "Dreamland," *Middle East Report* 210 (Spring 1999): 32.

115. Islamist doctors argue that male doctors are allowed to examine a female patient. The segregation of the sexes is preferred but not required in a professional medical capacity.

116. Many Egyptians I interviewed also commented that they assumed an Islamic clinic would be for Muslims only. I found that no clinics I visited had a "Muslims only" policy. None of the clinics I or my research assistants visited had Christians on staff, although one did mention a former Christian doctor. However, many clinics receive Christian patients, and in some clinics the percentage of Christian patients can reach as high as 35 percent. *Al-Ahram,* April 4, 1990.

117. Nandakumar, Chawla, and Khan, "Utilization of Outpatient Care in Egypt," 193, 195. The researchers surmise that the low rate of those seeking health care must be due to cost and lack of access. This survey does not into account take the number and availability of Islamic clinics.

118. Tekce, Oldham, and Shorter, *A Place to Live,* 50–52, 153. These statistics varied slightly depending on the age and sex of the patient.

119. Evelyn Early and Nayra Atiya (see below) both conducted their fieldwork in the early 1980s, prior to the intense privatization of medicine in Egypt. However, while folk medicine has declined as a proportion of medical care, it is still thriving. See Sonbol, *Creation of a Medical Profession in Egypt,* 3.

120. Evelyn A. Early, "Fertility and Fate: Medical Practices among Baladi Women in Cairo," in *Everyday Life in the Muslim Middle East,* ed. Donna Lee Brown and Evelyn A. Early (Bloomington: Indiana University Press, 1993), 104.

121. Evelyn A. Early, "Catharsis and Creation: The Everyday Narratives of Baladi Women of Cairo," *Anthropological Quarterly* 58, no. 4 (October 1985): 176.

122. Evelyn A. Early, "The Logic of Well Being: Therapeutic Narratives in Cairo, Egypt," *Social Science Medicine* 16 (1982): 1493–1494. In another case, a mother took her son to a clinic, then to the hospital, then to a Christian clinic, and then to another clinic. "Catharsis and Creation," 174; and, "Logic of Well Being," 1494.

123. Nayra Atiya, *Khul Khaal: Five Egyptian Women Tell Their Stories* (London: Virago Press, 1988), 55–57. Similarly, Dunya visits Farouk Hospital (government), a doctor in a private clinic, and a government hospital in Abassiyya (124–127). And Om Naeema, who cannot conceive, relies on a variety of folk prescriptions and visits numerous doctors, Qasr al-Aini hospital, and a local religious *shaykh* (153–158).

124. The answers of respondents are listed in terms of the answers received most frequently to the answers received least frequently. Respondents could give unlimited responses.

125. It must be noted that in the majority of cases, doctors are not in their associations' general assemblies or on their boards of directors. This is due both to the part-time (and often temporary) nature of most doctors' employment and the fact that the doctors are too busy for such extra responsibilities. They are, however, regularly consulted by their boards of directors on various technical and budgetary priorities.

126. Larger wealthier clinics are not without their problems. The Islamic Association of Huda and Noor, located in Giza, provides an extreme (and relatively rare) example of corruption. In 1991, the president of the board of directors of the Association was arrested for embezzling money from a fund established to help devout Muslims make the pilgrimage to Mecca. He stole over 100,000 LE and put the money in accounts under the names of his children. Sullivan and Abed-Kotob, *Islam in Contemporary Egypt,* 35. See also Sullivan, "Islam and Development," 224–225.

127. The fact that the poor turn to numerous forms of health care appears to confirm research elsewhere that the poor have neither the time to socially invest in these networks nor the economic security to place all their eggs in one Islamic basket. Survival dictates that the poor employ numerous and broad-based strategies which include using state, Islamic, and other sources of social welfare services such as food, medicine, clothing, and training. See, for example, Homa Hoodfar, *Between Marriage and the Market: Intimate Politics and Survival in Cairo* (Berkeley: University of California Press, 1997); Nadia Khouri-Dagher, "The State, Urban Households, and the Management of Daily Life: Food and Social Order in Cairo," in *Development, Change and Gender in Cairo,* ed. Diane Singerman and Homa Hoodfar (Bloomington: Indiana University Press, 1996), 110–133; James Scott, *Weapons of the Weak* (New Haven, Conn.: Yale University Press, 1985); Singerman, *Avenues of Participation;* and Tekce, Oldham, and Shorter, *A Place to Live.*

3. THE ISLAMIC CENTER CHARITY SOCIETY IN JORDAN

1. The director explained that there was no senior school for girls because the public school for girls was a good one. The ICCS felt that a senior school was needed for boys to

provide an environment without some of the bad influences, such as smoking, they would be exposed to at the public school.

2. The center used to have a medical clinic, but it was closed because it was difficult to keep prices down and because there are sufficient medical options, particularly a large government-run hospital, available in the region.

3. ICCS, *ICCS Executive Council Report for 1997.*

4. These fees ranged from $168 to $225 US, and the transportation fees ranged from $77 to $105 US.

5. ICCS Mafraq, interview with the author, Mafraq, Jordan, December 15, 1998.

6. For in-depth detail on Islamists' objections to the state-run education system, see Anne Sofie Roald, *Tarbiya: Education and Politics in Islamic Movements in Jordan and Malaysia* (Stockholm: Almquist and Wiksell, 1994), 172; and Marion Boulby, *The Muslim Brotherhood and the Kings of Jordan, 1945–1993* (Atlanta, Ga.: Scholars Press, 1999), 84–85.

7. The Islamic Hospital in Amman has a Fund for the Sick and Poor that subsidizes the medical costs of designated groups.

8. Laurie A. Brand, *Jordan's Inter-Arab Relations: The Political Economy of Alliance Making* (New York: Columbia University Press, 1994), 2, 277.

9. Boulby, *Muslim Brotherhood and the Kings of Jordan,* 74.

10. For an in-depth discussion of the founding of the Brotherhood in Jordan, see Boulby, *Muslim Brotherhood and the Kings of Jordan;* Shmuel Bar, *The Muslim Brotherhood in Jordan* (Tel Aviv: Tel Aviv University and The Moshe Dayan Center for Middle Eastern and African Studies, 1998), 10–11; and Ali Abdul Kazem, "The Historic Background of the Muslim Brotherhood and Its Ideological Origins," in *Islamic Movements in Jordan,* ed. Hani Hourani (Amman, Jordan: Al-Urdun al-Jadid Research Center and the Friedrich Ebert Stiftung, 1997), 13–46.

11. The first branch was established in Palestine in 1934. Hanna Freij and Leonard Robinson, "Liberalization, the Islamists, and the Stability of the Arab State: Jordan as a Case Study," *Muslim World* 96, no. 1 (January 1996): 5–6.

12. Hani Hourani, Taleb Awad, Hamed Dabbas, and Sa'eda Kilani, *Islamic Action Front Party* (Amman, Jordan: Al-Urdun al-Jadid Research Center, 1993), 9.

13. Boulby, *Muslim Brotherhood and the Kings of Jordan,* 45–47, 49.

14. Ibid., 37–38, 50–58, 103. First quote on 50–51; second quote on 51, quoting Manfred Halpern, *Politics of Social Change in the Middle East and North Africa* (Princeton, N.J.: Princeton University Press, 1963), 56.

15. Boulby, *Muslim Brotherhood and the Kings of Jordan,* 38–39. See also Abdel Kazem, "The Historic Background of the Muslim Brotherhood," 26–30. Kazem notes that the Jordanian Brotherhood ideology was very similar to that of the Egyptian Muslim Brotherhood and that of Hassan al-Banna.

16. Hourani, Awad, Dabbas, and Sa'eda, *Islamic Action Front Party,* 11.

17. From 1957 to 1989, the Brotherhood was the sole legal nongovernmental (and quasi-political) social organization after the suspension of multiparty competition.

18. For greater details, see Boulby, *Muslim Brotherhood and the Kings of Jordan,* 88.

19. A *waqf* (pl. *awqaf*) is a religious endowment, often in the form of land. The revenues of the *waqf* are to be used for charitable or religious purposes.

20. Hourani, Awad, Dabbas, and Sa'eda, *Islamic Action Front Party,* 12. For a list of influential Brothers who were once in the Ministry of Education, see 13–14.

21. Bar, *Muslim Brotherhood in Jordan,* 32. For more information on the cooperative relationship between the Jordanian regime and the Brotherhood, see Quintan Wiktorowicz, *The Management of Islamic Activism: Salafis, the Muslim Brotherhood, and State Power in Jordan* (Albany: State University of New York Press, 2001), 95–101.

22. Glenn E. Robinson, "Can Islamists Be Democrats? The Case of Jordan," *Middle East Journal* 51, no. 3 (Summer 1997): 381.

23. Waleed Hammad, "Islamists and Charitable Work," in *Islamic Movements in Jordan,* ed. Hani Hourani (Amman, Jordan: Al-Urdun al-Jadid Research Center, 1997), 169. Two hundred million JD is approximately $288 million US.

24. For details on the IMF riots and the introduction of democratic elections, see Freij and Robinson, "Liberalization, the Islamists, and the Stability of the Arab State"; Rex Brynen, "Economic Crisis and Post-Rentier Democratization in the Arab World," *Canadian Journal of Political Science* 25, no. 1 (March 1992): 69–97; Curtis R. Ryan, "Peace, Bread and Riots: Jordan and the International Monetary Fund," *Middle East Policy* 6, no. 2 (Oct. 1998): 55–57, 60; Katherine Rath, "The Process of Democratization in Jordan," *Middle Eastern Studies* 30, no. 3 (July 1994): 535–536; and Glenn E. Robinson, "Defensive Democratization in Jordan," *International Journal of Middle East Studies* 30, no. 3 (August 1998): 387–410.

25. Robinson, "Can Islamists Be Democrats?" 374. The number of seats won by the Islamists almost equaled the number won by the regime's loyalists—mostly Bedouins, rural tribal leaders, and former government officials—and greatly outnumbered the combined eleven seats won by leftist and liberal candidates. Freij and Robinson, "Liberalization, the Islamists, and the Stability of the Arab State," 10.

26. Boulby, *Muslim Brotherhood and the Kings of Jordan,* 73. The advantage of the Brothers was strengthened by the very short campaign period of twenty-five days—a period too short for other candidates to fill the gap. Furthermore, the Brothers fielded only a limited number of candidates (thirty); this ultimately meant that they were more organized and disciplined than many of the secular parties, who fielded as many as 700 candidates from other secular groups. Linda Shull Adams, "Political Liberalization in Jordan: An Analysis of the State's Relationship with the Muslim Brotherhood," *Journal of Church and State* 38, no. 3 (Summer 1996): 511. See also Malik Mufti, "Elite Bargains and the Onset of Political Liberalization in Jordan," *Comparative Political Studies* 32, no. 1 (February 1999): 110.

27. Boulby, *Muslim Brotherhood and the Kings of Jordan,* 104.

28. For more details, see Lawrence Tal, "Dealing with Radical Islam: The Case of Jordan," *Survival* 37, no. 3 (Autumn 1995): 139–156; and Freij and Robinson, "Liberalization, the Islamists, and the Stability of the Arab State."

29. Robinson, "Can Islamists Be Democrats?" 377.

30. Boulby, *Muslim Brotherhood and the Kings of Jordan,* 149–150.

31. Mufti, "Elite Bargains," 120.

32. In Arabic, *sawt wahid.* In addition, the distribution of electoral seats in the Chamber of Deputies favors pro-regime constituencies. Seats are allocated according to regime interests, not population size. Areas with large numbers of Palestinians are granted relatively few seats compared with those areas with Bedouin tribes. The government introduced the new electoral law before the 1993 elections. See Quintan Wiktorowicz, "The Limits of Democracy in the Middle East: The Case of Jordan," *Middle East Journal* 53, no. 4 (Autumn 1999): 619.

33. Overall, the law was viewed across the political spectrum as a conscious effort by the regime to reduce the number of seats won by Islamists in the next Parliament—due largely, but not solely, to their uncompromising stance against peace negotiations with Israel. See Bar, *Muslim Brotherhood in Jordan,* 43; Robinson, "Can Islamists Be Democrats?" 383; Boulby, *Muslim Brotherhood and the Kings of Jordan,* 138; Ibrahim Gharaibeh, "The Political Performance and the Organization of the Muslim Brotherhood," in *Islamic Movements in Jordan,* ed. Hani Hourani (Amman, Jordan: Al-Urdun al-Jadid Research Center and the Friedrich Ebert Stiftung, 1997), 51–52; and Laurie A. Brand, *Women, The State, and Political Liberalization: Middle Eastern and North African Experiences* (New York: Columbia University Press, 1998), 112–113. However, in post-election discussion and analy-

sis, many IAF members also pointed to reasons above and beyond the new electoral law as contributory factors to the Party's loss of parliamentary seats; in particular, the Muslim Brotherhood representatives' performance in Parliament between 1989 and 1993. For example, the Muslim Brotherhood sought to pass several pieces of legislation that did not have widespread public support. Much of this proposed legislation focused on issues of segregation and women's rights, including a ban on male hairdressers in women's beauty salons and an attempt to prevent fathers from attending sports events in which their daughters participated. As Mufti states, the Brotherhood went too far with what was considered by many Jordanians to be petty legislation instead of dealing with more pressing issues concerning the economy, for example. Gharaibeh argues that the Brothers quite simply failed to introduce any new visions or proposals for solving the country's problems (50–51). While the Brotherhood was vocal in highlighting Jordan's economic and political woes, it did little to advance solutions or policies. Despite its intense criticism of the unemployment problem in Jordan, it had no specific suggestion, much less a program, to deal with the issue. Boulby, *Muslim Brotherhood and the Kings of Jordan*, 123, 150–151. Additionally, the Muslim Brotherhood's hard-line approach toward Israel (rejection of peace and the demand for Israel's dismantlement) was not embraced by most Jordanians. Although criticism of Israel remains strong, one opinion poll showed that more than 70 percent of the population supported negotiations with Israel. The Islamists' intransigence on the issue seemed to hurt them at the polls. Brotherhood support of Saddam Hussein during the Gulf War further hurt the Party deeply—when Hussein lost so decisively, the Brotherhood partook of his failure as well. In fact, mosque attendance dropped significantly during the months following Iraq's defeat. Mufti, "Elite Bargains," 117–118. The Brotherhood also was regularly outmaneuvered by the monarchy through vetoes, the absence of Brotherhood representation in cabinet reshufflings, the firing of cabinet members, and ultimately the suspension of Parliament, thus contributing to the public image that the Brotherhood is as impotent as any other political party. By 1993, many analysts argued, the Brothers had squandered their unsullied political image. Boulby, *Muslim Brotherhood and the Kings of Jordan*, 116, 153–154. See also Laurie Brand, "'In the Beginning was the State . . . ': The Quest for Civil Society in Jordan," in *Civil Society in the Middle East*, ed. Augustus Richard Norton (Leiden: E. J. Brill, 1995), 1: 165. Quoting the director of the Center for Strategic Studies at Jordan University, Brand states that after the 1993 elections the Brotherhood was no longer viewed as the "Party of God" as it had been prior to serving in the government. Similarly, Robinson notes that while the Brotherhood still enjoyed a strong core of support in society, just under 25 percent (according to a survey conducted by the Center for Strategic Studies in 1993), the aura that surrounded it in 1989 had been somewhat dispelled by its members' less-than-impressive performance in Parliament, especially from January to June 1991, when it held several cabinet posts. Once in Parliament, a pattern was established whereby the Islamist parliamentarians would raise an issue only to be turned back by the king or by the successive prime ministers appointed by the king. Robinson, "Can Islamists Be Democrats?" 375. To a large extent, this seeming neglect of middle-class economic and political demands is a result of inexperience and interparty disputes between factions about the Party's understanding of *how* Islam should be implemented in society. See Janine A. Clark and Jillian Schwedler, "Who Opened the Window? Women's Activism in Islamist Parties," *Comparative Politics* (forthcoming).

34. However, a polarization emerged between those IAF members who felt that participation in the elections was necessary and those who supported the boycott. The split went so deep that six Islamists broke from the IAF and ran as independents in the 1997 elections. Robinson, "Defensive Democratization," 404.

35. Al-Urdun al-Jadid Research Center, "Jordan's Parliamentary Elections: Facts and Figures," unpublished report, Al-Urdun al-Jadid Research Center, Amman, Jordan, November 24, 1998.

36. Zaid Ayadat, "The Islamic Movement and Political Participation," in *Islamic Movements in Jordan,* ed. Hani Hourani (Amman, Jordan: Al-Urdun al-Jadid Research Center, 1997), 158.

37. Al-Urdun al-Jadid Research Center, interview with the author, Amman, Jordan, November 24, 1998.

38. Ibid. Based on a study carried out by the Public Opinion Poll Unit at the Center for Strategic Studies at the University of Jordan, Moaddel confirms that IAF supporters tend to be educated, they tend to have a professional-class background, and they are more likely to be married than the general population. Mansoor Moaddel, *Jordanian Exceptionalism: A Comparative Analysis of State-Religion Relationships in Egypt, Iran, Jordan, and Syria* (New York: Palgrave, 2002), 121–122.

39. Quoting a study conducted by the Center for Strategic Studies at the University of Jordan, Moaddel states that Palestinians in Jordan either tend to support the IAF or to remain politically noncommittal. Approximately 40 percent of IAF supporters are Palestinian. Approximately 27 percent of supporters of other parties are Palestinian; Moaddel, *Jordanian Exceptionalism,* 117, 119. In addition, Palestinians dominate the leadership of the IAF. There are a variety of reasons for the dominance of Palestinians in the Brotherhood. Boulby notes that the weakening of the Palestine Liberation Organization when it was ousted from Jordan in the early 1970s worked to the advantage of the Brothers; Boulby, *Muslim Brotherhood and the Kings of Jordan,* 92–95. Similarly, Robinson notes that the Palestinians in Jordan have no other party besides the IAF to represent their interests; Robinson, "Defensive Democratization," 400.

40. Musa Shteiwi, "Class Structure and Inequality in the City of Amman," in *Amman: The City and Its Society,* ed. J. Hannoyer and S. Shami (Beirut and Amman: Centre d'Études et de Recherches sur le Moyen-Orient Contemporain, 1996), 408–409, 414, 419–420.

41. Rula Majdalani, "The Changing Role of NGO's [*sic*] in Jordan: An Emerging Actor in Development," *Jordanies* 2, no. 12 (1996): 121.

42. Jocelyn DeJong, "The Urban Context of Health during Economic Crisis," in *Amman: The City and Its Society,* ed. J. Hannoyer and S. Shami (Beirut and Amman: Centre d'Études et de Recherches sur le Moyen-Orient Contemporain, 1996), 271–272.

43. General Union of Voluntary Societies, *A History of Projects Programs* (Amman, Jordan: General Union of Voluntary Services, General Union of Voluntary Societies, 1996), 1. In 1958 there were ninety NGOs, including those in the West Bank.

44. General Union of Voluntary Services, interview with the author, September 13, 1998. Until August 1987, GUVS's statistics included the West Bank.

45. Wiktorowicz, *Management of Islamic Activism,* 23.

46. General Union of Voluntary Societies, *Executive Council Report: The Financial and Administrative Report for 1997; Estimate Budget for 1998* (Amman, Jordan: GUVS, 1997), 91, 92, 94.

47. The law was originally established in 1933 and was revised in 1956 and in 1965. It reached its present form in 1966. In its essence, Law 33 is very similar in its procedures, regulations and restrictions to Egypt's Law 32.

48. For details, see Wiktorowicz, *Management of Islamic Activism,* 26–33.

49. GUVS is the "NGO of all NGOs." It is a state-created umbrella NGO to which all other charitable NGOs must belong. GUVS was formed in 1958 (its creation was mandated by law in 1956), ostensibly to coordinate the activities of NGOs and enhance their performance. GUVS collects accurate statistical data on all charitable NGOs in the country and provides financial assistance to NGOs. It provides approximately 30 percent of all investments (through infrastructure, services, subsidies, and donations) made by charitable NGOs in Jordan, most of which is raised through donations and a lottery run by GUVS. At

the same time, GUVS is itself an NGO with its own activities and must abide by the rules of the Ministry of Social Development. It is run by an executive council elected by the National Assembly. NGO representatives from the various governorate unions constitute the membership of the National Assembly. All NGOs must belong to their respective local/governorate union and thus have representation in the General Assembly of GUVS. NGOs are able to use this mechanism to bring their interests to the attention of the Ministry of Social Development. In this manner, GUVS acts as an intermediary and spokesperson for NGOs. Most important, however, GUVS, through this same hierarchical system, is an arm of state control and effectively regulates NGO activities. It does so through its collection of statistical data, its role in the registration process, and its surveillance of NGOs. Its financial role plays an important part in the regulation of NGOs. See Wiktorowicz, *Management of Islamic Activism,* 33–36.

50. Ibid., 28.

51. Ibid., 84. For a description of the various ISIs, see Hamed Dabbas, "Islamic Organizations and Societies in Jordan," in *Islamic Movements in Jordan,* ed. Hani Hourani (Amman, Jordan: Al-Urdun al-Jadid Research Center, 1997), 195–162.

52. Wiktorowicz, *Management of Islamic Activism,* 84–85.

53. Hammad, "Islamists and Charitable Work," 182. These figures do not include the revenues and expenditures of the Fund for the Sick and Poor or the revenues and expenditures of the Islamic Hospital.

54. In an interview, one Islamist complained that Islamists do not do any real development work, only charity. This is partially due, he argued, to the fact that the middle class has a different mentality than the poor and does not know the needs of the poor or how to meet them. Ibrahim Gharaibeh, interview with the author, Amman, Jordan, September 27, 1998.

55. Hammad, "Islamists and Charitable Work," 191, 214.

56. Ibid., 214.

57. Brand, "'In the Beginning,'" 164; Wiktorowicz, *Management of Islamic Activism,* 104.

58. Brand, "'In the Beginning,'" 164.

59. Wiktorowicz also found a general lack of coordination. Wiktorowicz, *Management of Islamic Activism,* 91–92.

60. In her study of Islamic NGOs in Palestine, Sara Roy found that Islamic NGOs are very competitive and territorial and that there appears to be very little collaboration and few partnerships among them. Islamic NGOs compete for limited funding for social, community, and development projects. The common, and perhaps only, form of cooperation was the sharing of information about people applying for relief in order to avoid a duplication of benefits. In general, one institution did not know what another was doing. Sara Roy, "The Transformation of Islamic NGOs in Palestine," *Middle East Report* 214 (Spring 2000): 26.

61. ICCS, *ICCS Executive Council Report for 1997.*

62. ICCS, *ICCS 1998 Agenda.* (A daytime planner for public distribution with data regarding the ICCS. One of the many ICCS public-relations publications.)

63. Islamic schools follow the government curriculum (by law), but while the state-run schools have three religious classes per week, Dar al-Arqam has four. General Director, Dar al-Arqam Amman, interview with the author, Amman, Jordan, September 22, 1998.

64. Roald, *Tarbiya,* 173.

65. ICCS, *ICCS Executive Council Report for 1997.*

66. List of services for 1998 provided to me during an interview with the director. Ali al-Hawamdeh, General Director, Islamic Hospital, interview with the author, Amman, Jordan, October 10, 1998. See also the Islamic Hospital brochures.

67. E-mail communication from the medical director, Islamic Hospital, July 18, 2001.

68. Islamic Hospital, *The Islamic Hospital, Amman-Jordan: A Philanthropic Model of Health Promotion in Jordan* (Amman, Jordan: Islamic Hospital, 1998). Hospital brochure in English.

69. See Hammad, "Islamists and Charitable Work," 171. The second ICCS hospital, which was built in Aqaba in 1992, is significantly smaller than the one in Amman; it has approximately forty beds and cares for between 300 and 400 patients per month. The hospital also has an outpatient clinic that serves 900 to 1,000 patients per month. It offers all basic services, such as internal medicine; general surgery; pediatrics; obstetrics and gynecology; orthopedic surgery; urology; otology; laryngology; rhinology; radiology; and anesthesiology. It also has a well-equipped coronary care unit; 24-hour emergency services; 24-hour pharmacy services; three operating rooms; and 24-hour laboratory services. Specialists such as neurologists, however, are only in Amman. As one of a limited number of hospitals serving the entire south, the hospital serves an important need in the region. General Director, Islamic Hospital, interview with the author, Aqaba, Jordan, December 1, 1998. See Islamic Hospital, *The Islamic Hospital.*

70. Roald, *Tarbiya,* 206–207.

71. Wiktorowicz, *Management of Islamic Activism,* 103.

72. ICCS, *ICCS 1998 Agenda.* See also the ICCS 1998 pocket calendar entitled *ICCS: 33 Years of Giving.*

73. ICCS, *ICCS Executive Council Report for 1997.*

74. ICCS, *ICCS 1998 Agenda;* ICCS, *ICCS: 33 Years of Giving.*

75. ICCS, *ICCS Executive Council Report for 1997.*

76. Although located in Zarqa, the College does not technically belong to the Zarqa branch of the ICCS but to the central headquarters.

77. Islamic Community College, interview with the author, Zarqa, Jordan, November 25, 1998.

78. ICCS, *ICCS Executive Council Report for 1997.*

79. Ibid. Outside the city, but still in the governorate of Zarqa, there are six additional centers.

80. Director, Merkaz Mahqat Sweilah, interview with the author, Amman, Jordan, November 24, 1998.

81. Merkaz Mahqat Sweilah helped eighty-nine orphans and eleven poor families in 1997. ICCS, *ICCS Executive Council Report for 1997.*

82. Director, ICCS Baqa'a camp, interview with the author, December 7, 1998. See also ICCS, *ICCS Executive Council Report for 1997.*

83. The center offers tutoring to children and classes in sewing for women. It also offers seasonal events and services, such as assistance with home repair, religious feasts, and various day trips for children. The center has seventeen employees, including its medical staff.

84. Merkaz Nusayba was established shortly after the Gulf War and is located on the outskirts of Zarqa in a newly developed area. It has two main goals. The first is to increase the role of women economically within society and within the family. The second is to provide charity for needy families. The center offers a variety of programs for women, including sewing, Qur'an-singing, hair-salon lessons, handwork and crafts, and sports (there is a sports hall in the basement). These programs and courses require fees and are therefore self-sustaining. In 1998, there were fifteen students taking courses (eight in sewing and seven in Qur'an-singing); in total, the center has seventy-four graduates. It also offers lectures on issues such as health care and child care. Director, ICCS Merkaz Nusayba, interview with the author, Zarqa, Jordan, November 21, 1998; and fax from Director, ICCS Merkaz Zarqa Headquarters, December 12, 1998.

85. Ramadan is the month of fasting required by all Muslims to commemorate the first revelation of the Qur'an. It is a time of heightened religious reflection and charity.

86. Wiktorowicz, *Management of Islamic Activism,* 86–87.

87. ICCS, *ICCS 1998 Agenda.*

88. World Bank, Population and Human Resources Operations Division, Country Department II, Middle East and North Africa Region, *Hashemite Kingdom of Jordan: Poverty Assessment,* vol. 1, *Main Report,* Report no. 12675-JO (Washington, D.C.: World Bank, 1994), 13.

89. Wiktorowicz, *Management of Islamic Activism,* 86.

90. Hammad, "Islamists and Charitable Work," 173, 176–180. See also ICCS, *ICCS Executive Council Report for 1997.*

91. ICCS, *ICCS Executive Council Report for 1997.* In the year 2000, the number of inpatients rose to 33,251 and the number of outpatients to 166,613. E-mail communication from the medical director, Islamic Hospital, July 18, 2001.

92. Director General, Islamic Hospital, interview with the author, Amman, Jordan, October 10, 1998; ICCS, *ICCS Executive Council Report for 1997.*

93. The Farah Hospital is considered to be the finest in the country; its prices are substantially more than 200 JD for a delivery.

94. The government also runs a variety of other hospitals catering to different constituencies. The University Hospital is a public hospital with some of the finest equipment and teaching facilities. It charges 180 JD for a delivery and overnight stay. Similarly, the Medical City Center, a hospital established for military families, is 150 JD. The Jordan Hospital, which is also considered to be "five star" hospital, comparable to the Islamic Hospital, charges 200 JD for similar services. DeJong found the same discrepancy in prices. De-Jong, "The Urban Context of Health during Economic Crisis," 278.

95. Approximately 50 percent of the Islamic Hospital's work is done for companies and educational facilities—that is, patients with health insurance through their employers. The other 50 percent is done with individual families. Approximately 20 percent of the families are patients from abroad, primarily from Yemen, Egypt, Turkey, and Kuwait. Islamic Hospital, interview with the author, Amman, Jordan, October 10, 1998.

96. This practice takes place at many, but not all, of the private hospitals in Jordan.

97. DeJong, "The Urban Context of Health during Economic Crisis," 277. The figure of 32 percent excludes Palestinians in camps who are covered by United Nations Relief and Works Agency (UNRWA) services—although the UNRWA health facilities are few in number and are overcrowded.

98. World Bank, *Poverty Assessment,* 113–114.

99. Ibid, 12, 167. For a discussion of the different methods for measuring poverty in Jordan, see pages 8–12. The health expenditures are based on a Employment, Unemployment, Returnees and Poverty Survey (EURPS) conducted by the Jordanian Department of Statistics in 1991. The figure of 15.88 JD was calculated based on the total expenditures of Jordan's lowest quintile, which spends 294 JD or less per capita per year (13). An earlier survey, the Income and Expenditure Survey (IES), conducted in 1986–1987 by the Department of Statistics, found that the medical expenditures of the lowest 16 percent of the population was 1.5 percent of expenditures, which translates into 3.5 JD per capita per year (191).

100. UNDP, *Human Development Report 2000* (New York: United Nations Development Programme, 2000), 169.

101. E-mail communication from medical director, Islamic Hospital, July 18, 2001.

102. ICCS, *ICCS Executive Council Report for 1997.* This amount rose to approximately 4.5 million JD in 2002. The current annual budget of the Fund is 300,000 JD. Ra'if Nijim, former director of the Fund for the Sick and Poor, interview with Rana Taha, Amman, Jordan, August 10, 2002.

103. For smaller bills, qualifying patients receive a subsidy of a maximum of 25 percent of the total costs; for larger bills, patients are granted a maximum 10 percent subsidy. Ra'if Nijim, former director of the Fund for the Sick and Poor, interview with Rana Taha, Amman, Jordan, August 10, 2002.

104. Ibid.

105. Hammad, "Islamists and Charitable Work,"171.

106. The Brotherhood first began discussing the creation of a charitable hospital in the late 1960s. The original plan was to establish a hospital that would charge little to no fees; one based entirely on donations. It original name was to have been The Grand Charitable Islamic Hospital. A German charitable organization provided the plans and drawings for the hospital for free—the cost of which was valued at 70,000 JD at the time. This generosity was supposedly inspired after members of the organization viewed the appalling conditions of Palestinians in the refugee camps. Donations for the operating costs of the hospital were raised throughout the Arab world. As the opening of the hospital approached in the late 1970s, it became clear that the annual operating budget of the hospital would run at approximately 10 million JD—all of which was based on donations. The ICCS therefore decided to register and open the hospital as a nonprofit hospital and to change the name to The Islamic Hospital. All the revenues must be invested back into the hospital. The hospital does not pay taxes. Ra'if Nijim, former director of the Fund for the Sick and Poor, interview with Rana Taha, Amman, Jordan, August 10, 2002. Also Qandil Shaker, current director of the ICCS, interview with Rana Taha, Amman, Jordan, July 30, 2002; and Ali al-Hawamdeh, founder and general director of the Islamic Hospital, interview with Rana Taha, Amman, Jordan, July 28, 2002.

107. ICCS, *ICCS Executive Council Report for 1997.*

108. Ibid.

109. Ibid.

110. Ibid. In 1997, the ICCS also gave out seventeen scholarships, unrelated to economic status, for boys who excelled at Qur'an memorization. The total cost to the ICCS for the scholarships for the poor and scholarships for multiple siblings (families receive discounts if multiple children attend the ICCS schools) was 40,000 JD in 1997.

111. World Bank, *Poverty Assessment,* 167. The education expenditures are based on EURPS. According to EURPS, the annual per-capita expenditures of the lowest quintile on education are 6.8 percent of expenditures. Using the total expenditures of Jordan's lowest quintile (294 JD or less per capita per year), we arrive at a figure of 19.99 JD per person per year for education. The IES records the education expenditures of the lowest 16 percent of the population as 0.8 percent of expenditures, which translates into 1.9 JD per capita per year (191)

112. Roald, *Tarbiya,* 173.

113. General Director, Dar al-Arqam, interview with the author, Amman, Jordan, September 22, 1998.

114. Interview with Rana Taha, Amman, Jordan, September 18, 2001.

115. ICCS, *ICCS Executive Council Report for 1997.*

116. Director, ICCS Zarqa, fax to author, December 12, 1998.

117. Wiktorowicz, *Management of Islamic Activism,* 107–108. Confirmed in Ra'if Nijim, former director of the Fund for the Sick and Poor, interview with Rana Taha, Amman, Jordan, August 10, 2002.

118. Roald, *Tarbiya,* 173.

119. The dentist explained to me that the biggest challenge he faces is that of educating the public about oral hygiene and care. Many patients, he stated, only go to the dentist when they are in pain and then demand that the tooth simply be removed. He often faces the dilemma of whether or not to remove a relatively healthy tooth when he knows that if he refuses the patient will go elsewhere to have the extraction.

120. *Al-Ra'y,* August 15, 2001; *Al-Arab al-Youm,* July 8, 2001. According to a 2001 Social Survey conducted by the Jordanian government, the government considers the poverty line to be 190 JD in expenditures for a family of six individuals. This is a family that owns its own home and does not pay rent.

121. World Bank, *Poverty Assessment,* 167. This data is based on a 1991 EURPS survey. The 1986/1997 IES survey states that the lowest 16 percent of the population spends 51.4 percent of their expenditures, or 118.2 JD per capita per year, on food (191).

122. The average Jordanian family spends 2,149.70 JD a year on food, beverages, and tobacco. This translates to 179.14 JD per month—an amount well above the 50 JD a lucky family may receive. These figures obviously do not include rent, clothing, schooling, or medical expenses. According to the Jordanian Department of Statistics, the average total of all expenses per household is 4,850.10 JD per year, or 404.18 JD per month.

123. While it is difficult to tell, since these cutoff marks are different at each ICCS center, it appears that the cutoff mark has lowered in recent years. Although unconfirmed, this appears to be due to the fact that the ICCS is receiving fewer donations from Palestinians and Jordanians living in the Gulf and because there are growing numbers of poor in Jordan.

124. Wiktorowicz, *Management of Islamic Activism,* 65, 67.

125. Recent allegations of corruption at the Islamic Hospital must certainly be aggravating this perception that the hospital is "un-Islamic." Several prominent managers of the Islamic Hospital, all of whom are Muslim Brothers, were dismissed by the Hospital and the ICCS. Ibrahim Gharaibeh, interview with Rana Taha, Amman, Jordan, July 22, 2002; Qandil Shaker, current director of the ICCS, interview with Rana Taha, Amman, Jordan, July 30, 2002; Ali el-Hawamdeh, founder of the Islamic Hospital and general director, interview with Rana Taha, Amman, Jordan, July 28, 2002. Ra'if Nijim attributed the problems to the patronage problem. While it is beyond the scope of this study, the expulsion of the managers, who were "hawks" (those who take a less compromising stance about cooperating with the government) within the Brotherhood, is having further repercussions with the Brotherhood itself.

126. This is the second largest number of poor families to be helped by any one center. ICCS, *ICCS Executive Council Report for 1997.*

4. THE ISLAH CHARITABLE SOCIETY IN YEMEN

1. Yemen is a largely segregated society; women cover their heads and often their faces, with the exception of their eyes, in the presence of men to whom they are not closely related.

2. Prior to being a colony, Aden was incorporated into the British Empire under the administration of the Indian government. In order to ensure the city's stability, Britain forged separate treaties with the warring *shayookh* and sultans in Aden's rural hinterland.

3. Carapico argues that civic activism in the two Yemens underwent three periods of political opening during which civil society was able to develop and expand. The first period was in the mid-twentieth century under British rule in colonial Aden. The second period was during the 1970s and early 1980s in North Yemen. The third, and most important, period for the purposes of this book, was in the 1990s, particularly between 1990 and 1994, after the creation of the united Republic of Yemen. See Sheila Carapico, *Civil Society in Yemen: The Political Economy of Activism in Modern Arabia* (Cambridge: Cambridge University Press, 1998), 16.

4. Prior to the creation of the YAR, the north of Yemen had been occupied by Ottoman forces in the seventeenth century and then again in the nineteenth century.

5. Despite the historical presence of religious minorities, north Yemen is almost wholly Muslim. Other than the southern mountains and the Red Sea coastal region where

primarily Shafi (Sunni) Muslims live, the population is largely Zaydi, a branch of Shi'ite Islam. Burrowes states that the Zaydi branch of Shiism is more similar to the rationalist schools of Sunnism than to the mystical millenarian sects that are typical of Shiism. Like Sunnism in general, Zaydi Islamism is an establishment religion, not one born out of defeat and dissent. Robert Burrowes, *The Yemen Arab Republic: The Politics of Development, 1962–1986* (Boulder, Colo.: Westview Press, 1987), 8. With the eventual fall of the imamate and in reaction against it, Zaydi learning became increasingly marginalized; for example, Zaydi boys were increasingly taught in schools to pray in the Sunni style. This marginalization was propagated in the public schools and religious institutes. The curriculum for both—which taught a generic nonsectarian Sunnism—came more or less under the control of Wahhabi neo-Islamists, including prominent members of the future Islah Party, as early as the 1970s. See Paul Dresch, *A History of Modern Yemen* (Cambridge: Cambridge University Press, 2000), 142, 173–174.

6. Much of this activity was subsidized by remittances from Yemenis working abroad in the oil-rich neighboring states.

7. For detailed sources concerning the unification process, see Ursula Braun, "Yemen: Another Case of Unification," *Aussenpolitik* 2, no. 2 (1992): 174–184; Robert D. Burrowes, "Prelude to Unification," *International Journal of Middle East Studies* 23 (1991): 483–506; Carapico, *Civil Society in Yemen*; Charles Dunbar, "The Unification of Yemen," *Middle East Journal* 46, no. 3 (Summer 1992): 456–476; and Joseph Kostiner, *Yemen: Tortuous Quest for Unity 1990–94* (Great Britain: Royal Institute for International Affairs for Chatham House, 1996).

8. Carapico, *Civil Society in Yemen,* 52.

9. Braun, "Yemen: Another Case of Unification," 179; see also Renaud Detalle, "Esquisse d'une sociologie électorale de Sana," in *Sanaa hors les murs,* ed. Gilbert Grandguillaume, Franck Mermier, and Jean-François Troin (Sana'a and Tours, France: Centre Francais d'Études Yémenites and URBAMA, 1995), 73.

10. The Islah Party has roots going back to 1979 with the creation of the Islamic Front (which was originally formed in opposition to groups, including leftists, against the new Republic). The Front was supported by al-Ahmar, who is now leader of the Islah Party. After unification, al-Ahmar, the head of one of Yemen's most powerful tribes, the Hashid, joined forces with Abd al-Majid al-Zindani (a man of deep Wahhabi tendencies and now the supreme religious guide of Islah), to form the Islah Party. Al-Ahmar and al-Zindani have historically shared a deep antipathy for the imamate, particularly for its traditions and religious interpretations that privilege *sayyid* (descendants of the Prophet) aristocrats; they also share an antipathy for socialism. Both have also long been identified as clients of the Saudis and strong supporters of President Salih, under whom they have both prospered economically. See Carapico, *Civil Society in Yemen,* 143–144; and Dresch, *History of Modern Yemen,* 186–187.

11. Falah al-Mdaires, "Political Islamic Movements in Modern Yemen," *Journal of South Asian and Middle Eastern Studies* 14, no. 2 (Winter 2001): 80.

12. Ibid. The Brotherhood stream is under the leadership of Sheikh Abd al-Majid al-Zindani, Abd al-Wahhab al-Anisi, and Abdel al-Aziz Yasen.

13. This third stream is represented by Mohamad Abd al-Wahhab al-Jabbari.

14. Al-Mdaires, "Political Islamic Movements in Modern Yemen," 81.

15. Ibid.

16. Associated Press, 1 May 1997.

17. The war erupted for a number of factors, including the personal animosity between the president and the vice president, failed attempts to merge the two armies; an imbalance in population and economic distribution in the former North's favor, and a large number of political killings and attempts to assassinate YSP leaders. This resulted in Vice President al-Bayd's declaration of secession from the union and the formation of a new

southern state in May 1994. Amy W. Hawthorn and Ronald G. Wolfe, *Pollworker Training and the Parliamentary Elections in Yemen: 1997 Final Report* (Washington, D.C.: International Foundation for Election Systems, 1997), 9.

18. Upon the creation of a new GPC–Hizb al-Islah ruling coalition, Islah immediately called for the revision of the Constitution to make Islamic Law the only source of law and for the introduction of Islamic punishments. Maxine Molyneux, "Women's Rights and Political Contingency: The Case of Yemen, 1990–1994," *Middle East Journal* 49, no. 3 (Summer 1995): 430.

19. Associated Press, 1 May 1997. The GPC increased its seats to 183. The shift was due in part to the elimination of the YSP from the political scene after its defeat in the 1994 civil war, which ironically gradually weakened the political standing of the Islah Party on the political scene. Once the YSP no longer challenged the authority of the northern political elite, President Salih did not need the Islah Party to offset its strength. Thus, by the time of the 1997 elections, the relative influence of the Islah Party in political affairs had dramatically decreased.

20. Statistics from "Yemen Overview," The World Bank. Available online at http://www.worldbank.org.ye. Accessed February 2000.

Broadly speaking, NGOs in Yemen consist of six types: social-welfare associations, friendship societies, unions and syndicates, sports clubs, specialized societies, and cultural or artistic organizations. S. Beatty, A. No'man al-Madhaji, and R. Detalle, *Yemeni NGOs and Quasi-NGOs: Analysis and Directory,* Part I: *Analysis* (Sana'a, Yemen: The Embassy of the Netherlands, 1996), 29, 31. While the number and types of NGOs seem impressive, a close analysis reveals a much more modest picture. The registration of NGOs occurs at the governorate branches of MSA, not at the central ministry. This means that the registration procedure varies from branch to branch, that the collection of data differs, and that MSA has difficulty keeping information up to date. Delays of up to a year may occur before a registration (or a closure) is recorded in the central ministry files. This entails a significant loss in accuracy of NGO numbers, and the actual number of functioning NGOs is unknown. Most observers agree that a large percentage of NGOs are defunct. Associations may split, merge, or cease activities and not inform MSA. Many NGOs do not renew their licenses and operate illegally. Some of the most successful NGOs have been working for years without ever renewing their registration.

21. United Nations Development Programme, *Human Development Report 2000* (New York: UNDP, 2000), 225, 170, 188, 159, 163, 257. These statistics are from 1998.

22. Detalle, "Esquisse d'une sociologie électorale de Sana," 78. See also Yemen Institute for the Development of Democracy, "The Experience of Yemeni Women in the Democratic Elections of April 1993" (unpublished report in Arabic, Sana'a, Yemen Institute for the Development of Democracy), 8; Mohammed al-Mikhlafi, "Inclusion of Women's Issues in the 1997 Electoral Programs" (paper presented in Arabic at the conference Challenges of the 21st Century to Women and Democracy, Women's Candidate Fund, Sana'a, May 27–29, 1997).

23. Helen Lackner, "Women and Development in the Republic of Yemen," in *Gender and Development in the Arab World,* ed. Nabil F. Khoury and Valentine M. Moghadam (Atlantic Highlands, N.J.: Zed Books, 1995), 76–77.

24. Linda Boxberger, "From Two States to One: Women's Lives in the Transformation of Yemen," in *Women in Muslim Societies: Diversity within Unity,* ed. Herbert L. Bodman and Nayereh Tohidi (Boulder, Colo.: Lynne Rienner, 1998), 119.

25. Amat al-Alim as-Suswa, ed., *Democratic Developments in Yemen* (Sana'a, Yemen: Professors World Peace Academy, 1994), 170; Women's National Committee, *National Report on the Status of Women in the Republic of Yemen* (Sana'a, Yemen: Women's National Committee, August 1995), 9. Women were first able to exercise their right to vote in the 1988 GPC elections; however, in these elections they were still unable to run as candidates.

26. Women's National Committee, *National Report,* 10.

27. Deborah Dorman, Ahmed No'man al-Madhaji, Mohammed Aidarus, Sharon Beatty, Zarina Ismael, and Marina de Regt, *Yemeni NGOs and Quasi-NGOs: Analysis and Directory,* Part II, *Directory* (Sana'a, Yemen: The Embassy of the Netherlands, 1996), 82.

28. Sheila Carapico, "Gender and Status Inequalities in Yemen: Honor, Economics, and Politics" (unpublished paper, Richmond, October 1992), 12.

29. Sheila Carapico, "Women and Public Participation in Yemen," in *Arab Women: Between Defiance and Restraint,* ed. Suha Sabbagh (New York: Olive Branch Press, 1996), 62. See also Sheila Carapico, "The Dialectics of Fashion: Gender and Politics in Yemen," in *Women and Power in the Middle East,* ed. Suad Joseph and Susan Slyomovics (Philadelphia: University of Pennsylvania Press, 2001), 183–190. Almost all Islamist women in Yemen wear the *niqab.* However, the majority of Islamist women in Jordan and Egypt do not cover their faces.

30. Five women were nominated to the first Supreme People's Council in 1970, and six women won seats in the first elected SPC in 1978. Helen Lackner, *P.D.R. Yemen: Outpost of Socialist Development in Arabia* (London: Ithaca Press, 1985), 118; Tareq Y. Ismael and Jacqueline S. Ismael, *The People's Democratic Republic of Yemen, Politics, Economics and Society: The Politics of Socialist Transformation* (London: Frances Pinter, 1986), 47, 126. By the time of Yemeni unification in 1990, women held 3 percent of the South's SPC. Women also held seats in the local councils of the governorates.

31. The General Union of Yemeni Women was founded in 1968 and recognized as a mass organization under the direction of the secretary of mass organizations of the Yemeni Socialist Party in 1970.

32. Ismael and Ismael, *The People's Democratic Republic of Yemen,* 55–56.

33. South Yemen boasted female judges, lawyers, doctors, nurses, university professors, teachers, and secretaries. Women worked in state farms, cooperatives, and industries. Ismael and Ismael, *The People's Democratic Republic of Yemen,* 127.

34. Lackner, *P.D.R. Yemen,* 108.

35. Carapico, *Civil Society in Yemen,* 155. See also Sheila Carapico, "Yemen between Civility and Civil War," in *Civil Society in the Middle East,* Part 2, ed. Richard Augustus Norton (Leiden: E. J. Brill, 1996), 310.

36. Individuals are sometimes members of both the Islah Party and the Islah Charitable Society. Sometimes Party members informally ask Society members to coordinate complementary events on the same day or week that the Party is hosting a particular event. While the two are independent of one another, certainly confusion about whether (and accusations that) the Society belongs to the Party is well founded.

37. Dorman et al., *Yemeni NGOs and Quasi-NGOs,* 13. The largest concentrations of poor residents are in the governorates of Sana'a, Taiz, and Ibb, while the highest percentage of total residents that are poor is found in the governorates of Dhamar, al-Baidha, and al-Mahweet.

38. The government is presently considering a change in the laws governing NGOs. NGOs from across Yemen participated in a conference aimed at promoting dialogue on the draft law. *Yemen Times,* May 25, 1998.

39. Law 11 does not specify the form and type that organizations under the scope of its jurisdiction must take, nor does it exclude from its precepts any type of association.

40. Tariq Abu Lahoom is a member of the president's party, the GPC, although he formerly supported the Islah Party.

41. It is a large multistoried building with offices and meeting rooms attached to a mosque near the new campus of Sana'a University.

42. The Society establishes projects and donates items and services to the needy; it does not organize the needy to initiate, contribute to, or create projects or services.

43. Tariq Abu Lahoom, interview with the author, Sana'a, Yemen, March 13, 1996.

44. Data presented at a fund-raising event sponsored by the Women's Committee of the Islah Charitable Society, February 3, 1996.

45. Although the president of the Islah Charitable Society is responsible for deciding where the regional branches of the Society will be located, each branch chooses the activities it feels are most necessary in its respective community. The Hodeidah branch is one of the largest branches, with ten employees and nineteen permanent volunteers (and far more temporary volunteers). It focuses on six primary activities: 1) support in the form of allowances, clothing, and food to orphans; 2) meals and clothing to the poor during the month of Ramadan; 3) two health care centers for the poor located in the slum areas of Salakhana and Al Baidha; 4) mass marriages; 5) lectures and activities for poor women and girls; and 6) a private school and day care center. The Hodeidah branch of the Society supports approximately 1,200 orphans and hopes to add another 400 orphans to the list of recipients (an orphan is defined as a child without a father). Representatives from the Society visit poorer neighborhoods in order to identify orphans and widows in need of help. Those eligible families receive 700 to 800 Yemeni riyal (YR) each month. The Society is also in the process of building both a third health care center (providing free services to the poor) and a hospital. Medicine is bought from the budget of the NGO as well as from the city of Hodeidah's Health Department. Marina de Regt, "Yemen NGOs: Perspectives on Women and Development," in *Women and Development in the Middle East: Perspectives of Arab NGOs and Project Participants,* ed. Inge Arends (Amsterdam: Middle East Research Associates, 1995), 109. The Hodeidah branch collects its funds and food mainly from local merchants who support the work of the Society. In addition, it receives income from the private school and day care center it runs.

46. Recently, an official from the government's Social Fund for Development visited the Society's five literacy centers in Hodeidah's poor areas. According to researcher Marina de Regt, the official was extremely impressed by the organization and activities of the centers and the number of women being taught. The official decided to finance the purchase of chairs and desks on the condition that the classes move from open spaces into proper rooms with roofs. In addition, the Fund found a literacy teacher in order to train the cadre of instructors at the centers in functional literacy. Director, Women's Committee of the Islah Charity Society, interview with Marina de Regt, Hodeidah, Yemen, April 22, 2002.

47. Dorman et al., *Yemeni NGOs and Quasi-NGOs,* 12.

48. At this hospital, there is a concerted attempt to have an all-female staff.

49. The biggest challenge facing the Society is its ability to better reach remote and rural areas of the country.

50. Director, Women's Committee of the Islah Charity Society, interview with the author, Hodeidah, Yemen, October 26, 1998.

51. As stated in the Society's leaflets and brochures, the Neighborhood Activities Committee establishes assistance centers through which it collects donations and assists the needy in designated neighborhoods. The Special Projects Committee engages in projects that do not fall under the purview of the other committees. For example, it plans to initiate local credit systems whereby the poor can establish their own income-generating projects. The Orphanage Care and Sponsorship Committee supports orphanages and provides monthly allowances to identified orphans. The Basic Health Services Committee runs primary health care centers and food distribution centers, particularly in rural areas. It also established Yemen's first hospital for mentally ill women. The Emergency Relief Committee primarily devotes its energies to assisting emigrant returnees from the Gulf War region with their housing, clothing, and food crises. The Women's Committee responds to the needs of women by working jointly with the other committees and by running centers for women and children where they can learn reading, writing, and sewing skills.

52. A relative of Shaykh al-Ahmar, speaker of the House and head of Hizb al-Islah, funded the building.

53. The area, which was built for workers at the port, is called Medinat al-Umal. It borders Hay al-Tigari, a commercial area in Hodeidah dominated by affluent families. In the past few years more and more wealthier families have moved to Medinat al-Umal and are building villas there. The new center is essentially a large hangar bought and donated to the Women's Committee by one of Hodeidah's largest merchants and a Member of Parliament for the GPC, Abdelgalil Thabet. Impressed by the women's work, he decided to personally support them. The new center replaces the old, and substantially smaller, center that had been located in a popular (*sha'abi*) part of Hodeidah on the second floor of an old building. The old center was closed in 2002 when the Women's Center completed its move to the new location.

54. Director, Islah Charitable Society Women's Committee, Central Headquarters, interview with the author, Sana'a, Yemen, March 16, 1996. Interestingly, in an interview with researcher Marina de Regt, the director of the Women's Committee in Hodeidah noted that the Committee decided to operate more independently from the central headquarters because the work was becoming increasingly routine for the men and the men suffered from what the women perceived to be a lack of commitment and activity. Previously, the Women's Committee contributed the donations they received toward the support of 1,500 orphans who were registered with the male-run central headquarters; now they independently support thirty-five orphans who are registered with the Women's Committee alone. Director, Women's Committee of the Islah Charity Society, interview with Marina de Regt, Hodeidah, Yemen, April 22, 2002. I noted this same attitude toward the male-dominated headquarters of the Islah Charitable Society among the women in Sana'a.

55. The event was by invitation only and was a relatively elegant affair; most of the women wore evening dresses. The evening was loosely modeled along the lines of a Western fund-raising event. Entertainment and food were provided, and an appeal was made for donations, with one donation reaching as much as 20,000 YR (two or three times the monthly salary of a junior civil servant).

56. Most activities conducted in the headquarters are held in the late afternoon and early evening when poorer women are available (except for day care services for children). In Sana'a, at the time of the interview, there were approximately sixty women enrolled in sewing classes and twenty students participating in the handicraft workshop.

57. One of the center's most exciting projects is its Braille lessons for blind girls. While various NGOs in Sana'a offer programs for the blind, this is the only option for blind girls in Hodeidah. Because of a lack of transportation, the center presently has only five students. However, the Society hopes to raise the funds to purchase a bus and to build separate facilities for the blind in the vacant plot of land adjacent to the center. Many of the courses offered at the center are intensive and are only available in the summer, when teachers and pupils are free. Other programs, such as sewing, are offered throughout the year during the evenings. I personally did not see any students when visiting the centers and cannot verify how large any of these classes are or how regularly they are held.

58. The sewing machines were purchased by the Women's Committee with funds donated by three prominent merchants in Sana'a.

59. At the time of the interview, a large number of well-made children's school uniforms were waiting to be sold.

60. A junior civil servant with a university degree earns approximately 8,000 YR per month. The average house rent in Sana'a is a minimum of 5,000 YR per month, although it can easily be 9,000 YR per month. Electricity, water, and telephone bills cost around 1,500 YR each month. Daily transportation to and from work costs about 1,200 YR per month. Food for the average family costs approximately 15,000 YR, for a monthly total of approximately four times his official salary. When other expenses, such as medical costs, are factored in, the average civil servant needs about 32,000 YR each month to cover the minimum living expenses. Families who want to lead a middle-class life (owning a car, decently

clothing their children, sending their children to school) in Sana'a need the salaries of two full-time civil servants as well as evening jobs to cover their costs. *Yemen Times,* 8 December 1997 and 24 August 1998; Dresch, *History of Modern Yemen,* 206.

61. De Regt, "Yemen NGOs," 109.

62. Sheila Carapico, "Gender and Status Inequalities in Yemen: Honor, Economics and Politics," in *Trajectories of Patriarchy and Development,* ed. Valentine Moghadam (Oxford: Clarendon Press, 1996), 81–83.

63. Ismael and Ismael, *The People's Democratic Republic of Yemen,* 126.

64. Mouna Hashem, "The Role and Status of Women in Social and Economic Development in the Yemen Arab Republic" (report prepared for the United States Agency for International Development, Yemen, January 1990), 30–31.

65. UNDP, *Human Development Report 2000,* 257.

66. Much of the women's work is done on an ad hoc basis and addresses needs as they arise.

67. In some *nadawat,* passages are read from a learned scholar's book and then discussed. In other cases, a speaker (female) is brought in to talk or "preach" on a religious topic. *Nadawat* vary in the level and amount of discussion.

68. Women over the age of 40 are the exception rather than the rule.

69. This is not to say that uneducated or poorer women never attend. Occasionally, poorer women from various charity events might be encouraged by someone in the Society to come to a *nadwa* as a way to learn more about Islam.

70. Organizationally, the Party is composed of the Majlis al-Shura (the Supreme Board), the secretariat general (the judicial apparatus of the organization), and the councils and apparatuses of the local organizational or executive units. The secretariat general consists of nine executive bodies or departments: political, mobilization and recruitment, information and propaganda, education and culture, economics, social affairs, labor unions and organizations, financial and administrative affairs, and planning, statistics, and research. The Party structure is replicated in local units at various administrative levels throughout the country: at the capital and provincial level, in provincial capitals and their districts, and in villages, neighborhoods, and wards. The departmental divisions within the Party as a whole are present within the Women's Sector. Therefore, the women technically have their own representatives in social and political affairs and economic and budgetary matters. In this organizational sense, women in Hizb al-Islah are independent. At the regional level, the segregation is less pronounced. In Taiz, the Party operates far more informally. This is due to the distance from Sana'a, the lack of funds and, as a consequence, the reduced number of activities. The women in the Taiz branch generally conduct activities with the men, in addition to a few specific activities geared toward women, such as religious lectures.

71. In 1998, the General Assembly voted in favor of allowing women to be on the Majlis al-Shura. Seven women were nominated, and all seven were then voted onto the Majlis. The decision to nominate the seven women to the Majlis al-Shura surprised most observers, including Yemenis. When the Party was first founded, it strongly opposed women's rights to act in politics. This view was forcefully expounded by many of the female members of the Party. During united Yemen's first elections in 1993, voices within Islah questioned whether it was acceptable for women to vote because they would have to reveal their faces to a stranger to be photographed for their voter registration card. (According to some interpretations of Islam, notably the Wahhabi interpretation that is strongly supported by Shaykh Abd al-Majid al-Zindani, women should be seen only by their husbands and immediate family.) Aware of the potentially pivotal role female voters might play in the elections, various Islah officials urged the Party's (elected) supreme spiritual leader, al-Zindani, to issue a *fatwa* (a religious opinion issued by a learned religious scholar) stating that it was acceptable for women to be photographed in order to vote. The need to mobilize voters and win seats to enable the Party to realize its goals, they argued, far outweighed other concerns.

Zindani eventually did issue a *fatwa*, though he emphasized the religious obligation of women to be obedient to their husbands (and, presumably, to vote for their husband's choice of candidates). In 1993 as well as in 1997, the Islah Party was one of the few parties in Yemen that forbade its female members from running. Various reasons were put forth, notably the idea that since women cannot occupy any position superior to that of a man, female parliamentarians are necessarily unacceptable. Many women within Islah defended the ban, arguing that since Yemeni society was not ready for female leadership, premature candidacy would actually hinder women's struggle for a greater voice. Consequently, Islamist women have never been represented in parliament. The Party, however, has never opposed women's role in public life in general, as long as it is limited to "gender-appropriate" fields, such as charity work. The decision to nominate women to the Majlis al-Shura came as a result of strategic concerns, ideological differences within the Party, and interparty tensions over the loss of seats in the 1997 national elections. See Janine A. Clark and Jillian Schwedler, "Who Opened the Window? Women's Struggle for Voice within Islamist Political Parties," in *Comparative Politics* (forthcoming).

72. Women are bused to the voting centers if they need transportation. The main Party, not the Women's Sector, pays for the buses; however, the women organize and help with the busing.

73. Socializing in northern Yemen is to a large extent conducted during the late afternoon and early evening during *qat*-chewing sessions and other forms of get-togethers such as tea parties or *nadawat*. (*Qat* is a mildly narcotic shrub that is legally chewed in social gatherings for its stimulating effects.) However, as women have more household and child-rearing duties than men, they cannot chew *qat* for as long or as often as men can (and more women than men are opposed to *qat*-chewing).

74. *Nadawat* are very popular on university campuses, particularly in the dormitories. Islahi women come to the dorms on a regular basis and the word is spread to the students that a *nadwa* will be held at a specific time. Some of these are relatively spontaneous; others are conducted at a routine time and place. Special *nadawat* are also organized and announced ahead of time in honor of specific events and often draw large numbers. It is far less common for a speaker to attend a *qat*-chew. While hosting *nadawat* at the university enables the SMO to target large numbers of women, sending speakers to homes to talk at *nadawat* or *qat*-chews enables the Women's Sector to target or select women with education, professional skills, financial resources, and personal contacts. Since the 1997 elections, women within the Party have focused more and more on attracting women with resources and, most important, personal ties. In interviews with members of the Women's Sector, Party women indicated that the primary lesson they learned from the electoral losses of 1997 was the need to target women with wide-ranging and influential personal ties in terms of prospective members and possible suppliers of resources. Interviews with female members of the Islah Party, November 1998.

75. At the *nadawat* and lectures within the university and at the headquarters of the Women's Sector of the Islah Party, Islahi women rarely mention the Party directly (with the exception of during election times). Rather, they focus on Islam as the proper and comprehensive path. Educating women about Islam, regardless of whether or not they become Party members, is in itself a useful strategy. By doing so, Party members are creating a sympathetic environment in which Islah's ideas and political ascent are made more possible. The focus on education furthermore serves to provide access to those women who would normally shy away from political discussion or political work; tribal tradition generally prevents women from entering politics and, given the history of political violence in Yemen, many women are wary of formally joining a party. (Since the 1997 student elections, political activities have been banned at Sana'a University. Since that time, student councils have generally devoted their efforts to assisting students by such activities as selling books at reduced prices.)

76. In Aden, Islahi women are considered to be less educated in the teachings of Islam and less politically aware. Most interviewees also confirm that Islahi women in Aden are generally most fervent. While a discussion of the reasons for these regional differences is beyond the scope of this chapter, to a large degree this is due to the unique history of Aden, in contrast to the history of the North, where Islam was violently suppressed and has now returned with a ferocity. Too young to have been influenced by the former socialist regime in terms of women's rights and consciousness and political awareness, Islahi women in the city of Aden have not had the same opportunities to study Islam as have the women in the North.

77. The relative youth of Islahi women is partially due to the fact that the Party targets younger women. These are the women who are going to be mothers, who are going to be teachers, who are going to influence the next generation. The women's page of the Party's newspaper, *Al-Sahwa,* is written by and primarily directed to an audience of younger women. The women also tend to be the product of the government schools. Until 1997, Islah controlled the Ministry of Education. The curriculum thus reflected an increased emphasis on Islam, and the hiring of principles and teachers often reflected Islah's biases. The religious socialization of these institutions among girls clearly renders them predisposed to *nadawat* and *da'wa.*

78. In Yemen, photocopied versions of Egyptian Islamist Heba Rauf's research on Islam and feminism (University of Cairo) were circulated among Islamist women. Heba Rauf has an M.A. from the University of Cairo and is now a Ph.D. student in England.

79. The degree to which a *nadwa* becomes political is also dependent upon the interests and education of the women in attendance. For example, a discussion concerning cleanliness could potentially evolve into a discussion of health policies and institutions.

80. In her study of Islamist women in Egypt, Soraya Duval notes that Islamic duties such as *nadawat* are deemed by both husband and wife to take precedence over other issues, such as housecleaning. Duval, "New Veils and New Voices: Islamist Women's Groups in Egypt," in *Women and Islamization: Contemporary Dimensions of Discourse on Gender Relations,* ed. Karen Ask and Marit Tjomsland (New York: Berg, 1998), 63.

81. This is not to discount the fact that the religious discussion within a *nadwa* may support one particular understanding of Islam or another. However, strictly speaking, there is a distinction between the act and the ideology.

82. Robert D. Putnam, *Making Democracy Work: Civic Traditions in Modern Italy* (Princeton, N.J.: Princeton University Press, 1993), 173.

83. Dresch, *History of Modern Yemen,* 200.

5. THE SIGNIFICANCE OF BEING MIDDLE CLASS

1. Diane Singerman, *Avenues of Participation: Family, Politics, and Networks in Urban Quarters of Cairo* (Princeton, N.J.: Princeton University Press, 1995), 254.

2. This is confirmed by other research conducted on ISIs. In her study of Islamic NGOs in Palestine, Sara Roy confirms that the managers and staff of Islamic NGOs are typically well educated, highly trained, and professional; many individuals hold advanced degrees from Western universities. Roy, "The Transformation of Islamic NGOs in Palestine," *Middle East Report* 214 (Spring 2000): 26. Similarly, Hale notes that the National Islamic Front in Sudan is middle class, educated, and heavily urban and has developed a culture and an economy to serve that class. Sondra Hale, *Gender Politics in Sudan: Islamism, Socialism, and the State* (Boulder, Colo.: Westview Press, 1996), Chapter 6.

3. Doug McAdam and Ronnelle Paulsen, "Specifying the Relationship between Social Ties and Activism," *American Journal of Sociology* 99, no. 3 (August 1987): 644.

4. Doug McAdam, "Micromobilization Contexts and Recruitment to Activism," in *International Social Movement Research,* vol. 1, *From Structure to Action: Comparing Move-*

ment Participation across Cultures, ed. Bert Klandermans, Hanspeter Kriesi, and Sydney Tarrow (Greenwich, Conn.: JAI Press, 1988), 135.

5. Debra Friedman and Doug McAdam, "Collective Identity and Activism: Networks, Choices, and the Life of a Social Movement," in *Frontiers in Social Movement Theory,* ed. Aldon D. Morris and Carol McClurg Mueller (New Haven, Conn.: Yale University Press, 1992), 161.

6. Catharina Raudvere, "Female Dervishes in Contemporary Istanbul: Between Tradition and Modernity," in *Women and Islamization: Contemporary Dimensions of Discourse on Gender Relations,* ed. Karin Ask and Marit Tjomsland (New York: Berg, 1998), 137.

7. Harik's study of Shiites in Lebanon also found that material rewards played an important role in "luring and securing" participants in Hizballah. Of the 405 respondents in her survey, 63 percent were from the low economic stratum, 28 percent from the middle stratum, and 9 percent from the upper class. When asked about their political preferences, 53 percent of the middle stratum stated that they supported Hizballah. This was the highest percentage of middle-stratum participants for any party, including Amal, the reputed party of the Shiite bourgeoisie. (Among the low and high strata, 47 percent and 44 percent preferred Hizballah, respectively.) Contrary to expectations, many professionals, lawyers, engineers, and teachers are Party members or strong supporters of Hizballah. According to one Hizballah adherent interviewed by Harik, this is due to the fact that this middle stratum does not benefit from the Amal party in any real sense, whereas Hizballah's social and economic projects affect Shiites of all classes. For example, agricultural engineers in Hizballah provide free services to farmers whether they are landowners or tenant farmers. Judith Palmer Harik, "Between Islam and the State: Sources and Implications of Popular Support for Lebanon's Hizballah," *Journal of Conflict Resolution* 40, no. 1 (March 1996): 48 and 55. Similarly, in her study of Palestinian NGOs, Rema Hammami notes that the pay scales of NGOs are higher than professional and semiprofessional salaries in the public sector (particularly the salaries of teachers, social workers, and the police). As she states, NGOs have become desirable workplaces for a new generation of middle-class professionals who view NGO employment as a stepping-stone to more lucrative salaries and prestigious jobs in international companies. Rema Hammami, "Palestinian NGOs Since Oslo: From NGO Politics to Social Movements?" *Middle East Report* 214 (Spring 2000): 27. For examples outside the Middle East, see Rodney Stark and William Sims Bainbridge, "Networks of Faith: Interpersonal Bonds and Recruitment to Cults and Sects," *American Journal of Sociology* 85, no. 6 (1980): 1393–1394.

8. Asef Bayat, "Revolution without Movement, Movement without Revolution: Comparing Islamic Activism in Iran and Egypt," *Society for Comparative Study of Society and History* 40, no. 1 (January 1998): 164.

9. Carrie Rosefsky Wickham, "Interests, Ideas, and Islamist Outreach in Egypt," in *Islamic Activism: A Social Movement Theory Approach,* ed. Quintan Wiktorowicz (Bloomington: Indiana University Press, forthcoming), 268.

10. Interestingly, Munson notes that a key ingredient of the success of the early Muslim Brotherhood in Egypt was that its organizational structure allowed the Brotherhood to tap in to many social beliefs and levels of commitment and did not immediately demand that potential members alter their lifestyles or circumstances. It had a three-tiered membership structure that allowed the organization to incorporate new members with a variety of different beliefs and degrees of commitment. Only at the second tier were ideological responsibilities placed upon members. Potential recruits could therefore commit at their own time and pace. Ziad Munson, "Islamic Mobilization: Social Movement Theory and the Egyptian Muslim Brotherhood," *Sociological Quarterly,* 42, no. 4 (2001): 499–500.

11. In her study on Islamists in Egypt, Wickham observes precisely this type of networking and the development of horizontal linkages between state employees and Islamists based on prior ties of kinship or acquaintance, mutual economic interest, or shared ideo-

logical commitments. Carrie Rosefsky Wickham, "Political Mobilization under Authoritarian Rule: Explaining Islamic Activism in Mubarak's Egypt" (Ph.D. diss., Princeton University, 1996), 475–476. Sullivan also notes that civil servants often independently act on these informal and formal (private) affiliations, often in contradiction to their prescribed roles as public servants. Denis Sullivan, *Private Voluntary Organizations in Egypt* (Gainesville: University Press of Florida, 1994), 44.

12. For information on the Afaf Marriage Society, see Quintan Wiktorowicz and Suha-Taji Farouki, "Islamic NGOs and Muslim Politics: A Case from Jordan," *Third World Quarterly* 21, no. 4 (August 2000): 685–699.

13. 1 JD equaled $1.41 US at the time of the interview (September 2001). The dollar equivalents for the cost of a delivery are $25.38 for the al-Bashir Hospital and $267.90 for the Islamic Hospital (in 2001 dollars).

14. Waleed Hammad, "Islamists and Charitable Work," in *Islamic Movements in Jordan,* ed. Hani Hourani (Amman, Jordan: Al-Urdun al-Jadid Research Center, 1997), 171.

15. In her study of Kuwaiti women's organization, including Islamic organizations, Haya al-Mughni takes this argument one step further. She found that not only did the activities of the organizations not act to bring about changes in poor women's status, they also served to defend and reproduce class relations. Charity work does little, she argues, to improve the situation of poor women. Rather, "philanthropy is part of a process through which the upper classes reproduce themselves. It keeps the lower classes under control and helps to maintain the status quo." Al-Mughni, *Women in Kuwait: The Politics of Gender* (London: Saqi Books, 2001), 119–200.

16. Vickie Langohr, "The Organization of a Religious Movement in the Countryside: A Study of Muslim Brotherhood Branches in Rural Towns in Egypt, 1930–1952" (paper presented to the Middle East Studies Association Annual Conference, Washington, D.C., December 1995). Ziad Munson confirms Langohr's findings. In his study of the Egyptian Muslim Brotherhood in the 1930s, 1940s, and 1950s, he provides data from the U.S. State Department on the distribution of occupations among Muslim Brotherhood members tried for crimes or wanted by the police in 1954. He found that the bulk of the Brotherhood's supporters came from the most Westernized and modernized segments of the population—students, engineers, doctors, and government bureaucrats. Out of 179 members in the population he studied, sixty-one were students, thirty were civil servants, eighteen were teachers, ten were professionals, and four were army and police officers. Only nine were workers, two were farmers, and fourteen were "other"—mostly unemployed. This pattern, Munson continues, is corroborated by data on the composition of the Brotherhood's 1953 Consultative Assembly. Of the 1,950 members, only twenty-two were not from the modern European class—the new educated middle class. Munson, "Islamic Mobilization," 492.

17. Vickie Langohr, "The Problems of Practicing What They Preached: How Hindu Movements in India and Muslim Movements in Egypt in the Pre-Independence Period Dealt with the Underprivileged in Their Ranks" (paper presented at the American Political Science Association Annual Conference, San Francisco, Calif., September 1996).

18. Bayat "Revolution without Movement," 157.

19. Ibid., 151.

20. Asef Bayat, *Street Politics: Poor People's Movements in Iran* (New York: Columbia University Press, 1997), 39.

21. Nancy Elizabeth Gallagher, *Egypt's Other Wars: Epidemics and the Politics of Public Health* (Syracuse, N.Y.: Syracuse University Press, 1990, 1993), 10.

22. Director, Association of Imam ʿAbu al-ʿAzm, interview with the author, Cairo, Egypt, May 12, 1991.

23. My research indicates that not all those who work in ISIs are religious, and some may actually be opposed to Islamism. Interestingly, in her study of Shiites in Lebanon, Harik found that individuals of secular tendencies are not the only group to object to Is-

lamization. A considerable portion of the highly and moderately religious opposed it as well. Harik, "Between Islam and the State," 58.

24. This contrasts with Craisatti's findings on secular health clinics in Palestine. See Dina Craissati "Social Movements and Democracy in Palestine: Politicization of Society or Civilization of Politics?" *Orient* 37, no. 1 (1996): 111–136.

25. Soheir Morsy, "Islamic Clinics in Egypt: The Cultural Elaboration of Biomedical Hegemony," *Medical Anthropology Quarterly* 2, no. 4 (December 1988): 355, 358, quote on 358.

26. Sylvia Chiffoleau, "Le désengagement de l'État et les transformations du système de santé," *Maghreb-Machrek* 127 (janvier–mars 1990): 102.

27. In Egypt, *zakat* money is collected and distributed in three ways: through direct private donations, through private Islamic banks, and through the Islamic Bank Nasr, which is a quasi-state organization originally established by former president Sadat. As does Jordan, Bank Nasr both collects and redistributes *zakat* through voluntary *zakat* committees located in most mosques and associations. For more details, see Sarah Ben Nefissa-Paris, "Zakat officielle et zakat non-officielle aujourd'hui en Égypte," *Égypte Monde Arabe* 7 (3e trim. 1991): 105–120.

28. Quintan Wiktorowicz, *The Management of Islamic Activism: Salafis, the Muslim Brotherhood, and State Power in Jordan* (Albany: State University of New York Press, 2001), 65, 67.

29. Ibid., 85.

30. Other researchers have noticed that the differences between Islamic and non-Islamic institutions are barely distinguishable. Karen Pfeiffer's examination of Islamic and non-Islamic businesses in Egypt found that there were no meaningful differences in business practices between the two other than with regard to two factors—neither of which she could attribute to the fact that the firms were "Islamic." The first is that Islamic firms had on average a lower rate of profit and paid higher wages; they were also more inclined to share profits. This, however, could be attributed to Egypt's profit-sharing regulations rather than to the "Islamic" nature of the businesses. The second difference is that some of the Islamic firms had policies of not hiring women—however, this could be explained by the nature of their work. In all other regards—treatment of workers and customers; employee benefits, such as healthcare and transportation; and business practices—the two groups of firms were indistinguishable. Timur Kuran concurs; he argues that Islamic firms appear to do business much like their secular counterparts—both seek profits equally aggressively and both have similar levels of quality control and productivity. See Karen Pfeiffer, "Islamic Business and Business as Usual: A Study of Firms in Egypt," *Development in Practice* 11, no. 1 (February 2001): 20–33. See also Karen Pfeiffer, "Is There an Islamic Economics?" in *Political Islam: Essays from Middle East Report*, ed. Joel Beinin and Joe Stork (New York: I. B. Tauris, 1997), 163; and Timur Kuran, "Islamic Economics and the Islamic Subeconomy," *Journal of Economic Perspectives* 9 (1995): 153–173. Hammad notes that the ICCS seeks to meet the direct and ordinary needs of people and distances itself from direct involvement in politics. Hammad, "Islamists and Charitable Work," 171.

31. Alberto Melucci, *Nomads of the Present: Social Movements and Individual Needs in Contemporary Society*, ed. John Keane and Paul Mier (Philadelphia: Temple University Press, 1989).

32. Susan D. Phillips, "Meaning and Structure in Social Movements: Mapping the Network of National Canadian Women's Organizations," *Canadian Journal of Political Science* 24 (December 1991): 758, 756.

33. Phillips paraphrasing Bert Klandermans. Ibid., 757.

34. Bayat, "Revolution without Movement," 165.

35. Timothy Mitchell, "Dreamland: The Neoliberalism of Your Desires," *Middle East Report* 210 (Spring 1999): 32.

36. Ninette S. Fahmy, "The Performance of the Muslim Brotherhood in the Egyptian Syndicates: An Alternative Formula for Reform?" *Middle East Journal* 52, no. 4 (Autumn 1998): 554.

37. Sullivan, *Private Voluntary Organizations in Egypt,* 27.

38. In 1986–1987, only 37.5 percent of Egypt's associations received financial aid, an increase over past levels of government support. Sarah Ben Nefissa-Paris, "Le mouvement associatif égyptien et l'islam," *Maghreb-Machrek* 135 (janvier–mars 1992): 22. Berger notes that in 1970, only 25 percent of associations received government funding. Morroe Berger, *Islam in Egypt Today* (Cambridge: Cambridge University Press, 1970), 104.

39. Sullivan, *Private Voluntary Associations in Egypt,* 27–28.

40. Sarah Ben Nefissa-Paris, "Le mouvement associatif," 26.

41. Director of Dar al-Arqam, interview with the author, Amman, Jordan, September 22, 1998.

42. Sami Zubaida, "Islam, the State and Democracy," *Middle East Report* 179 (November–December 1992), 8.

43. Morsy, "Islamic Clinics in Egypt," 355, 360, 366. Quote on page 360.

44. Wiktorowicz, *The Management of Islamic Activism,* 89–91. Quote on page 85.

45. Yesim Arat, "Islamic Fundamentalism and Women in Turkey," *Muslim World* 80 (1990): 21, 22. See also Mark Tessler and Jolene Jesse, "Gender and Support for Islamist Movements," *Muslim World* 86, no. 2 (April 1996): 206.

46. Bayat, "Revolution without Movement," 165.

47. Ibid., 142. For a fuller discussion, see pages 139–142. In her study of Islamic NGOs in Palestine, Roy found that, similarly, there is no comprehensive social program or master plan at the macro level among Islamists or within the Islamic movement that serves as a framework for institutional development or program planning. She argues that the lack of an organizing vision linking social programs to a social plan reveals the absence of long-range thinking or planning. The projects and programs of Islamic NGOs are the initiatives of individuals and the institutions with which they belong. Roy, "Transformation of Islamic NGOs," 26.

48. Bayat, "Revolution without Movement," 141.

49. Ra'if Nijim, former director of the Fund for the Sick and Poor, interview with Rana Taha, Amman, Jordan, August 10, 2002.

50. Hammad, "Islamists and Charitable Work," 171.

51. Almost without exception, the ICIs and IWIs in this study work independently— the profits of one are not given to the other.

BIBLIOGRAPHY

ARABIC SOURCES

ʿAbd al-Halim, Mahmud. *Muslim Brotherhood: Events That Made History.* Part 3, *Cairo.* Cairo: Dar al-Daʿwa, 1971.

ʿAbdallah, Ismaʿil Sabri, et al. *Contemporary Islamic Movement in the Arab Nation.* Beirut: The Center for Arab Unity Studies, 1989.

ʿAbu al-Magd, Ahmad Kamal. *No Confrontation Dialogue.* Cairo: Dar al-Sharuq, 1988.

ʿAbu as-Saʿud, Mahud. *Islamic Movement: Future Vision and Papers on Self-Criticism.* Cairo: Madbuli Library, 1989.

al-Alim as-Suswa, Amat. *Yemeni Women in Numbers.* Sanaʿa: Embassy of the Netherlands, 1996.

ʿAmara, Muhammad. *Islam and Human Rights: Necessities. . . . Not Rights.* Cairo: Dar al-Sharuq, 1989.

al-ʿAwwa, Muhammad Salim. *In the Political System for an Islamic State.* Cairo: Dar al-Sharuq, 1989.

al-Banna, Hassan. *Memoirs of the Call and the Caller.* Cairo: Islamic Publishing and Distribution House, 1966.

al-Bayumi, Ghanim Ibrahim. *The Political Thought of Imam Hassan al-Banna.* Cultural Studies Series. Cairo: Islamic Publishing and Distribution House, 1992.

Egypt between the Religious and the Civil State: The Famous Debate at the Cairo International Book Exhibition Debate. Cyprus: Al Dar al-Masria Publishing and Distribution House, 1992.

Farhan, Izhaq Ahmed. *The Islamic Action Front in Jordan: Justifications and Principles and the Lawful.* Amman: Islamic Action Front, 1994.

General Union of Voluntary Societies. *Directory of Charitable Societies.* Amman: General Union of Voluntary Societies, 1995.

———. *Executive Council Report: The Financial and Administrative Report for 1997; Estimated Budget for 1998.* Amman: General Union of Voluntary Societies, 1997.

———. *A History of Projects Programs.* Amman, Jordan: General Union of Voluntary Societies, 1996.

Gharaibeh, Ibrahim. *The Muslim Brotherhood in Jordan.* Amman. Al Urdun al-Jadid Research Center, 1997.

al-Ghazali, Muhammad. *The Crisis of Shura in Arabic and Islamic Communities.* Cairo: Middle East Publishers, 1990.

al-Hudaybi, Hassan. *Propagandists, Not Judges.* Cairo: Islamic Publishing and Distribution House, 1977.

Huwaydi, Fahmi. *The Quran and Power: Contemporary Islamic Concerns.* 3d ed. Cairo: Dar al-Sharuq, 1991.

Islamic Charitable Center Society. *ICCS 1998 Agenda.* Amman: ICCS, n.d.

———. *ICCS Executive Council Report for 1997.* Amman: ICCS, n.d.

———. *Pocket Calendar: ICCS: 33 Years of Giving.* Amman: ICCS, n.d.

Kandil, Amani, and Sarah Ben Nefissa. *Civil Associations in Egypt.* Cairo: Al-Ahram, 1994.

al-Mikhlafi, Mohammed. "Inclusion of Women's Issues in the 1997 Electoral Programs." Paper presented at the conference Challenges of the 21st Century to Women and Democracy, Women's Candidate Fund, Sana'a, Yemen, May 27–29, 1997.

Muru, Muhammed. "Shaykh Mahmoud Khattab al-Sobky: Founder of Al-Jam'iya al-Shar'iya." *Manbar al-Sharq* 2 (June 1992): 199–203.

al-Qaradawi, Yusuf. *The Islamic Solution: Necessity and Duty.* Cairo: Wahba Library, 1987.

Shawqi. Muhammad. *The Muslim Brotherhood and the Egyptian Society.* Cairo: Dar al-Ansar, 1980.

Republic of Yemen. Central Statistical Organization. *Statistical Yearbook.* Sana'a: Central Statistical Organization, Republic of Yemen, 1994.

———. National Committee for Women. *The Situation of Women in Yemen.* Sana'a: National Committee for Women, 1998.

Yemen Institute for the Development of Democracy. "The Experience of Yemeni Women in the Democratic Elections of April 1993." Sana'a: Yemen Institute for the Development of Democracy, 1993.

Yemeni Congregation for Reform. *Political Organization of the Yemeni Congregation for Reform.* Sana'a: Yemeni Congregation for Reform, 1994.

———. *Program for Political Work.* Sana'a: Yemeni Congregation for Reform, 1994.

ENGLISH, FRENCH, AND GERMAN SOURCES

Abdalla, Ahmed. "Egypt's Islamists and the State." *Middle East Report* 183 (1993): 28–31.

Abdelnasser, Walid M. "Islamic Organizations in Egypt and the Iranian Revolution of 1979: The Experience of the First Few Years." *Arab Studies Quarterly* 19, no. 2 (Spring 1997): 25–39.

Abed-Kotob, Sana. "The Accommodationists Speak: Goals and Strategies of the Muslim Brotherhood of Egypt." *International Journal of Middle East Studies* 27, no. 3 (August 1995): 321–339.

Abou-Zeid, O. W., et al. *Dossiers du CEDEJ: Âge liberal et néo-liberal.* Paris: Centre d'Études et de Documentation Économiques, 1996.

Aclimandos, Tewfick. "Les ingenieurs militaires égyptiens." *Maghreb-Machrek* 146 (October–December 1994): 7–25.

Adams, Linda Shull. "Political Liberalization in Jordan: An Analysis of the State's Relationship with the Muslim Brotherhood." *Journal of Church and State* 38, no. 3 (Summer 1996): 507–528.

Adams, Richard H., Jr. "Evaluating the Process of Development in Egypt, 1980–97." *International Journal of Middle East Studies* 32 (2000): 255–275.

Ahmed, Leila. "Feminism and Feminist Movements in the Middle East, A Preliminary Exploration: Turkey, Egypt, Algeria, People's Democratic Republic of Yemen." *Women's Studies International Forum* 5, no. 2 (1982): 153–168.

———. *Women and Gender in Islam: Historical Roots of a Modern Debate.* New Haven, Conn.: Yale University Press, 1992.

Albrecht, Kirk. "Hussein Gets a Loyal Legislature." *The Middle East* 273 (December 1997): 15.

al-Alim as-Suswa, Amat, ed. *Democratic Developments in Yemen.* Sana'a: Professors World Peace Academy, 1994.

Aly, Abdel Monem Said. "Democratization in Egypt." *American-Arab Affairs* 22 (Fall 1987): 11–27.

Amawi, Abla. "Poverty and Vulnerability in Jordan." *Jordanies* 1 (June 1996): 89–93.

———. "The 1993 Elections in Jordan." *Arab Studies Quarterly* 16, no. 3 (Summer 1994): 15–27.

Anderson, Roy R., Robert F. Seibert, and Jon G. Wagner. *Politics and Change in the Middle East: Sources of Conflict and Accommodation.* 6th ed. Englewood Cliffs, N.J.: Prentice Hall, 2001.

Andoni, Lamis. "King Abdallah: In His Father's Footsteps." *Journal of Palestine Studies* 29, no. 3 (Spring 2000): 77–89.

Anheier, Helmut K., and Lester M. Salamon, eds. *The Nonprofit Sector in the Developing World: A Comparative Analysis.* Manchester and New York: Manchester University Press, 1998.

Antonius, Rachad. *The Development NGO Sector in the Middle East: An Overview with Suggestions for Future Research.* Ottawa: International Development Research Center, 1993.

Arab Republic of Egypt, General Agency for Public Mobilization and Statistics, Central Agency for Public Mobilization and Statistics. *Statistical Year Book: Arab Republic of Egypt.* Cairo: General Agency for Public Mobilization and Statistics, Central Agency for Public Mobilization and Statistics, 1994.

Arat, Yesim. "Islamic Fundamentalism and Women in Turkey." *Muslim World* 80, no. 21 (1990): 17–23.

Arends, Inge, Ada Ruis, Maja van der Velden, and Marina de Regt. *Women and Development in the Middle East: Perspectives of Arab NGOs and Project Participants.* Amsterdam: Middle East Research Associates, 1995.

Arjomand, Said Amir, ed. *From Nationalism to Revolutionary Islam.* London: Macmillan Press, 1984.

Ask, Karin, and Marit Tjomsland, eds. *Women and Islamization: Contemporary Dimensions of Discourse on Gender Relations.* New York: Berg, 1998.

Atiya, Nayra. *Khul-Khaal: Five Egyptian Women Tell Their Stories.* Syracuse, N.Y.: Syracuse University Press, 1988.

Aveni, Adrian F. "Organizational Linkages and Resource Mobilization: The Significance of Linkage Strength and Breadth." *Sociological Quarterly* 19 (Spring 1978): 185–202.

Bainbridge, William Sims. *Sociology of Religious Movements.* New York: Routledge, 1977.

Bar, Shmuel. *The Muslim Brotherhood in Jordan.* Tel Aviv: Tel Aviv University/The Moshe Dayan Center for Middle Eastern and African Studies, 1998.

Barakat, Halim. *The Arab World: Society, Culture and State.* Los Angeles: University of California Press, 1993.

Bayat, Asef. "Activism and Social Development in the Middle East." *International Journal of Middle East Studies* 34, no. 1 (February 2002): 1–28.

———. "Revolution without Movement, Movement without Revolution: Comparing Islamic Activism in Iran and Egypt." *Society for Comparative Study of Society and History* 40, no. 1 (January 1998): 136–169.

———. *Street Politics: Poor People's Movements in Iran.* New York: Columbia University Press, 1997.

———. "Who's Afraid of Ashwaiyyat? Urban Change and Politics in Egypt." *Environment and Urbanization* 12, no. 2 (October 2000): 185–200.

Beatty, Sharon, Ahmed No'man al-Madhaji, and Renaud Detalle, eds. *Yemeni NGOs and Quasi-NGOs: Analysis and Directory.* Part I: *Analysis.* Sana'a: The Embassy of the Netherlands, 1996.

Behdad, Sohrab. "Winners and Losers of the Iranian Revolution: A Study in Income Distribution." *International Journal of Middle Eastern Studies* 21 (1989): 327–358.

Beinin, Joel, and Joe Stork, eds. *Political Islam: Essays from Middle East Report.* New York: I. B. Tauris, 1997.

Ben Nefissa-Paris, Sarah. "L'Association al-Nida' Al Gadid: Un nouvel acteur sur la scène politique égyptienne." *Égypte/Monde Arabe* 20 (4ème trimestre 1994): 155–166.

———. "Associations égyptiennes: Une liberalisation sous contrôle." *Monde Arabe/Maghreb-Machrek* 150 (octobre–decembre 1995): 40–56.

———. "L'état égyptien et le monde associatif." *Égypte/Monde Arabe* 8 (4ème trimestre 1991): 107–124.

———. "Les lignes régionales et les associations islamiques en Égypte: Deux formes de regroupements à vocation sociale et caritative." *Revue Tiers Monde* 36, no. 141 (janvier–mars 1995): 163–177.

———. "Le mouvement associatif égyptien et l'islam." *Maghreb-Machrek* 135 (janvier–mars 1992): 19–36.

———. "Ramadan 1991: Les pages religieuses des grands quotidiens pendant le Ramadan." *Égypte/Monde Arabe* 6 (2ème trimestre 1991): 143–176.

———. "Zakat officielle et zakat non officielle aujourd'hui en Égypte." *Égypte/Monde Arabe* 7 (3ème trimestre 1991): 105–120.

Benford, Robert D. "Frame Disputes within the Nuclear Disarmament Movement." *Social Forces* 71, no. 3 (March 1993): 677–701.

Benthall, Jonathan. "The Red Cross and Red Crescent Movement and Islamic Societies, with Special Reference to Jordan." *British Journal of Middle Eastern Studies* 24, NO. 2 (1997): 157–177.

Berger, Morroe. *Islam in Egypt Today.* Cambridge: Cambridge University Press, 1970.

Bianchi, Robert. "Businessmen's Associations in Egypt and Turkey." *Annals of the American Academy* 482 (November 1985): 147–159.

———. "The Corporatization of the Egyptian Labor Movement." *Middle East Journal* 40, no. 3 (Summer 1986): 429–444.

———. "The Strengthening of Associational Life and Its Potential Contributions to Political Reform in Egypt, Turkey and Lebanon." Paper presented at the Conference on Political Liberalization and Democratization in the Arab World, Montreal, May 7–8, 1993.

———. *Unruly Corporatism: Associational Life in Twentieth-Century Egypt.* New York: Oxford University Press, 1989.

Bidwell, Robin. *The Two Yemens.* Boulder, Colo.: Westview Press, 1983.

Bill, James A., and Robert Springborg. *Politics in the Middle East.* 5th ed. New York: Longman, 2000.

Billings, Dwight B. "Religion as Opposition: A Gramscian Analysis." *American Journal of Sociology* 96, no. 1 (July 1990): 1–31.

Bocco, Riccardo, Blandine Destremau, and Jean Hannoyer, eds. *Les cahiers du CERMOC: Palestine, palestiniens: Territoire national, espaces communautaires.* Vol. 17. Beirut, Lebanon: Centre d'Études de Recherches sur le Moyen-Orient Contemporain, 1997.

Bodman, Herbert L., and Nayereh Tohidi, eds. *Women in Muslim Societies.* Boulder, Colo.: Lynne Rienner Press, 1998.

Boulby, Marion. *The Muslim Brotherhood and the Kings of Jordan, 1945–1993.* Atlanta, Ga.: Scholars Press, 1999.

Bowen, Donna Lee, and Evelyn A. Early, eds. *Everyday Life in the Muslim Middle East.* Bloomington and Indianapolis: Indiana University Press, 1993.

Brand, Laurie A. "The Effects of the Peace Process on Political Liberalization in Jordan." *Journal of Political Studies* 28, no. 2 (Winter 1999): 52–67.

———. *Jordan's Inter-Arab Relations: The Political Economy of Alliance Making.* New York: Columbia University Press, 1994.

———. *Women, the State, and Political Liberalization: Middle Eastern and North African Experience.* New York: Columbia University Press, 1998.

Braun, Ursula. "Yemen: Another Case of Unification." *Aussenpolitik* 11, no. 2 (1992): 174–184.

Brindle, Simon. "Egypt: A High Rise Economy." *The Middle East* (January 1995): 25–26.

Bromley, David G. *Moonies in America: Cult, Church, and Crusade.* London: Sage Publications, 1979.

Brumberg, Daniel. "The Political Economy of Survival Strategies in the Arab World." Paper presented at the Conference on Political Liberalization and Democratization in the Arab World, Montreal, May 7–8, 1993.

Brynen, Rex. "Economic Crisis and Post-Rentier Democratization in the Arab World." *Canadian Journal of Political Science* 25, no. 1 (March 1992): 69–97.

Buechler, Steven M. "Beyond Resource Mobilization: Emerging Trends in Social Movement Theory." *Sociological Quarterly* 34, no. 2 (1993): 217–235.

———. *Social Movements in Advanced Capitalism: The Political Economy and Cultural Construction of Social Activism.* New York: Oxford University Press, 2000.

Burgat, François, and William Dowell. *The Islamic Movement in North Africa.* Austin: Center for Middle Eastern Studies, University of Texas at Austin, 1993.

Burke, Edmund, III, and Ira M. Lapidus, eds. *Islam, Politics and Social Movements.* London: I. B. Tauris, 1988.

Burrowes, Robert D. "Prelude to Unification: The Yemen Arab Republic, 1962–1990." *International Journal of Middle Eastern Studies* 23 (1991): 483–506.

———. *The Yemen Arab Republic: The Politics of Development 1962–1986.* Boulder, Colo. and London: Westview Press and Croom Helm, 1987.

———. "The Yemen Arab Republic's Legacy and Yemeni Unification." *Arab Studies Quarterly* 1, no. 4 (Fall 1992): 41–68.

Cantori, Louis J., ed. "Democratization in the Middle East." *American-Arab Affairs* 36 (Spring 1991): 1–30.

Caplan, Lionel, ed. *Studies in Religious Fundamentalism.* London: Macmillan, 1987.

Carapico, Sheila. *Civil Society in Yemen: the Political Economy of Activism in Modern Arabia.* Cambridge: Cambridge University Press, 1998.

———. "From Ballotbox to Battlefield: The War of the Two 'Alis.'" *Middle East Report* 190 (September/October 1994): 27.

———. "The Economic Dimension of Yemen Unity." *Middle East Report* 184 (September/October 1993): 9–14.

———. "Elections and Mass Politics in Yemen." *Middle East Report* 185 (November–December 1993): 2–6.

———. "Gender and Status Inequalities in Yemen: Honor, Economics, and Politics." Richmond, Va., October 1992.

———. "NGOs, INGOs, GO-NGOs and DO-NGOs: Making Sense of Non-Governmental Organizations." *Middle East Report* 214 (Spring 2000): 12–15.

———. "Women and Participation in Yemen." *Middle East Report* 173 (November/December 1991): 15.

Carapico, Sheila, and Cynthia Myntti. "A Tale of Two Families: Change in North Yemen 1977–1989." *Middle East Report* 170 (May/June 1991): 24–29.

Cardiff, Patrick W. "Poverty and Inequality in Egypt." *Research in Middle East Economics* 2 (1997): 3–38.

Cassandra. "The Impending Crisis in Egypt." *Middle East Journal* 49, no. 1 (Winter 1995): 9–27.

Chiffoleau, Sylvia. "Le deséngagement de l'État et les transformations du système de santé." *Maghreb-Machrek* 127 (janvier–mars 1990): 84–103.

———. "Itineraires Médicaux en Egypte." *Revue Tiers-Monde* 36, no. 143 (juillet–septembre 1995): 515–530.

———. "Le monopole national d'exercice d'une profession libérale: Le cas de la médecine." *Monde Arabe* 11 (3ème trimestre 1992): 59–75.

———. "Reinventer une 'médicine pour tous': Les médecins à la recherche d'une nouvelle crédibilité." *Monde Arabe* 26 (2ème trimestre 1996): 81–109.

Choudhury, Masudul Alam. "Principles of Islamic Economics." *Middle Eastern Studies* 19, no. 1 (January 1983): 93–103.

Chwe, Michael Suk-Young. "Structure and Strategy in Collective Action." *American Journal of Sociology* 105, no. 1 (July 1999): 128–156.

Clark, Janine A. "Islamic Social Welfare Organizations in Cairo: Islamization from Below?" *Arab Studies Quarterly* 17, no. 4 (Fall 1995): 11–28.

———. "Women and NGOs in Yemen." *Najda Newsletter* (Spring 1997): 4–6.

Clark, Janine A., and Schwedler, Jillian. "Who Opened the Window? Women's Struggle for Voice within Islamist Political Parties." *Comparative Politics* (forthcoming, April 2003).

Coleman, James S. *Education and Political Development*. Princeton, N.J.: Princeton University Press, 1965.

Craissati, Dina. "Social Movements and Democracy in Palestine: Politicization of Society or Civilization of Politics?" *Orient* 37, no. 1 (1996): 111–136.

Curmi, Brigitte, and Sylvia Chiffoleau, eds. *Les cahiers du CERMOC: Médicins et protection sociale dans le monde arabe*. Vol. 5. Beirut: Centre d'Études de Recherches sur le Moyen-Orient Contemporain, 1993.

Cuthell, David, Philip Stoddard, and Margaret Sullivan, eds. *Change and the Muslim World*. Syracuse, N.Y.: Syracuse University Press, 1981.

Dalton, Russell J., and Manfred Kuechler, eds. *Challenging the Political Order: New Social and Political Movements in Western Democracies*. Oxford: Polity Press, 1990.

Daum, Werner, ed. *Yemen: 300 Years of Art and Civilization in Arabia Felix*. Innsbruck: Penguin, 1988.

DeJong, Jocelyn. "The Urban Context of Health during Economic Crisis." In *Amman: The City and Its Society*, ed. J. Hannoyer and S. Shami. Beirut and Amman: Centre d'Études et de Recherches sur le Moyen-Orient Contemporain, 1996.

della Porta, Donatella. "Recruitment Processes in Clandestine Political Organizations: Italian Left-Wing Terrorism." *Research in Social Movements, Conflicts and Change* 1 (1988): 155–169.

Denoeux, Guilain. *Urban Unrest in the Middle East: A Comparative Study of Informal Networks in Egypt, Iran and Lebanon*. Albany: State University of New York Press, 1993.

Dessouki, Ali E. Hillal, ed. *Islamic Resurgence in the Arab World*. New York: Praeger Publishers, 1982.

Detalle, Renaud. "Yémen. Les élections législatives du 27 Avril 1993." *Monde Arabe/Maghreb-Machrek* 141 (July–September 1993): 3–26.

Diamond, Larry Jay, ed. *Political Culture and Democracy in Developing Countries*. Boulder, Colo.: Lynne Rienner, 1993.

Diani, Mario, and Giovanni Lodi. "Three in One: Currents in the Milan Ecology Movement." *Research in Social Movements, Conflicts and Change* 1 (1988): 103–124.

Dorman, Deborah, Ahmed No'man al-Madhaji, Mohammed Aidarus, Sharon Beatty, Zarina Ismael, and Marina de Regt. *Yemeni NGOs and Quasi-NGOs: Analysis and Directory*. Part II, *Directory*. Sana'a: The Embassy of the Netherlands, 1996.

Douglas, J. Leigh. *The Free Yemeni Movement 1935–1962*. Beirut: The American University of Beirut, 1987.

Dresch, Paul. *A History of Modern Yemen*. Cambridge: Cambridge University Press, 2000.

———. *Tribes, Government and History in Yemen*. New York: Oxford University Press, 1989.

Dresch, Paul, and Bernard Haykel. "Stereotypes and Political Styles: Islamists and Tribesfolk in Yemen." *International Journal of Middle East Studies* 27, no. 4 (November 1995): 405–431.

Dunbar, Charles. "The Unification of Yemen: Process, Politics, and Prospects." *Middle East Journal* 46, no. 3 (Summer 1992): 456–475.

Dunn, Michael Collins. "Islamist Parties in Democratizing States: A Look at Jordan and Yemen." *Middle East Policy* 2, no. 2 (1993): 16–27.

Early, Evelyn A. "Catharsis and Creation: The Everyday Narratives of Baladi Women of Cairo." *Anthropological Quarterly* 58, no. 4 (October 1985): 172–181.

———. "The Logic of Well Being: Therapeutic Narratives in Cairo, Egypt." *Social Science Medicine* 16 (1982): 1491–1497.

Eckstein, Susan, ed. *Power and Popular Protest: Latin American Social Movements.* Los Angeles: University of California Press, 1989.

"Egypt: Democratic Safeguards for Professional Associations." *International Labour Review* 132, no. 2 (1993): 129–130.

"Egypt: Parliament Pushes Union Law Through." *Civil Society* 15 (March 1993): 3–7.

Egyptian Preparatory Committee for the 1995 International Women's Forum. *Report of the Egyptian NGOs for the Forum on Women Beijing 1995: Egyptian Women's Status From Nairobi to Beijing.* Cairo: Egyptian Preparatory Committee with the cooperation of UNICEF, USAID, and the Social Fund, 1995.

Eickelman, Dale F., and James Piscatori. *Muslim Politics.* Princeton, N.J.: Princeton University Press, 1996.

Ekland-Olson, Sheldon, David A. Snow, and Louis A. Zurcher, Jr. "Social Networks and Social Movements: A Microstructural Approach to Differential Recruitment." *American Sociological Review* 45, no. October (1980): 787–801.

Economic and Social Commission for Western Asia (ESCWA). *Arab Women: Statistical Database.* Beirut, Lebanon: ESCWA, 1995.

Esim, Simel, and Dilek Cindoglu. "Women's Organizations in 1990s Turkey: Predicaments and Prospects." *Middle Eastern Studies* 35, no. 1 (January 1999): 178–188.

Esposito, John L., ed. *The Oxford Encyclopedia of the Modern Islamic World.* New York: Oxford University Press, 1995.

Evans, John H. "Multi-Organizational Fields and Social Movement Organization Frame Content: The Religious Pro-Choice Movement." *Sociological Inquiry* 67, no. 4 (November 1997): 451–469.

Evans, Sara. *Personal Politics.* New York: First Vintage Books, 1979.

Fahmy, Ninette S. "The Performance of the Muslim Brotherhood in the Egyptian Syndicates: An Alternative Formula for Reform." *Middle East Journal* 52, no. 4 (1998): 551–562.

Fandy, Mamoun. "Regional Revenge." *Middle East Journal* 48, no. 4 (Autumn 1994): 607–625.

———. "Tribe vs. Islam: The Post-colonial Arab State and the Democratic Imperative." *Middle East Policy* 3, no. 2 (1994): 40–51.

Farhan, Ishaq Ahmad. *The Islamic Stand towards Political Involvement.* Translated by Basma Nayef Sa'd. Amman: Dar al-Furqan, 1997.

Faris, Hani A., ed. *Arab Nationalism and the Future of the Arab World.* AAUG Monograph Series 22. Belmont, Mass.: Association of Arab-American University Graduates, 1987.

Farschid, Olaf. "Hizbiya: Die Neuorientierung der Muslimbrüderschaft Ägyptens in den Jahren 1984 bis 1989." *Orient* 30 (1989): 59–73.

Fergani, Nader. "Médecins et ingénieurs sur le marché du travail en Égypte." *Maghreb-Machrek* 146 (octobre–decembre 1994): 40–47.

Fernando, Jude L., and Alan W. Heston. "NGOs between States, Markets, and Civil Society." *Annals of the American Academy of Political and Social Science* 554 (November 1997): 8–20.

Ferree, Myra Max, and Frederick D. Miller. "Mobilization and Meaning." *Sociological Inquiry* 55, no. 1 (Winter 1985): 38–61.

Forstner, Martin. "Auf dem legalen Weg zur Macht? Zur politischen Entwicklung der Muslimbrüderschaft Ägyptens." *Orient* 29, no. 3 (1988): 386–422.

Freij, Hanna Y., and Leonard C. Robinson. "Liberalization, the Islamists, and the Stability of the Arab State: Jordan as a Case Study." *Muslim World* 136, no. 1 (January 1996): 1–32.

Gaffney, Patrick. *Prophet's Pulpit: Islamic Preaching in Contemporary Egypt*. Los Angeles: University of California Press, 1994.

Gallagher, Nancy. *Egypt's Other Wars: Epidemics and the Politics of Public Health*. Syracuse, N.Y.: Syracuse University Press, 1993.

Gibb, Hamilton, Alexander Rosskeen, and Harold Bowen. *Islamic Society and the West: Islamic Society in the Eighteenth Century*. Part II, vol. 1. London: Oxford University Press, 1957.

Giugni, Marco, Doug McAdam, and Charles Tilly, eds. *How Social Movements Matter*. Vol. 10, *Social Movements, Protest, and Contention*. Minneapolis: University of Minnesota Press, 1999.

Glosemeyer, Iris. "The First Yemeni Parliamentary Elections in 1993: Practicing Democracy." *Orient* 34, no. 3 (1995): 439–451.

Gopolan, Pritha. "The Trust Factor in Participation and Social Education." *Annals of the Academy of Political and Social Science* 554 (November 1997): 178–192.

Gould, Roger V. *Insurgent Identities: Class, Community and Protest in Paris from 1848 to the Commune*. Chicago: University of Chicago Press, 1995.

———. "Multiple Networks and Mobilization in the Paris Commune, 1871." *American Sociological Review* 56 (December 1991): 716–729.

———. "Trade Cohesion, Class Unity, and Urban Insurrection: Artisanal Activism in the Paris Commune." *American Journal of Sociology* 98, no. 4 (January 1993): 721–754.

Gran, Peter. "Medical Pluralism in Arab and Egyptian History: An Overview of Class Structures and Philosophies of the Main Phases." *Social Science and Medicine* 13B (1979): 339–348.

Grandguillaume, Gilbert, Franck Mermier, and Jean-Francois Troin, eds. *Sanaa hors les murs*. Sana'a and Tours, France: Centre Français d'Études Yemenites and URBAMA, 1995.

Green, Andrew, and Ann Matthias. *Non-Governmental Organizations and Health in Developing Countries*. New York: St. Martin's Press, 1997.

Guenena, Neimat. "The Islamic Alternative in Egypt Today." *Civil Society* 7 (July 1992): 4–7.

———. *The Jihad: An "Islamic Alternative" in Egypt*. 2d ed. Cairo: The American University in Cairo Press, 1988.

el-Guindi, Fadwa. "Veiling Intifah with Muslim Ethic: Egypt's Contemporary Islamic Movement." *Social Problems* 28, no. 4 (April 1981): 465–485.

Gusfield, Joseph R. "Social Movements and Social Change: Perspectives of Linearity and Fluidity." *Research in Social Movements, Conflicts and Change* 4 (1981): 317–339.

Hashem, Mouna. "The Role and Status of Women in Social and Economic Development in the Yemen Arab Republic." A report prepared for the United States Agency for International Development, Yemen, January 1990.

Haggag, Karim. "A Civil Society in the Arab World?" *Civil Society* 6 (June 1992): 11–18.

———. "One Year after the Storm." *Civil Society* 5 (May 1992): 9–12.

Hale, Sondra. *Gender Politics in Sudan: Islamism, Socialism, and the State*. Boulder, Colo.: Westview Press, 1996.

———. "'The New Muslim Woman': Sudan's National Islamic Front and the Invention of Identity." *Muslim World* 86, no. 2 (April 1996): 176–199.

Halpern, Manfred. *Politics of Social Change in the Middle East and North Africa*. Princeton, N.J.: Princeton University Press, 1963.

Hammady, Iman Roushdy. "Religious Medical Clinics in Cairo." M.A. thesis, no. 885, American University of Cairo, 1990.

Hammami, Rema. "Palestinian NGOs Since Oslo: From NGO Politics to Social Movements?" *Middle East Report* 214 (Spring 2000), 16–19, 27, 48.

Hamzeh, A. Nizar. "Lebanon's Islamists and Local Politics: A New Reality." *Third World Quarterly* 21, no. 5 (2000): 739–759.

Hannoyer, J., and S. Shami, eds. *Amman: ville et societe.* Beirut and Amman: Centre d'Études et de Recherches sur le Moyen-Orient Contemporain, 1996.

Harders, Cilja. "Transition from Below? Poverty and Participation in Cairo Neighborhoods." Paper presented at the Middle East Studies Association, Providence, Rhode Island, 1996.

Harik, Judith Palmer. "Between Islam and the State: Sources and Implications of Popular Support for Lebanon's Hizballah." *Journal of Conflict Resolution* 40, no. 1 (March 1996): 41–67.

Hashemite Kingdom of Jordan, Coordinating Office for the Beijing Conference. *Arab Women: Facts and Prospects, 1995.* Amman: Coordinating Office for the Beijing Conference, 1995.

Hawthorn, Amy W., and Ronald G. Wolfe. *Pollworker Training and the Parliamentary Elections in Yemen: 1997 Final Report.* Washington, D.C.: International Foundation for Election Systems, 1997.

Heilman, Bruce, and John Lucas. "A Social Movement for African Capitalism? A Comparison of Business Associations in Two African Cities." *African Studies Review* 40, no. 2 (September 1997): 141–171.

Hobsbawm, Eric, and Terence Ranger, eds. *The Invention of Tradition.* Cambridge: Cambridge University Press, 1983.

Hoodfar, Homa. *Between Marriage and the Market: Intimate Politics and Survival in Cairo.* Los Angeles: University of California Press, 1997.

Hopkins, Nicholas S., and Saad Eddin Ibrahim, eds. *Arab Society: Class, Gender, Power and Development.* 3d ed. Cairo: The American University in Cairo Press, 1997.

Hourani, Hani, ed. *Islamic Movements in Jordan.* Amman, Jordan: Al-Urdun al-Jadid Research Center, 1997.

Hourani, Hani, Taleb Awad, Hamed Dabbas, and Saʿeda Kilani. *Islamic Action Front Party.* 1st ed. Translated by Saʿeda Kilani. Amman: Al-Urdun al-Jadid Research Center, September 1993.

Ibrahim, Fathi. "Quelques caractéristiques de l'évolution économique de l'Égypte depuis 1991." *Monde Arabe* 21 (1er trimestre 1995): 11–18.

Ibrahim, Saad Eddin. "Anatomy of Egypt's Militant Islamic Groups: Methodological Note and Preliminary Findings." *International Journal of Middle East Studies* 12 (1980): 423–453.

———. "The Betrayal of Democracy by Egypt's Intellectuals." *Civil Society* 2 (February 1992): 1.

———. "The Changing Face of Islamic Activism." *Civil Society* 4, no. 41 (May 1995): 4–8.

———. "Egyptian Law 32 of 1964 on Egypt's PVOs and PFs: A Critical Assessment." Cairo: Ibn Khaldoun Center for Development Studies, 1994.

———. "Egypt's Civil Society: A Big Step Backward . . . a Small Step Forward." *Civil Society* 15 (March 1993): 2.

———. "Egypt's Islamic Activism in the 1980's." *Third World Quarterly* 19 (1988): 632–657.

———. *Governance and Structural Adjustment: The Egyptian Case.* Cairo: Ibn Khaldoun Center for Development Studies, November 1994.

———. "Islamic Activists Take Over Egypt's Fortress of Liberalism." *Civil Society* 10 (October 1992): 2.

Ibrahim, Saad Eddin, and Nicholas S. Hopkins, eds. *Arab Society: Social Science Perspectives.* 2d ed. Cairo: The American University in Cairo Press, 1987.

Ibrahim, Saad Eddin, Amani Kandil, Moheb Zaki, Nagah Hassan, Ola El-Ramly, Sahar Al-Ga'arah, Mohammad Sami, and Ahmed Abu Al-Yazid, eds. *An Assessment of Grassroots Participation in the Development of Egypt.* Cairo: The American University in Cairo Press, 1996.

Islamic Hospital. *The Islamic Hospital, Amman-Jordan: A Philanthropic Model of Health Promotion in Jordan.* Amman: Islamic Hospital, 1998.

Ismael, Tareq Y., and Jacqueline S. Ismail. *The People's Democratic Republic of Yemen: Politics, Economics, and Society.* Boulder, Colo.: Lynne Rienner, 1986.

Jaber, Kamel Abu, Matthes Buhbe, and Mohamma Smadi, eds. *Income Distribution in Jordan.* Boulder, Colo.: Westview Press, 1990.

Jansen, W. "Contested Identities: Women and Religion in Algeria and Jordan." Paper presented at the Middle East Studies Association of North America, Phoenix, Arizona, 1994.

Jasper, James M. *The Art of Moral Protest: Culture, Biography, and Creativity in Social Movements.* Chicago: University of Chicago Press, 1997.

Johnston, Hank, and Bert Klandermans, eds. *Social Movements and Culture.* Minneapolis: University of Minnesota Press, 1995.

Joseph, Suad, ed. *Gender and Citizenship in the Middle East.* Syracuse, N.Y.: Syracuse University Press, 2000.

Joseph, Suad, and Susan Slyomovics, eds. *Women and Power in the Middle East.* Philadelphia: University of Pennsylvania Press, 2001.

Judah, J. Stillson. *Hare Krishna and the Counterculture.* New York: John Wiley and Sons, 1974.

Kandela, Peter. "Egypt: Control of Professional Organizations." *The Lancet* 341 (February 27 1993): 549–550.

Kandil, Amani. *Civil Society in the Arab World: Private Voluntary Organizations.* Washington, D.C.: CIVICUS, 1995.

———. "Some Features of Egypt's Civil Society." *Civil Society* 1 (January 1992): 3–4.

———. "The Status of the Third Sector in the Arab Region." In *Citizens: Strengthening Global Civil Society,* ed. Miguel Darcy de Oliveira and Rajesh Tandon. Washington, D.C.: CIVICUS World Alliance for Citizen Participation, 1994.

Kandiyoti, Deniz, ed. *Women, Islam and the State.* Philadelphia: Temple University Press, 1991.

Katzenstein, Mary Fainsod. "Organizing against Violence: Strategies of the Indian Women's Movement." *Pacific Affairs* 62, no. 1 (Spring 1989): 53–71.

Kepel, Gilles. *Muslim Extremism in Egypt: The Prophet and Pharaoh.* Los Angeles: University of California Press, 1984.

Khadduri, Majid, and Herbert J. Liebesny, eds. *Law in the Middle East: Origin and Development of Islamic Law.* Vol. 1. Washington, D.C.: The Middle East Institute, 1955.

Khouri, Nicole. "Acteurs islamistes et modernite dans l'Égypte des vingt dernières années." *Revue Tiers Monde* 36, no. 141 (janvier–mars 1995): 145–161.

Khoury, Nabil F., and Valentine M. Moghadam, eds. *Gender and Development in the Arab World.* Atlantic Highlands, N.J.: Zed Books and United Nations University Press, 1995.

Kim, Hyojoung, and Peter S. Bearman. "The Structure and Dynamics of Movement Participation." *American Sociological Review* 62 (February 1997): 70–93.

Kitts, James A. "Not in Our Backyard: Solidarity, Social Networks, and the Ecology of Environmental Mobilization." *Sociological Inquiry* 69, no. 4 (1999): 551–574.

Klandermans, Bert. "The Formation and Mobilization of Consensus." *Research in Social Movements, Conflicts and Change* 1 (1988): 173–196.

———. "Introduction: Interorganizational Networks." *International Social Movement Research* 2 (1989): 301–314.

Klandermans, Bert, Hanspeter Kriesi, and Sydney Tarrow, eds. *International Social Movement Research.* Vol. 1, *From Structure to Action: Comparing Movement Participation across Cultures.* Greenwich, Conn.: JAI Press, 1988.

Klandermans, Bert, and Dirk Oegema. "Potentials, Networks, Motivations, and Barriers: Steps towards Participation in Social Movements." *American Sociological Review* 52 (August 1987): 519–531.

Knoke, David. *Political Networks: The Structural Perspective.* New York: Cambridge University Press, 1990.

Kostiner, Joseph. *The Struggle for South Yemen.* London: Croom Helm, 1984.

———. *Yemen: Tortuous Quest for Unity, 1990–94.* London: Chatham House, 1996.

Kotb, Sayed. *Social Justice in Islam.* Translated by John B. Hardie. New York: Octagon Press, 1970.

Kramer, Gudrun. "The Change of Paradigm: Political Pluralism in Contemporary Egypt." *Peuples Meditérranéens* 41–42 (October 1987–March 1988): 283–302.

———. "Islamist Notions of Democracy." *Middle East Report* 183 (July–August 1993): 2–8.

———. "Liberalization and Democracy in the Arab World." *Middle East Report* 174 (January–February 1992): 22–25, 35.

Kriesberg, Louis, ed. *Research in Social Movements, Conflicts and Change.* Vol. 11. London: JAI Press, 1989.

Kuhnke, Laverne. *Lives at Risk: Public Health in Nineteenth-Century Egypt.* Berkeley: University of California Press, 1990.

Kuran, Timur. "The Economic System in Contemporary Islamic Thought: Interpretation and Assessment." *International Journal of Middle Eastern Studies* 18 (1986): 135–164.

———. "Islamic Economics and the Islamic Subeconomy." *Journal of Economic Perspectives* 9 (Fall 1995): 155–173.

———. "On the Notion of Economic Justice in Contemporary Islamic Thought." *International Journal of Middle Eastern Studies* 21 (1989): 171–191.

Kurzman, Charles. "Structural Opportunity and Perceived Opportunity in Social-Movement Theory: The Iranian Revolution of 1979." *American Sociological Review* 61 (February 1996): 153–170.

———. "Who Are the Islamists?" Unpublished paper. University of North Carolina at Chapel Hill, 1996.

Lackner, Helen. *P.D.R. Yemen: Outpost of Socialist Development in Arabia.* London: Ithaca Press, 1985.

Langohr, Vickie. "Do Clients of Clinics Become Cadres? Critiquing Some Assumptions about Islamist Social Welfare." Paper presented at the Middle East Studies Association, San Francisco, California, 1997.

———. "The Organization of a Religious Movement in the Countryside: A Study of Muslim Brotherhood Branches in Rural Towns in Egypt, 1930–1952." Paper presented at the Middle East Studies Association, Washington, D.C., 1995.

———. "The Problems of Practicing What They Preached: How Hindu Movements in India and Muslim Movements in Egypt in the Pre-Independence Period Dealt with the Underprivileged in Their Ranks." Paper presented at the Annual Meeting of American Political Science Association, San Francisco, California, 1996.

Larana, Enrique, Hank Johnston, and Joseph R. Gusfield, eds. *New Social Movements: From Ideology to Identity.* Philadelphia: Temple University Press, 1994.

Latowsky, Robert J., Tarek Abdel Ghany, and Hussein Tamaa. *Egypt PVO Sector Study: Financial Profile of Egypt's PVO Sector.* Washington, D.C.: The World Bank, June 1994.

Lefresne, Bernard. "Les islamistes yéménites et les élections." *Maghreb-Machrek* 141 (juillet–août 1993): 27–36.

Lesch, Ann M. "Democracy in Doses: Mubarak Launches His Second Term as President." *Arab Studies Quarterly* 11, no. 4 (Fall 1989): 87–107.

Lofgren, Hans. "Egypt's Program for Stabilization and Structural Adjustment: An Assessment." *Cairo Papers* 16 (1993): 20–37.

Lofland, John. "'Becoming a World-Saver' Revisited." *American Behavioral Scientist* 20, no. 6 (1977): 805–818.

———. *Doomsday Cult.* New York: Irvington Publishers, 1981.

———. *Social Movement Organizations: Guide to Research on Insurgent Realities.* New York: Aldine de Gruyter, 1996.

Lofland, John, and Rodney Stark. "Becoming a World-Saver: A Theory of Conversion to a Deviant Perspective." *American Sociological Review* 30, no. 6 (1965): 862–875.

Lone, Saahir. "Economic and Social Roots of Religious Movements." *Civil Society* 4, no. 41 (May 1995): 23–24.

———. "Government Cracks Down on Militants." *Civil Society* 4, no. 39 (March 1995): 6–9.

Longuenesse, Élisabeth. "Ingénieurs et médecins dans le changement social: Égypte, Syrie, Jordanie." *Maghreb-Machrek* 146 (octobre–decembre 1994): 3–6.

———. "Le 'Syndicalisme Professionnel' en Égypte: entre identités socio-professionnelles et corporatisme." *Monde Arabe* 24 (4ème trimestre 1995): 139–187.

Longuenesse, Elisabeth, ed. *Santé, Médecine et Société dans le Monde Arabe.* France: L'Harmattan and Maison de l'Orient Méditeranéen, 1995.

Lynch, Marc. *State Interests and Public Spheres: The International Politics of Jordan's Identity.* New York: Columbia University Press, 1999.

Mackie, Alan. "Private Hospital Quickens Interest of Private Investors." *Middle East Economic Digest* 29 (September 1978): 10.

Majdalani, Rula. "The Changing Role of NGO's [*sic*] in Jordan: An Emerging Actor in Development." *Jordanies* 2, no. 12 (1996): 119–135.

Makram-Ebeid, Mona. "From Single Party Rule to One Party Domination: Some Aspects of Pluralism without Democracy." *Civil Society* 3 (March 1992): 5–7.

———. "Political Opposition in Egypt: Democratic Myth or Reality?" *Middle East Journal* 143, no. 3 (1989): 423–436.

Marty, Martin, and Scott R. Appleby, eds. *Fundamentalism and the State: Remaking Polities, Economies and Militance.* Chicago: University of Chicago Press, 1993.

Marwell, Gerald, and Pamela E. Oliver. "Collective Action Theory and Social Movements Research." *Research in Social Movements, Conflict and Change* 7 (1984): 1–28.

Marwell, Gerald, Pamela E. Oliver, and Ralph Prahl. "Social Networks and Collective Action." *American Journal of Sociology* 94, no. 3 (November 1988): 502–534.

Massis, Maher J. "Jordan: A Study of Attitudes toward Democratic Changes." *Arab Studies Quarterly* 20, no. 3 (Summer 1998): 37–63.

McAdam, Doug, John D. McCarthy, and Mayer N. Zald. *Comparative Perspectives on Social Movements: Political Opportunities, Mobilizing Structures and Cultural Framings.* Cambridge: Cambridge University Press, 1996.

McAdam, Doug, and Ronnelle Paulsen. "Specifying the Relationship between Social Ties and Activism." *American Journal of Sociology* 99, no. 3 (November 1993): 640–667.

McAdam, Doug, and David A. Snow, eds., *Social Movements: Readings on Their Emergence, Mobilization, and Dynamics.* Los Angeles: Roxbury, 1997.

McCarthy, John D., and Mark Wolfson. "Resource Mobilization by Local Social Movement Organizations: Agency, Strategy, and Organization in the Movement against Drinking and Driving." *American Sociological Review* 61 (December 1996): 1070–1088.

al-Mdaires, Falah. "Political Islamic Movements in Modern Yemen." *Journal of South Asian and Middle Eastern Studies* 24, no. 2 (Winter 2001): 73–86.

el-Mehairy, Theresa. *Medical Doctors: A Study of Role Concept and Job Satisfaction—The Egyptian Case.* Social, Economic and Political Studies of the Middle East, vol. 33. Leiden: E. J. Brill, 1984.

Meier, Gitta. "Providing Affordable Medical Care in a Third World Country: The Case of Egypt." *Inquiry* 19 (Winter 1982): 346–356.

Meijer, Roel. "The Problems of Integration: The State and Moderate Islamic Movements in Egypt, Jordan and Palestine." *The Japanese Institute of Middle Eastern Economics* (Spring 1996): 19–34.

Melucci, Alberto. *Nomads of the Present: Social Movements and Individual Needs in Contemporary Society.* Edited by John Keane and Paul Mier. Philadelphia: Temple University Press, 1989.

Middle East and North Africa Program of the Lawyers Committee for Human Rights and The Egyptian Organization for Human Rights. "Restricting the Human Rights Movement in Egypt: Legal Restrictions on Independent Non-Governmental Organizations." *Civil Society* 5 (May 1992): 6–9.

Migdal, Joel S., Atul Konti, and Vivienne Shue, eds. *State Power and Social Forces: Domination and Transformation in the Third World.* Cambridge: Cambridge University Press, 1994.

el-Mikawy, Noha. "Conceptions of the Social Role of the State in Egypt." Paper presented at the Middle East Studies Association, Chicago, Illinois, 1998.

Mitchell, Richard P. *The Society of Muslim Brotherhood.* 2d ed. New York: Oxford University Press, 1993.

Mitchell, Timothy. "Dreamland: The Neoliberalism of Your Desires." *Middle East Report* 210 (Spring 1999): 28–33.

Moaddel, Mansoor. *Jordanian Exceptionalism: A Comparative Analysis of State-Religion Relationships in Egypt, Iran, Jordan and Syria.* New York: Palgrave, 2002.

Moen, Matthew C., and Lowell S. Gustafson, eds. *The Religious Challenge to the State.* Philadelphia: Temple University Press, 1992.

Moghadam, Valentine, ed. *Trajectories of Patriarchy and Development.* Oxford: Clarendon Press, 1996.

Mohieldin, Mahmoud. "On Formal and Informal Islamic Finance in Egypt." Paper presented at the Middle East Studies Association of North America, Washington, D.C., 1995.

Molyneux, Maxine. "Legal Reform and Socialist Revolution in Democratic Yemen: Women and the Family." *International Journal of the Sociology of Law* 13 (1985): 147–172.

———. "Women's Emancipation under Socialism: A Model for the Third World?" *World Development* 9, no. 9/10 (1981): 1019–1037.

———. "Women's Rights and Political Contingency: The Case of Yemen, 1990–1994." *Middle East Journal* 49, no. 3 (Summer 1995): 418–431.

Moore, Clement Henry. *Images of Development.* Cambridge, Mass.: MIT Press, 1980.

Morris, Aldon D., and Carol McClurg Mueller, eds. *Frontiers in Social Movement Theory.* New Haven, Conn.: Yale University, 1992.

Morris, Timothy. *The Despairing Developer: Diary of an Aid Worker in the Middle East.* London: I. B. Tauris, 1991.

Morsy, Soheir A. "Islamic Clinics in Egypt: The Cultural Elaboration of Biomedical Hegemony." *Medical Anthropology Quarterly* 2, no. 4 (December 1988): 355–369.

Moustafa, Tamir. "Conflict and Cooperation Between the State and Religious Institutions in Contemporary Egypt." *International Journal of Middle East Studies* 32, no. 1 (February 2000): 3–22.

Mufti, Malik. "Elite Bargains and the Onset of Political Liberalization in Jordan." *Comparative Political Studies* 32, no. 1 (February 1999): 100–129.

al-Mughni, Haya. *Women in Kuwait: The Politics of Gender.* London: Saqi Press, 2001.

Munck, Gerardo L. "Actor Formation, Social Co-ordination, and Political Strategy: Some Conceptual Problems in the Study of Social Movements." *Sociology* 29, no. 4 (November 1995): 667–685.

Mundy, Martha. *Domestic Government: Kinship, Community, and Polity in North Yemen.* London: I. B. Tauris, 1995.

Munson, Ziad. "Islamic Mobilization: Social Movement Theory and the Egyptian Muslim Brotherhood." *Sociological Quarterly* 42, no. 4 (2001): 487–510.

Murphy, Caryle. "The Business of Political Change." *Current History* 94, no. 588 (January 1995): 18–22.

Mustafa, Hala. *Les forces islamistes et l'expérience démocratique en Égypte, in Démocratie et démocratisations dans le monde arabe.* Cairo: Dossiers du Centre d'Études et de Documentation Économiques, 1992.

Mutalib, Hussin, and Taj ul-Islam Hashmi, eds. *Islam, Muslims, and the Modern State.* New York: St. Martin's Press, 1994.

Muth, Annmarie, ed. *Statistical Abstract of the World.* 3d ed. Detroit: Gale Research, 1997.

Nandakumar, A. K., Mukesh Chawla, and Maryam Khan. "Utilization of Outpatient Care in Egypt and Its Implications for the Role of Government in Health Care Provision." *World Development* 28, no. 1 (2000): 187–196.

Nandakumar, A. K., Michael R. Reich, Mukesh Chawla, Peter Berman, and Winnie Yip. "Health Reform for Children: The Egyptian Experience with School Health Insurance." *Health Policy* 50 (2000): 155–170.

Nasr, Seyyed Vali Reza. "Islamic Economics: Novel Perspectives." *Middle Eastern Studies* 25, no. 4 (October 1989): 516–530.

Newman, David, and Tamar Hermann. "A Comparative Study of Gush Emunim and Peace Now." *Middle Eastern Studies* 28, no. 3 (July 1992): 509–530.

Niknam, Azadeh. "The Islamization of Law in Iran: A Time of Disenchantment." *Middle East Report* 212 (Fall 1999): 17–21.

Norton, Augustus Richard. *Civil Society in the Middle East.* Vols. I and II. New York: E. J. Brill, 1995–1996.

———, ed. "The Future of Civil Society in the Middle East." *Middle East Journal* 47, no. 2 (Spring 1993): 205–216.

Oberschall, Anthony. "Loosely Structured Collective Conflict: A Theory and an Application." *Research in Social Movements, Conflicts and Change* 3 (1980): 45–68.

Okasha, A., and T. Okasha. "Mental Health in Cairo (Al-Qahira)." *International Journal of Mental Health* 28, no. 4 (Winter 1999–2000): 62–68.

Oliver, Pamela. "Bringing the Crowd Back In: The Nonorganizational Elements of Social Movements." *Research in Social Movements, Conflicts and Change* 11 (1989): 1–30.

———. "The Mobilization of Paid and Volunteer Activists in the Neighborhood Movement." *Research in Social Movements, Conflicts and Change* 5 (1983): 133–170.

de Oliveira, Miguel Darcy, and Rajesh Tandon, eds. *Citizens: Strengthening Global Civil Society.* World Assembly ed. Washington, D.C.: CIVICUS World Alliance for Citizen Participation, 1994.

Olson, Mancur. *The Logic of Collective Action: Public Goods and the Theory of Groups.* Cambridge, Mass.: Harvard University Press, 1980.

al-Omar, Fuad, and Mohammed Abdel-Haq. *Islamic Banking: Theory, Practice and Challenges.* Atlantic Highlands, N.J.: Zed Books, 1996.

"A One Minute Earthquake." *Civil Society* 11 (November 1992): 3–4.

Opp, Karl-Dieter, and Christiane Gern. "Dissident Groups, Personal Networks, and Spontaneous Cooperation: The East German Revolution of 1989." *American Sociological Review* 58 (October 1993): 659–680.

Oweiss, Ibrahim M., ed. *The Political Economy of Contemporary Egypt.* Washington, D.C.: Center of Contemporary Arab Studies, Georgetown University, 1990.

Pankhurst, David, and Nassib el-Husseini. "Review of NGO/NGI Activity in Egypt." Internal Report. Cairo: Canadian International Development Agency, December 1992.

Peixoto, Otavio. "Grassroots Associations, Non-Governmental Organisations, and the Growth of Civil Society in Egypt." *FORUM: Newsletter of the Economic Research Forum for Arab Countries, Iran and Turkey* 3, no. 1 (March 1996): 14–15.

Peterson, John E. *Yemen: The Search for a Modern State.* Baltimore: Johns Hopkins University Press, 1982.

Pfaff, Steven. "Collective Identity and Informal Groups in Revolutionary Mobilization: East Germany in 1989." *Social Forces* 75, no. 1 (September 1996): 91–118.

Pfeiffer, Karen. "How Tunisian, Morocco, Jordan and Even Egypt Became IMF 'Success Stories' in the 1990s." *Middle East Report* 210 (Spring 1999): 23–27.

———. "Islamic Business and Business as Usual: A Study of Firms in Egypt." *Development in Practice* 11, no. 1. (February 2001): 20–33.

Phillips, Susan D. "Meaning and Structure in Social Movements: Mapping the Network of National Canadian Women's Organizations." *Canadian Journal of Political Science* 24, no. 4 (December 1991): 755–782.

Piro, Timothy J. *The Political Economy of Market Reform in Jordan.* Lanham, Md.: Rowman and Littlefield, 1998.

Piven, Francis Fox, and Richard A. Cloward. *Poor People's Movements: Why They Succeed, How They Fail.* New York: Vintage Books, 1979.

Population Reference Bureau. *World Population Data Sheet: Demographic Data and Estimates for the Countries and Regions of the World.* Washington, D.C.: Population Reference Bureau, 1998.

Pridham, B. R. *Contemporary Yemen: Politics and Historical Background.* London: Croom Helm, 1984.

———. *Economy, Society, and Culture in Contemporary Yemen.* London: Croom Helm, 1985.

Putnam, Robert D. *Making Democracy Work: Civic Traditions in Modern Italy.* Princeton, N.J.: Princeton University Press, 1993.

Qandil, Amani. "Études des groupes d'intérêt en Égypte: aspect international et aspect particulier." In *Dossiers du CEDEJ: Études Politiques Du Monde Arabe.* ed. CEDEJ. Cairo: Centre d'Études et de Documentation Économiques, 1991.

Rath, Kathrine. "The Process of Democratization in Jordan." *Middle Eastern Studies* 30, no. 3 (July 1994): 530–557.

Reddy, Marlita A., ed. *Statistical Abstract of the World.* 2d ed. Detroit: Gale Research, 1996.

Reid, Donald M. "The Rise of Professions and Professional Organization in Modern Egypt." *Comparative Studies in Society and History* 16, no. 1 (January 1974): 24–57.

Richards, Alan, and John Waterbury. *A Political Economy of the Middle East: State, Class and Economic Development.* Oxford: Westview Press, 1990.

Roald, Anne Sofie. *Tarbiya: Education and Politics in Islamic Movements in Jordan and Malaysia.* Stockholm: Almqvist and Wiksell, 1994.

Robinson, Glenn E. *Building a Palestinian State: The Incomplete Revolution.* Bloomington: Indiana University Press, 1997.

———. "Can Islamists Be Democrats? The Case of Jordan." *Middle East Journal* 51, no. 3 (Summer 1997): 373–388.

———. "Defensive Democratization in Jordan." *International Journal of Middle East Studies* 30, no. 3 (August 1998): 387–410.

Rosenthal, Naomi. "Social Movements and Network Analysis: A Case Study of Nineteenth-Century Women's Reform in New York State." *American Journal of Sociology* 90, no. 5 (1985): 1022–1054.

Roussillon, Alain. "Entre al-Jihad et al-Rayyan: Phénoménologie de l'islamisme égyptien." In *Dossiers du CEDEJ: Modernisation et nouvelles formes de mobilisation sociale,* ed. CEDEJ, 39–80. Cairo: Centre d'Études et de Documentation Économiques, 1991.

———. "Islam, Islamisme et Démocratie: Recomposition du Champ Politique." *Peuples Méditérranéens* 41–42 (October–March 1987–1988): 303–339, 354.

———. "Le paradigme islamiste, généralisations et limites: le cas de l'Égypte." In *Dossiers du CEDEJ: Études Politiques du Monde Arabe,* ed. CEDEJ, 279–306. Cairo: Centre d'Études et de Documentation Économiques, 1991.

———. *Sociétés islamiques de placement de fonds et ouverture économique.* Cairo: Centre d'Études et de Documentation Économiques, 1988.

Roy, Oliver. *The Failure of Political Islam.* Translated by Carol Volk. Cambridge, Mass.: Harvard University Press, 1994.

Roy, Sara. "The Transformation of Islamic NGOs in Palestine." *Middle East Report* 214 (Spring 2000): 24–27.

Rucht, Dieter. "Themes, Logics, and Arenas of Social Movements: A Structural Approach." *Research in Social Movements, Conflicts and Change* 1 (1988): 305–328.

Ruechemeyer, Dietrich, Evelyn Huber Stephens, and John D. Stephens. *Capitalist Development and Democracy.* Cambridge: Polity Press, 1992.

Ryan, Curtis R. "Elections and Parliamentary Democratization in Jordan." *Democratization* 5, no. 4 (Winter 1998): 176–196.

———. "Peace, Bread, and Riots: Jordan and the International Monetary Fund." *Middle East Policy* 6, no. 2 (1998): 54–66.

Sabbagh, Suha, ed. *Arab Women: Between Defiance and Restraint.* New York: Olive Branch Press, 1996.

Sadowski, Christine M. "Resource Mobilization in a Marxist Leninist Society: The Case of Poland's Solidarity Movement." *Journal of Communist Studies* 4, no. 2 (June 1988): 181–201.

Sadowski, Yahya. "Egypt's Islamist Movement: A New Political and Economic Force." *Middle East Insight* 5 (November–December 1987): 37–45.

Saleebey, Dennis. "Culture, Theory, and Narrative: The Intersection of Meanings in Practice." *Social Work* 39, no. 4 (1994): 351–359.

Salem, A. Amir. "Law No. 32 for 1964 on Associations: A Deterrent against Participation." Paper presented at the Second Intellectual Forum on Human Rights in Egypt: The Right to Life . . . The Right to Participation, Cairo, 1990.

al-Sayyid, Mustapha Kamel. "Civil Society Concept and the Arab World." Paper presented at the Conference on Political Liberalization and Democratization in the Arab World, McGill University and University of Montreal, 1993.

———. "A Civil Society in Egypt?" *Middle East Journal* 47, no. 2 (Spring 1993): 228–242.

al-Sayyid Marsot, Afaf Lufti. "Religion or Opposition? Urban Protest Movement in Egypt." *International Journal of Middle East Studies* 16 (1984): 541–552.

el-Sayyid Said, Muhammed. *Modernisation et nouvelles formes de mobilisation sociale: Égypte-Brésil, Métamorphoses du champ societal à partir du renforcement des mouvements à référence religieuse en Égypte.* Cairo: Dossiers du Centre d'Études et de Documentation Économiques, 1991.

Schennink, Ben. "From Peace Week to Peace Work: Dynamics of the Peace Movement in the Netherlands." *Research in Social Movements, Conflicts and Change* 1 (1988): 247–279.

Schmitz, Chuck. "Civil War in Yemen: The Price of Unity." *Current History* 94 (January 1995): 33–36.

Schneirov, Matthew, and Jonathan David Geczik. "A Diagnosis for Our Times: Alternative Health's Submerged Networks and the Transformation of Identities." *Sociological Quarterly* 37, no. 4 (1996): 627–644.

Schulz, Markus S. "Collective Action across Borders: Opportunity Structures, Network Capacities, and Communicative Praxis in the Age of Advanced Globalization." *Sociological Perspectives* 41, no. 3 (1998): 587–616.

Schwedler, Jillian. "A Paradox of Democracy? Islamist Participation in Democratic Elections." *Middle East Report,* no. 209 (Winter 1998): 25–29.

Scott, James. *Weapons of the Weak.* New Haven, Conn.: Yale University Press, 1985.

Sela, Avraham, ed. *Political Encyclopedia of the Middle East.* New York: Continuum, 1999.

Silver, Ira. "Buying an Activist Identity: Reproducing Class through Social Movement Philanthropy." *Sociological Perspectives* 41, no. 2 (1998): 303–321.

Singerman, Diane. *Avenues of Participation: Family, Politics, and Networks in Urban Quarters of Cairo.* Princeton, N.J.: Princeton University Press, 1995.

Singerman, Diane, and Homa Hoodfar, eds. *Development, Change, and Gender in Cairo: A View from the Household.* Bloomington: Indiana University Press, 1996.

Smelser, Neil J., ed. *The Handbook of Sociology.* Newbury Park, Calif.: Sage Publications, 1988.

Snow, David Alan. *Shakubuku: A Study of the Nichiren Shoshu Buddhist Movement in America, 1960–1975.* New York: Garland Publishing, 1993.

Snow, David A., E. Burke Rochford, Jr., Steven K. Worden, and Robert D. Benford. "Frame Alignment Processes, Micromobilization, and Movement Participation." *American Sociological Review* 51 (August 1986): 464–481.

Snow, David A., and Susan E. Marshall. "Cultural Imperialism, Social Movements, and the Islamic Revival." *Research in Social Movements, Conflicts and Change* 7 (1984): 131–152.

Snow, David A., Louis A. Zurcher, Jr., and Sheldon Ekland-Olson. "Social Networks and Social Movements: A Microstructural Approach to Differential Recruitment." *American Sociological Review* 45 (October 1980): 787–801.

Sonbol, Amira el-Azhary. *The Creation of a Medical Profession in Egypt, 1800–1922.* Syracuse, N.Y.: Syracuse University Press, 1991.

Springborg, Robert. "Professional Syndicates in Egyptian Politics, 1952–1970." *International Journal for Middle East Studies* 9 (1978): 275–295.

Staggenborg, Suzanne. "Life-style Preferences and Social Movement Recruitment: Illustrations from the Abortion Conflict." *Social Science Quarterly* 68, no. 4 (December 1987): 779–797.

———. "Stability and Innovation in the Women's Movement: A Comparison of Two Movement Organizations." *Social Problems* 36, no. 1 (February 1989): 75–91.

Stark, Rodney. "Social Contexts and Religious Experience." *Review of Religious Research* 7, no. 1 (Fall 1965): 17–28.

Stark, Rodney, and William Sims Bainbridge. "Of Churches, Sects, and Cults: Preliminary Concepts for a Theory of Religious Movements." *Journal for the Scientific Study of Religion* 18, no. 2 (1979): 117–133.

———. "Networks of Faith: Interpersonal Bonds and Recruitment to Cults and Sects." *American Journal of Sociology* 85, no. 6 (1980): 1376–1395.

———. "Towards a Theory of Religion: Religious Commitment." *Journal for the Scientific Study of Religion* 19, no. 2 (1980): 114–128.

Stevens, Mark Power. *A Discussion of Jordan's 1993 Parliamentary Election.* Amman, Jordan: Al-Urdun al-Jadid Research Center, 1994.

Stoecker, Randy. "Community, Movement, Organization: The Problem of Identity Convergence in Collective Action." *Sociological Quarterly* 36, no. 1 (1995): 111–130.

Stookey, Robert W. *South Yemen: A Marxist Republic in Arabia.* Boulder, Colo.: Westview, 1982.

Stork, Joe. "Political Aspects of Health." *Middle East Report* 161 (November–December 1989): 4–10.

———. "Socialist Revolution in Arabia: A Report from the People's Democratic Republic of Yemen." *Middle East Research and Information Project* 15 (March 1973): 1–25.

Streeten, Paul. "Nongovernmental Organizations and Development." *Annals of the Academy of Political and Social Science* 554, no. November (1997): 193–210.

Suleiman, Ezra N., and John Waterbury, eds. *The Political Economy of Public Sector Reform and Privatization.* Boulder, Colo.: Westview Press, 1990.

Sullivan, Denis J. *Non-Governmental Organizations and Freedom of Association: Palestine and Egypt—A Comparative Analysis.* Jerusalem: Palestinian Academic Society for the Study of International Affairs, 1995.

Sullivan, Denis J., and Sana Abded-Kotob. *Islam in Contemporary Egypt: Civil Society vs. the State.* Boulder, Colo.: Lynne Rienner, 1999.

al-Suwadi, Jamal S., ed. *Private Voluntary Organizations in Egypt: Islamic Development, Private Initiative, and State Control.* Gainesville: University Press of Florida, 1994.

———. *The Yemeni War of 1994: Causes and Consequences.* London: The Emirates Center for Strategic Studies and Research, 1995.

Tabler, Andrew. "Another Year on the Civil Society Treadmill." *Cairo Times* 4, no. 14 (June 2000): 10–11.

Tachau, Frank, ed. *Political Parties of the Middle East and North Africa.* Westport, Conn.: Greenwood Publishing Group, 1994.

Tal, Lawrence. "Dealing with Radical Islam: The Case of Jordan." *Survival* 37, no. 3 (Autumn 1995): 139–156.

Taraki, Lisa. "Islam Is the Solution: Jordanian Islamists and the Dilemma of the Modern Woman." *British Journal of Sociology* 46, no. 4 (December 1995): 643–661.

———. "Jordanian Islamists and the Agenda for Women: Between Discourse and Practice." *Middle Eastern Studies* 32, no. 1 (January 1996): 140–158.

Tekce, Belgin, Linda Oldham, and Frederic C. Shorter. *A Place to Live: Families and Child Health in a Cairo Neighborhood.* Cairo: American University in Cairo Press, 1994.

Tessler, Mark, and Jolene Jesse. "Gender and Support for Islamist Movements: Evidence from Egypt, Kuwait and Palestine." *Muslim World* 86, no. 2 (April 1996): 200–228.

Tilly, Charles. *From Mobilization to Revolution.* Reading, Mass.: Addison-Wesley, 1978.

United Nations. *Statistical Yearbook 1994.* New York: United Nations, 1996.

———. *The World's Women, 1995: Trends and Statistics.* New York: United Nations, 1995.

United Nations Development Programme. "Making New Technologies Work for Human Development." *Human Development Report.* New York: Oxford University Press for the UNDP, 2001.

———. *United Nations Human Development Report 2000.* New York: Oxford University Press for the UNDP, 2000.

UNESCO. *World Education Report.* Paris: UNESCO Publishing, 1995.

Al-Urdun al-Jadid Research Center. *General Parliamentary Elections in Jordan, 8 November 1993: An Introduction, the Results and Future Prospects.* Amman, Jordan: Al-Urdun al-Jadid Research Center, 1995.

———. *Jordan's 1993 Elections: An Analytic Study.* Amman, Jordan: Al-Urdun al-Jadid Research Center, 1995.

———. "Jordan's Parliamentary Elections: Facts and Figures." Al-Urdun al-Jadid Research Center, Amman, Jordan, November 24, 1998.

Useem, Bert. "Solidarity Model, Breakdown Model, and the Boston Anti-Busing Movement." *American Sociological Review* 45 (June 1980): 357–369.

Utvik, Bjorn Olav. "Filling the Vacant Throne of Nasser: The Economic Discourse of Egypt's Islamist Opposition." Paper presented at the Middle East Studies Association of North America, Phoenix, Arizona, 1994.

Valibeigi, Mehrdad. "Islamic Economics and Economic Policy Formation in Post-Revolutionary Iran: A Critique." *Journal of Economic Issues* 27, no. 3 (September 1993): 793–811.

van Binsbergen, Wim, Filip Reyntjens, and Gerti Hesseling, eds. *State and Local Community in Africa.* Brussels: Centre d'Étude et de Documentation Africaines/Afrika Studieen Documentatiecentrum, 1986.

Waterbury, John. *Exposed to Innumerable Delusions: Public Enterprise and State Power in Egypt, India, Mexico and Turkey.* New York: Cambridge University Press, 1993.

Weir, Lorna. "Limitations of New Social Movement Analysis." *Studies in Political Economy* 40 (March 1993): 73–99.

Weir, Shelagh. *Qat in Yemen: Consumption and Social Change.* London: British Museum Publications, 1985.

———. "Religious Conflict in the Yemeni Highlands." Paper presented at the Middle East Studies Association of North America, Washington, D.C., 1995.

Wenner, Manfred W. *Modern Yemen, 1918–1966.* Baltimore: Johns Hopkins University Press, 1967.

White, Louise G. "Urban Community Organizations and Local Government: Exploring Relationships and Roles." *Public Administration and Development* 6 (1986): 239–253.

Wickham, Carrie Rosefsky. "Are the Islamists in Egypt Part of Civil Society?" Paper presented at the American Political Science Association Annual Meeting, Washington, D.C., 1993.

———. *Mobilizing Islam.* New York: Columbia University Press (forthcoming).

———. "Political Mobilization under Authoritarian Rule: Explaining Islamic Activism in Mubarak's Egypt." Ph.D. diss., Princeton University, 1996.

Wikan, Unni. *Life among the Poor in Cairo.* Translated by A. Henning. London: Tavistock, 1980.

———. "Living Conditions among Cairo's Poor: A View from Below." *Middle East Journal* 39, no. 1 (Winter 1985): 7–26.

Wiktorowicz, Quintan. "Civil Society as Social Control: State Power in Jordan." *Comparative Politics* 33, no. 1 (October 2000): 43–61.

———. "Islamists, the State, and Cooperation in Jordan." *Arab Studies Quarterly* 21, no. 4 (Fall 1999): 1–17.

———. "The Limits of Democracy in the Middle East: The Case of Jordan." *Middle East Journal* 53, no. 4 (Autumn 1999): 606–620.

———. *The Management of Islamic Activism: Salafis, the Muslim Brotherhood, and State Power in Jordan.* Albany: State University of New York Press, 2001.

———. "The Salafi Movement in Jordan." *International Journal of Middle East Studies* 32, no. 2 (May 2000): 219–240.

———. "State Power and the Regulation of Islam in Jordan." *Journal of Church and State* 41, no. 4 (Autumn 1999): 677–696.

———, ed. *Islamic Activism: A Social Movement Theory Approach.* Bloomington: Indiana University Press (forthcoming).

Wiktorowicz, Quintan, and Suha-Taji Farouki. "Islamic Non-Governmental Organizations and Muslim Politics: A Case from Jordan." *Third World Quarterly* 21, no. 4 (August 2000): 685–699.

Wilson, Rodney. *Economic Development in the Middle East.* New York: Routledge, 1995.

Women's National Committee. "National Report on the Status of Women in The Republic of Yemen." Sanaʿa, Women's National Committee, August 1995.

World Bank, The Population and Human Resources Operations Division, Country Department II, Middle East and North Africa Region. *Hashemite Kingdom of Jordan: Poverty Assessment.* Washington, D.C.: World Bank, 1994.

World Bank. *Social Indicators of Development.* Washington, D.C.: Johns Hopkins University Press, 1996.

———. *World Development Indicators 1997.* Washington, D.C.: International Bank for Reconstruction and Development/The World Bank, 1997.

Wuerth, Anna. "The Legal Status of Women in Yemen." A report submitted to CID/WID Project of the Bureau of Applied Research in Anthropology, Department of Anthropology, University of Arizona. Tucson, Ariz., March 1994.

———. "A Sanaʿa Court: The Family and the Ability to Negotiate." *Islamic Law and Society* 2, no. 3 (1995): 320–340.

"Year in Review: Rigged Elections, Terrorism and Stagnant Peace Process." *Civil Society* 7, no. 73 (February 1998): 5–17.

Yousef, Ahmed. "The State of Islamist Politics in Yemen: An Interview with a Representative of the Yemen Reform Assembly (Islah)." *Middle East Affairs* 2, no. 2–3 (Winter/Spring 1995): 119–137.

Zaki, Moheb. *Civil Society and Democratization in Egypt, 1981–1994.* Cairo: Ibn Khaldoun Center, 1994.

Zeghal, Malika. "Religion and Politics in Egypt: The Ulema of al-Azhar, Radical Islam, and the State (1952–1994)." *International Journal of Middle East Studies* 31, no. 3 (August 1999): 371–399.

Zubaida, Sami. "Islam, the State and Democracy." *Middle East Report* 179 (November–December 1992): 2–10.

Zuo, Jiping, and Robert D. Benford. "Mobilization Processes and the 1989 Chinese Democracy Movement." *Sociological Quarterly* 36, no. 1 (1995): 131–156.

Zygmunt, Joseph F. "Movements and Motives: Some Unresolved Issues in the Psychology of Social Movements." *Human Relations* 25, no. 5 (1972): 449–467.

REGULARLY CONSULTED ARAB PRESS

Al-Ahram (Egypt)

Al-Ahram al-Iqtisadi (Egypt)

Al-Akhbar (Egypt)

Akher Saʿaa (Egypt)

Al-Arab al-Youm (Jordan)

Al-Belad (Jordan)

Al-Belagh (Yemen)

Balkis (Yemen)

Al-Daʿwa (Egypt)

Al-Dustur (Jordan)

Al-Eslah (Yemen)

Al-Hawadeth (Yemen)

Jordan Times

Al-Jumhuriya (Egypt)

Maeen (Yemen)

Al-Mara (Yemen)

Al-Masa' (Egypt)
Al-Masa' Al Usbu'i (Egypt)
Masr al-Fatat (Egypt)
Al-Mustakillah (UK)
Al-Ra'y (Jordan)
As-Sabeel (Jordan)
As-Sahwa (Yemen)
Al-Sha'b (Egypt)
Al-Shoura (Yemen)
Al-Thawra (Yemen)
Al-Wafd (Egypt)
Al-Wahda (Yemen)
Yemen Times

INDEX

Janine A. Clark is Associate Professor of Political Science at the University of Guelph. She is co-editor (with Remonda Bensabat-Kleinberg) of *Economic Liberalization, Democratization, and Civil Society in the Developing World* and author of numerous articles on Islamism and politics.